JANET RUHL

COMPUTER
JOB
SURVIVAL
GUIDE

TECHNION Books

Published by Technion Books
P.O. Box 171
Leverett, MA 01054
technion@realrates.com

Portions of this book were previously published by: Prentice-Hall, Inc., under the title, *The Programmer's Survival Guide*.

Additional copies of this book may be ordered from the publisher. Please include $2.50 for postage and handling. For information about volume discounts please contact the publisher at the address above.

This publication is designed to provide accurate and authoritative information in regard to the subject matter covered. It is sold with the understanding that the publisher and author are not engaged in rendering legal, accounting, or other professional services. If legal advice or other expert assistance is required, the services of a competent professional person should be sought.

LIBRARY OF CONGRESS CATALOG CARD NUMBER: 00-190960
ISBN NUMBER: 0-9647116-4-8

Printed in the United States of America

10 9 8 7 6 5 4 3 2 1

ACKNOWLEDGMENTS

This book would not be here were it not for the substantial support Ed Yourdon gave me many years ago when I sent him the manuscript of my first computer career book, *The Programmer's Survival Guide*. Without his enthusiastic promotion of that book, which contributed greatly to its subsequent success, I probably would have just gone back to my cube and never have written another.

Thanks are also due to the many regulars at the Realrates.com Bulletin Board whose detailed reporting on the conditions they have experienced while working at their jobs and consulting contracts has kept me in daily contact with the realities of computer employment around the world. I'm particularly grateful for the many wonderful career tips and tricks that have been posted, often anonymously, on our board over the years.

Thanks, too, to the many thousands of contributors to the Real Salary Survey, who by supplying their data have given all of us the ability to *know*, rather than guess at, the salaries, skills, and experience required to fill today's computer jobs.

Special thanks to Pat Adams, Kristen Babineau, Eric Dew, Patrick McGovern, Scot Robertson, Tom Scott, Rob Taulton, and Don Wallace for their willingness to discuss their careers. Their observations have been very helpful in bringing this book up-to-date. I am also very grateful for Peter Atwood's painstaking copyediting and general all around good cheer.

And, as always, my heartfelt thanks goes out to my readers, whose feedback over the years has encouraged me to believe that my books do, in fact, help them succeed in their careers.

TABLE OF CONTENTS

CHARTS AND FACT SHEETS

Introduction

When my first book, *The Programmer's Survival Guide*, was published in 1988 the publisher printed up a mere 2,000 copies believing that the number of computer people willing to pay money to find out how to succeed in their field would not exceed that number.

How wrong they were! That book sold more than ten times that many copies in stores, was featured repeatedly by book clubs, and maintained its place on retail bookshelves for a good eight years — until it had long outlived the technology its pages described.

Along the way it achieved considerable critical acclaim. *CompuServe Magazine* called it "Required reading for anyone considering a career in the field" and *PC Week*'s reviewer said, "With *The Programmer's Survival Guide* computer professionals will be better equipped to survive both a debugging battle and a paycheck war." Even more gratifying were the many letters sent by enthusiastic readers who described themselves as professionals with ten or even twenty years in the business who wrote things like, "I felt as if you had been following me around at work for a couple of years" and "How I wish I had known about the things you write about back when I started out!"

The *Programmer's Survival Guide* was written when most serious professional programmers worked on mainframes and the PC was still making its transition from being a hacker's toy to a serious business tool. Back then, the word "online" referred to companies' in-house networks, which usually ran IBM's CICS software. Email in most companies was still experimental. But despite the changes that the passage of thirteen years has brought to the industry, the fundamental premises of *The Programmer's Survival Guide*, were, and continue to be, true.

The *Programmer's Survival Guide* taught that, for maximal success, Information Technology (IT) professionals should treat their first two or three years of salaried employment in the corporate world as an apprenticeship. The skills and real world experience they acquired during this apprenticeship could be used to qualify themselves for the most interesting and highly paid salaried jobs or to craft a more entrepreneurial career in either consulting, contracting, or software product development. This has certainly not changed. *The Programmer's Survival Guide* also explored the conflict between the worldview of the puzzle-solving, logical thinkers who become programmers and the reward-motivated managers and businesspeople that pay their salaries. That conflict continues — far more intensely now than it did a generation ago.

Finally, and most importantly, *The Programmer's Survival Guide* laid out simple but powerful principles to use in your job hunt to ensure that the job you get is the job you thought you were getting, and that the job you get is one that will improve your prospects for your next job hunt and for the one after that. The only thing that has really changed since 1987 when the *Guide* was written is that, because of the speed-up in the pace of technological change, it now takes a far shorter time for computer skills to become obsolete. This is significant because in today's more brutal business environment, no matter how good your skills, your intelligence, or your connections, the penalty for technical obsolescence will invariably be the termination of your computer career.

Because the technology described in the original book was so out-of-date while the advice that formed the meat of it was emphatically not, I have long wanted to revise *The Programmer's Survival Guide* for a new generation of computer professionals. But because the book's original publisher was acquired and changed its market strategy, this was not possible until the original edition of the book finally went out of print at the end of the 1990s. Only then was I able to rewrite the older book in a brand new, extensively updated version, one that would take into account the changes that had taken place both in technology and the IT marketplace while staying faithful to the original book's vision. It is that book which you now hold in your hands.

In writing this new *Computer Job Survival Guide* I have had the enormous advantage of being able to draw on resources unavailable to me when I wrote that first book so long ago. Among the most important of these is the data provided by the Real Salary Survey, an ongoing Web-based survey of the salaries and job conditions of thousands of salaried computer professionals who contribute detailed reports about their current jobs to my Web site, Realrates.com.

The contributors to the Real Salary Survey give us rich and explicit data about the software, hardware, and application area their current job involves. They tell us their job titles, their credentials, their number of years of experience, their age, gender and immigration status. They also tell us the location and industry of their current job and whether they got the job through a job placement agency, a consulting firm, or though their own efforts. Each Real Salary Survey report also gives the employee's salary, their salary on their previous job, and the amount of any bonus they may have received, and describes any unusual benefits they receive from their employers.

When I wrote the original version of *The Programmer's Survival Guide*, I could draw only upon the experiences of perhaps a hundred computer professionals—those I had encountered on the job—and upon the limited amount of information about salaries and skills that was available in the IT trade press. Because of the secrecy of employers and the lack of communication between computer professionals working in different companies back then, there was much that simply could not be known. Now, with the information available from thousands of Real Salary Survey contributions going back several years it is possible to present a much more accurate picture of the salaries, qualifications, and skills of the working computer professional. You'll see this data summarized in graphs throughout this book.

Another invaluable resource that is now available to me is the bulletin board that we run at `Realrates.com`. Though our focus on the site is computer consulting and contracting, our board attracts computer professionals at every stage of their careers as well as job placement recruiters and executives. Their posts—24,000 messages in the past year alone—have given me even more insight into the working conditions faced by computer professionals today all over the US and in other countries. They have also alerted me to news stories from around the world of importance to computer professionals.

With access to this wealth of new data, I have tried to blend the core advice found in the older book with the new facts and information that the Web has made available to us. From the many thousands of people who have contributed salary data to the Real Salary Survey, I selected a group of successful old-timers whose salaries range from $76,000 up to $150,000 and asked them to share with my readers their tips, their warnings, and their recommendations. Because most have asked that their names be kept private but that their opinions be shared you'll find their words quoted without attribution in special text boxes scattered around the book.

I have also extracted from the original *Programmer's Survival Guide* those portions describing the nature of an IT career and job hunting, and revised them to fit with today's IT environment. A few of the original anecdotes that cite mainframe-based technologies have been left in as they illustrate important points. In other cases, I've replaced references to outdated technologies with ones more up-to-date. I've also deleted the detailed discussions of the market value of specific languages and system software and which formed a part of the original book. Readers who want to know what's currently in demand can find the very latest data in the Real Salary Survey and Real Rate Survey available at my Web site, `Realrates.com`.

In writing this new book, I have limited its scope to the discussion of salaried computer work. The original book covered both salaried and entrepreneurial career options for computer professionals. However, since 1988 I have published three other books, two about computer consulting and one on computer contracting, which cover entrepreneurial career paths in far greater detail than can be done in a book of this type. I recommend that readers who wish to pursue a more entrepreneurial course in their careers read those. The discussion of contract consulting which you will find in these pages concentrates only on salaried contract consulting work.

It is still my very strong belief that the first five years of a computer professional's career are a critical period. After this period is over it is much harder to improve your credentials and pick up new skills. Unfortunately, by the time many computer professionals figure out what it is that they would like to concentrate on, it is too late. They are simply at too high a salary level and too closely identified with a specific niche to have an employer provide the training and opportunities they need to change course. That means that with every job you take, particularly at the start of your computer career, you are, whether you mean to or not, opening some possibilities for your future and shutting off others.

With that in mind I have organized this book as follows: The first section sketches out the various career paths that computer professionals most commonly follow. You'll see what it takes to get your first job, what you must learn in that job, and where you can go once that job is over. The second part of the book goes into great depth about how to manage your job hunt so that you land the job that will lead to the type of career you want. It is here you will find a host of details about the world of the working computer professional. Finally, at the end of the book you will find a list of twenty-five sets of questions you might ask at a job interview. These questions correspond to various points made throughout the book. You might want to browse these questions before reading the rest of the book and then return to them later to help you focus on the issues that will be most important to you as you evaluate new positions.

If you are thinking about becoming a computer professional, I hope this book can help you enter the field with realistic expectations and a strategy that gets you where you want to be in ten years. If you are already working in the field, I hope this book helps you sort out the features of your experience that are unique from those that are the common fate of computer professionals everywhere. I also hope it will help you fine-tune your job hunting skills and improve your long-term career satisfaction. Finally, if you are just a curious bystander or a computer professional's spouse, relative, or friend, I hope this book gives you a better idea of what it is computer professionals must deal with every day and what all those acronyms you see in the Sunday classifieds mean to them.

CHAPTER 1

The Many Kinds of Computer Jobs

Computer jobs are hot! According to the U.S. Bureau of Labor Statistics, between 1987 and 1998 the number of people employed in the United States in computer-related jobs rose from nearly one million to a whopping two and a half million. What's more, the Bureau predicted that for every computer-related job category except computer operations the number of people employed in the computer field during the next five years will rise at a greater than average rate.

It's also no secret that these computer jobs pay better than do those in almost every other field requiring similar amounts of education. Our Real Salary Survey data for computer professionals showed that the median salary for programmers with one or fewer years of experience was $45,000, while the actual salaries reported for people in the first year of their computer careers ranged from $22,000 to a whopping $62,000. By the time these same computer professionals had spent five years in their chosen career, their median salary was $60,000, though the Real Salary Survey has received reports of people with only five years of experience earning annual salaries as high as $150,000.

And the good news doesn't stop there. Unlike professionals in other high paying fields, most of the people earning these starting salaries do not have advanced degrees nor did they attend prestigious and expensive Ivy League colleges. In fact, the Bureau of Labor Statistics reported that, while 45.3 percent of programmers in 1998 had a bachelor's degree and 13.4 percent had a graduate degree, 31.1 percent had *no* college degree at all and another 10.2 percent had earned only an Associate degree.

Clearly, for people who have an aptitude for computer work, the computer field offers unparalleled opportunities for career success while demanding a far more modest investment of time and energy than just about any other career path.

But, as enticing as this sounds, there is no free lunch. Joining the ranks of those who make it into these high paying computer jobs takes study, planning, and persistence. There are plenty of shady businesses out there preying on your desire to earn big bucks in the computer field that will sell you worthless training programs or waste your time preparing you for marginal computer jobs that will take your career nowhere. There are also far too many high school and college guidance counselors who, unaware of the realities of life in the computer professions, will steer you in the wrong direction. Finally, even if you do manage to get to where you are an attractive candidate for a starting level computer job, recruiters and hiring managers may lure you into taking a first job that will make it difficult or even impossible to ever get one of the challenging, big money computer jobs you dream of.

You will need help to get to where you can qualify for the fulfilling and high paying jobs you want, and that is what this book will give you. We'll begin our journey towards your dream computer job here, by sketching out briefly the different kinds of jobs that computer professionals fill. In later chapters we'll examine this topic again in much greater detail.

Then we'll take a tour of the early years of your computer career, showing you what you'll need to do to get that all important very first job, what you have to achieve as you work in that first job, and what your career options will be if you stay a salaried corporate employee. Throughout these discussions we keep the focus on how aware computer professionals can use their first couple of years of paid experience to position themselves to get the most interesting and highest paying jobs. We'll also look at how mature computer professionals can keep their skills current no matter how swift the pace of technological change.

After completing our tour of your potential future, we'll spend a couple of chapters looking at the job hunting process in detail and showing you how you can go out and land the jobs you need to make your computer career dreams a reality.

What Do Computer Professionals Do?

Before you can start planning your computer career, you'll need to understand the different kinds of work that computer professionals do. Salaried computer professionals actually fall into several major groups. For simplicity's sake we'll call these groups here "programmers," "technical administrators", "technicians", and "other computer-related professionals." Each of these groups represents a complete career path that begins with an entry-level job that leads to more senior level technical jobs or to team leader and management positions. Some of these jobs also give you the skills you will need should you decide to pursue a more entrepreneurial career path and strike out on your own as a consultant or software product developer. On Page 7 you'll find charts that show you the median salary and the range in which salaries cluster for a selection of computer job descriptions.

Programmers

The Real Salary Survey data shows that more than half of all working computer professionals fall into the programmer category. This category includes several entry level job titles including "Jr. Programmer", "Programmer", "Programmer Analyst", "Developer", and "Systems Engineer", a title that is usually abbreviated as "SE". The United States Bureau of Labor Statistics reports that, in 1998, 648,000 people in the United States were employed as programmers, 617,000 were employed as computer systems analysts, and 299,000 were employed as computer engineers. The distinction between these various programmer categories can be subtle. At times they are simply different titles used by employers describe jobs involving the same work. But the SE title is more likely to be used in a high tech software development environment, while the titles containing the word "programmer" are more common in manufacturing, financial, and service industries.

What all these jobs have in common is that they involve writing or maintaining code. Programmers must master one or more computer languages and use them to design, develop, and maintain software that works with specific operating systems and databases. Programmers must also know how to use software development tools, such as code libraries and debuggers.

Experienced programmers can advance to jobs with titles such as "Senior Programmer", "Senior Analyst", "Senior Developer", and "Senior SE" where they continue to design, develop, or maintain software using their expertise with a specific set of software tools. Some Web site designers are also programmers.

The next step up from these senior technical positions are those that involve technical leadership. Some of these are "Team Leader" positions—entry-level management positions that involve assigning work to the programmers that make up the team. A different and more technically oriented leadership position is "Architect." A systems architect is a highly experienced technical person whose responsibility is to provide the overall design of a complex new system.

A final and very confusing job title that usually, but not always, describes experienced programmers, is "Consultant." The confusion comes in because the term is used to cover a variety of people who fill very different types of roles. A very small number of consultants are independent business people paid a flat fee, an hourly rate or on a retainer basis to advise management. But most of the people you will meet in IT who use the title fall into two other groups. These "consultants" are either programmers at any level of experience who are salaried employees of consulting firms or contractors working as hourly rate employees, sole proprietors, or even as employees of their own corporations. One last type of worker who is also given the title "consultant" is the highly experienced salaried employee who continues to do programming work but has a job class that ranks above "Sr. Developer" or "Sr. SE."

If you are looking for those with the best paying computer jobs, it is usually here among the ranks of experienced programmers that you will find them. While the entry level salaries of programmers may not be all that different from that of other kinds of computer professionals, most of the jobs titles held by computer professionals earning the highest salaries are held by programmers. You can see this clearly in the charts shown on Page 7.

Technical Administrators

Jobs falling into this category involve configuring operating systems, databases, and networks. The job titles that fall into this category include "Systems Programmer", "Systems Administrator," often abbreviated to "Sysadmin", "Database Administrators", abbreviated to "DBA", "Network Engineer" and "Network Administrator." The United States Bureau of Labor Statistics reports that, in 1998, 87,000 people were employed as database administrators and 97,000 were employed in the "other computer scientist" category that the Bureau uses to include network and systems administrators.

The professionals who fall into this category may have a programming background, particularly the database administrators. But most do not code at all. Their expertise lies in knowing how to install, configure, and maintain hardware, software products, databases and operating systems.

Some of these technical administrator jobs may be very highly paid positions involving a great deal of technical expertise. Many DBAs, Sysadmins, and Network Administrators fall into this category. Other jobs however, verge on the clerical and may merely involve updating control files, setting up new user accounts, or running backups.

These professionals may also work as contractor "consultants" or develop careers as self-employed entrepreneurial consultants.

Technicians

Technicians include people who repair hardware, install and upgrade software, and staff help desks. The United States Bureau of Labor Statistics reports that, in 1998, 429,000 people were employed as computer support specialists. Another 138,000 were employed repairing computers, automatic teller machines, and other office machinery. Technicians and help desk staff frequently have little formal academic computer education and their career paths rarely lead to the highest paying salaried jobs, although, as you can see from the graphs on Page 7, some technicians earn very good incomes. The aristocrats of the technician career paths are those with hardware backgrounds who get into network configuration and network engineering.

Technicians rarely fill high paying contract consultant jobs though some may fill jobs as temporary employees of consulting firms. Those with excellent hardware and network design and installation experience can also build successful entrepreneurial businesses.

Other Computer-Related Career Tracks

Business Analysts are usually employees who belong to user departments like accounting or sales whose job is to interface with the technical people who make up the IT staff. It is their job to define the user group's requirements when new software is being developed or when old software must be upgraded. They usually do not have a formal computer background but may have professional training and expertise in the user areas.

Testing and Quality Assurance staff have the responsibility of testing software during the development phase and certifying that it meets company or ISO 9000 quality standards. Testing and QA staff may have significant expertise in programming and be highly paid or they may simply function in a more clerical capacity. You'll find more QA jobs in software product development companies in high tech hotbeds like Silicon Valley than you will in companies where the IT staff supports traditional business functions like manufacturing or sales.

Technical Writers are responsible for producing system documentation and manuals. Traditionally theirs were not high paying jobs, however, with the advent of the Web, Technical Writers have been more in demand as they are now being called upon to produce Web content. Technical writers usually have a background that includes academic training in writing and research.

Trainers may provide in-house classes for company personnel or they may be employed by companies that sell training to customers. They may come from programming, technical administration, or technical backgrounds, but to succeed as trainers they must have excellent public speaking skills and an outgoing entertainer-like personality. Trainers who start out as salaried employees often branch out and start their own entrepreneurial training operations.

Webmasters design and maintain Web pages. Their work may be graphic design-oriented and involve producing professional layouts and images using tools like PhotoShop and FrontPage or they may be more technically oriented and do the sophisticated programming necessary to create dynamic pages (those that are produced by scripts running on the server) and to interface with databases. Because this career path is so new it is very open to anyone who has the skills to get the job done and there is currently no clear credential for entry, though many webmasters have professional training in graphic arts. Some webmasters also contribute content, which calls for professional writing skills.

All of these job classes except for Business Analysts may also work as entrepreneurial consultants. Webmasters often build very successful entrepreneurial businesses designing and maintaining Web sites. Many trainers start their own training businesses.

These then are the jobs that we'll be discussing in the pages that follow. Now it's time to look at what it takes to get one.

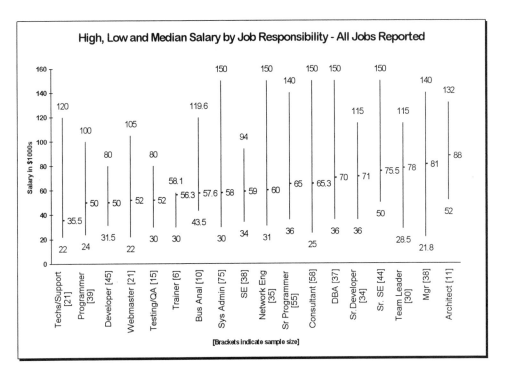

High, Low and Median Salary by Job Responsibility - All Jobs Reported

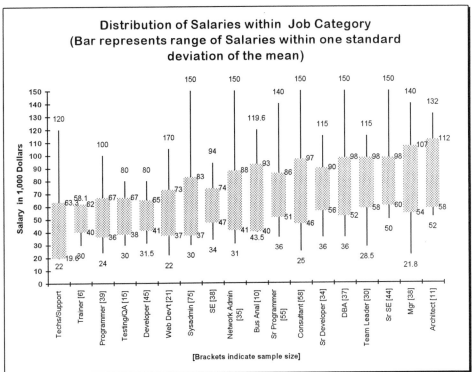

Distribution of Salaries within Job Category
(Bar represents range of Salaries within one standard deviation of the mean)

Source: January 2000 Real Salary Survey Report

CHAPTER 2

How to Break In

If you want to be a doctor, you go to medical school. If you want to be an accountant you get a four-year degree in accounting and then work to pass the CPA exam. Lawyers must go to Law school and pass the state bar exam. These are all professions that have been around for a while, and early in the twentieth century, as competition for jobs in these lucrative fields grew more intense, the people working in them erected stringent qualification procedures to limit the number of people who could compete for these coveted jobs. As a result, no matter how much medicine you know today you will go to jail if you claim to be a physician but haven't passed the necessary exams.

In contrast, the computer professions are relatively new, having evolved only during the past 35 years. Demand for those with computer skills has almost always outstripped the supply, so few barriers have been raised to bar entry to the field, and as a result the rules that govern who can call themselves a computer professional are far more flexible.

Do You Need a Degree?

Most advisors in the academic world or industry will tell you that a four-year computer science degree is a must for anyone who plans a serious computer career. This is not bad advice. In fact, if you can afford to get a Bachelor of Science in Computer Science, or a Bachelors degree in Management Information Science, you'd be well advised to do so. Earning such a degree does not guarantee you a high salaried job five years into your career, but it does make getting your first job far easier than it will be for people who lack this degree.

Four-year computer college degrees come in two major flavors. One, the Bachelors of Science in Computer Science degree (BSCS), tends to be heavier on theory and may require that you take many difficult classes in electronic engineering and higher math to graduate. Once you are working in the field, you may discover that much, if not all, of what you learned in college in this kind of curriculum is only marginally related to the actual work you will do, which often demands a lot more library research and verbal thinking than these math and engineering-heavy curricula do. However, this type of degree is the most prestigious entry-level computer degree and it is the one you will need if you'd like to be considered for the most glamorous jobs right out of college. (Whether you actually would want to be considered for these so-called glamorous jobs straight out of college is another issue entirely, and one that we will discuss in some detail in Chapter 12, "Your Place in the Systems Development Cycle").

Another degree that leads directly to entry-level computer jobs is the Bachelor's degree in either Management Information Science, or Information Technology. You will find both Bachelor of Science and Bachelor of Arts degrees issued in these majors. What these degrees have in common is that they are computer degrees that are conferred by the *business* division of the college rather than by the *engineering* divisions that usually grant the BSCS degrees.

The coursework in these business-oriented computer degree programs is intended to prepare you to work in the IT department of a major corporation rather than in a software development shop devoted to new software product development. These business-related curricula vary greatly in the amount of exposure they will give you to the computer languages, databases, and tools used in industry. However, the required coursework here will probably include more business classes, which are invaluable in preparing you to understand the culture of the work world you are about to enter.

What the Statistics Show about Credentials

The Real Salary Survey data shows that although the majority of those who found their first computer job in 1999 had one of these computer-related four-year college degrees, a significant number did not. Other credentials that entry-level computer professionals with one or less years of experience reported to the Real Salary Survey in 1999 were BS degrees in Math, Chemistry, and Business, and BA degrees in Philosophy, Anthropology, and even English. The Real Salary Survey also received salary reports from a handful of professionals working entry-level salaried computer jobs who reported having no degree at all. Several of these had completed Junior College certificate programs, a few had earned vendor certifications, and a surprising number reported having no recognized credential at all, although, of course, they did have strong self-taught computer skills. The graphs on Page 16 show how starting salaries correlated with credentials for a sample of 73 people with one or less years of experience who submitted salary reports to the Real Rate Survey between April 1, 1999 and April 3, 2000.

As should come as no surprise, the entry-level jobs of people with weak credentials paid lower salaries than those of people with shiny new computer science degrees. But they still paid excellent salaries for people just starting their careers: most paid salaries in the $30,000s. But whatever their starting salaries, these people with weak credentials got their foot in their door. And, as we shall see when we look at how computer careers evolve, by the time they reach the five year point some of the people who have started out at lower salaries in less impressive jobs may outstrip those with far better credentials because they will have made better career decisions at each step of their career.

The reason for this is that in computer work, unlike in most other career paths, your actual value in the marketplace is determined far more by what you can do right now than by what you might have done in the past. Once you are experienced, the employers who are desperate for competent programming and system support help don't care what college you attended or what your grades were. They care only that you can do their job, right now, and that you know the intimate details of the technologies to which they have committed their businesses' future.

To understand this better, let's take a look at the history of salaried computer employment.

A Brief History of the Computer Profession

The history of computer careers over the past half century has been one in which periods of great opportunity alternate with contractions where the barriers to entry get raised. During business downturns jobs become scarce and only with the strongest résumés can find work. But no sooner does this occur than technology seems to make a hairpin turn as it did when PCs hit the market in the early 1980s or when the World Wide Web erupted in the late 1990s. When the technology changes like this, the demand for people who can make use of the new technologies outstrips the number of people with impressive—but in view of the new technology irrelevant—credentials. This allows another influx of brilliant but informally credentialed people to build high-paying computer careers.

Computer-related work first became a significant career path in the late 1960s when American industry responded to the introduction of IBM's 360 and 370 series of mainframe computers—and the persuasiveness of its sales force—by computerizing its most vital functions. First banks and insurance companies committed their businesses to computerized systems. Then manufacturers computerized their accounting, payroll, and inventory systems. As more mainframes were installed, software products were developed that extended their capabilities. The result of this was an insatiable demand for programmers in a world where only a handful of colleges offered computer science courses.

To fill this need, business first turned to the people who had been exposed to the nascent technology in the military. Many of the oldest old-timers you will encounter in the field got their start in programming simply because they had some electronics exposure in the military of the Sixties. If you work with one of these gentlemen you will sooner or later be regaled with tales of the birth of the computer age. Old-timers are still around — and still too young to collect social security — who remember sitting at a system console keying in hexadecimal storage addresses and typing in information about which devices should be allocated to each program and then loading in punched cards containing the program's object code. Though it could take all night to run a single program the systems they used were far less powerful than the scientific calculator now on your desk.

Others who began their computer careers in this early period were technicians who made their living wiring accounting machines, devices halfway between a computer and the older generation of office accounting machinery. "Programming" one of these involved dealing with a Medusa-like tangle of wires which the programmer plugged into different sockets to achieve different effects.

In these early years a large number of programmers began their careers as mainframe computer operators. They started out doing the most menial tasks such as loading and tending printers. Often they had very long hair and short academic histories. If they showed up regularly and demonstrated some competence, their companies trained them for more sophisticated programming jobs.

In the 1960s and 1970s it was often hardware vendors, not universities, who provided the training that was the basis for a programming career. When businesses recruited college students for programming they usually took those with degrees in mathematics and in the process introduced into the business world a generation of women who would otherwise have faced a lifetime of teaching high school math.

At first business programmers drew little attention from the media. While computer engineering majors from schools like MIT commanded what were at the time princely salaries, the programmers working on insurance or billing applications were treated like any other group of technicians. They received modest salaries, many of which remained below $10,000 per year until the later part of the 1970s.

But as the 1970s progressed, the need for programmers became acute, especially for the IT-intensive insurance and banking industries. These companies traditionally paid low wages and could not compete for the small number of college graduates emerging from the few colleges that were teaching computer science. Consequently, these companies looked at their other departments for people they could train as programmers, picking people out of the areas that used the computer systems like accounting and from related areas like technical writing. When these people were insufficient to fill their needs they turned to the larger community, offering anyone who could get a high score on a programmer aptitude test the opportunity to enter an intensive programmer training program.

English majors, rock guitarists, and widows who had been getting by selling real estate answered the call. The training courses were comprehensive and intensive: in some companies the participants were informed that they would have jobs at the end of the course only if they achieved certain grade levels. Many old-timers remember these training courses as times of sheer personal terror. However, if the trainee survived the course, they entered the work force with a solid grounding in programming fundamentals — including more experience with low-level assembly language than many recent college graduates now command. Many of these people are now managers or consultants.

In 1980 the media discovered the programming shortage and publicized the whopping $20,000-a-year salaries being paid to entry-level new hires. Computer programmers were being paid a lot more than people starting out in most other fields. Graduating seniors with Comp. Sci. degrees were quoted as bragging about the companies that would fly them to headquarters, wine and dine them, and make them generous offers even though they were only maintaining C averages in their courses.

Suddenly it seemed as if every college was offering computer science courses. Computer science became a fad and students stood in line for days to register for required courses the way that, in earlier times, they had lined up for tickets to rock concerts.

As the number of people graduating with Computer Science and MIS degrees skyrocketed, companies could afford to become more selective about the qualifications of the programmers they hired. By 1987 an estimated 50,000 graduates were competing for some 25,000 open positions. The situation grew even tougher during the downsizing that took place during the recession of the late 1980s and early 1990s. Companies looking to get rid of "dead wood" fired a lot of live programmers, and "outsourcing" — the use of temporary contract workers rather than salaried employees — became the latest IT management fad.

The waves of downsizing hit computer professionals hard and took much of the glamour out of computer work by the mid-1990s, so college students looking for high paying careers began to major in other subjects. But no sooner had the market contracted like this, than the World Wide Web emerged. Suddenly anyone with $20 a month for Web host rental, a few "Teach Yourself" books, and a brilliant mind could set up a dot.com business. The technology behind Web site design, unlike the software used in the corporate world until then, was simple to understand and used open standards, allowing the Web site developer who had a home computer and a modem to compete on a near-equal basis with developers at the largest corporations.

So once again the world of professional software development was invaded by the talented, the brilliant, the innovative and, most significantly, the very young. The press once again began writing articles about the "programmer shortage" and this time US industry lobbied heavily to get Congress to grant an increase in the number of H-1B "Guest Worker" visas given to college educated foreigners so that they could fill the hundreds of thousands of unfilled jobs they claimed to have.

And so it goes. The majority of salaried computer workers today still work for traditional corporations: banks, manufacturing companies, and service companies of all types. And because these companies continue to be affected by the business cycle, you can expect that the demand for people with computer expertise will continue to rise and fall with that business cycle—until yet another major shift in technology opens the gates, once more, to anyone with talent.

Non-Academic Computer Career Credentials

As it stands today, beyond a four-year degree in Computer Science or MIS, there is still no commonly accepted qualification in data processing that would correspond to the CPA exam or the bar exam.

Over the years there have been many attempts to come up with a non-academic computer credential for working computer professionals. For the past 20 years the Institute for the Certification of Computer Professionals has offered several exam-based certifications open to programmers with five or more years of experience in the field, though these exams never attracted much attention or respect from anyone but the people who held the certification.

In the mid-to-late 1990s, software and hardware venders came up with a second set of credentials, which were much more popular. These credentials focussed on a single vendor's product line and sometimes on only a single product. They included the Novell CNE and CNA, and a whole host of Microsoft credentials, including the MCSE, MCP, and MCSD. The vendors promoted these programs with well-financed advertising campaigns. Each certification required that the applicant pay the vendor hefty fees for study guides and a series of exams also sold by the vendor. These vendor certifications were most attractive to people who lacked the traditional four-year college degrees who saw them as a way to qualify for high paying jobs that were otherwise closed to them.

But all too often people with no professional experience in computer work bought the guides, crammed for the tests, and passed them to earn the certification, without ever having gotten the real-world experience that they would need to do the jobs they were applying for. Because of the one-vendor or one-product concentration of these certifications and because of the lack of real world-experience, their subsequent performance on the job was often spotty since real world hardware and software environments are usually made up of a mix of many different vendors' products. As a result, the value of most of these certifications has become diluted.

In addition, any vendor certification that did prove to lead to higher paying jobs soon suffered from over-exposure as everyone and their best friend rushed to get it in the hopes of improving their salaries.

Our Real Salary Survey data displayed on Page 16 suggest that the credentials that correlate best with well-paid computer work continue to be Computer Science degrees followed by other four-year degrees, with all vendor certifications trailing behind.

Preparing To Get Your First Job

In the following pages we'll look at the steps you'll need to take to prepare yourself to get your first paid programming job depending on what kind of entry-level credential you have.

Four-year CS Degree with Good Grades

If you have a four-year college degree in computer science or one of the many other synonyms such as "information science" or "business data processing," you are a lucky dog. But it will take more than luck to build a good career. You can safely assume that you will get some kind of entry-level programming job. The challenge, however, is to make sure you get the job that will put you in the best position possible for the future you want to build for yourself. This means you need to develop a good understanding of what long-term career possibilities exist for your chosen career path. Furthermore, you need to have insight into your own strengths and weaknesses so that the long term career path you choose for yourself is one that you are temperamentally and intellectually suited for. Finally, you must be able to see through the heady haze of the interview situation and gauge the realities of the jobs that are offered to you. Only then will you be as excited by where you find yourself in your career ten years down the line as you are when you receive your diploma.

If you fall into this category, you must be very careful what programming and database courses you take. It is just as easy to complete coursework in a computer language that is in heavy demand in the workplace as it is in one that appeals to your professor but is used nowhere but in his lab. Unfortunately, all too many Computer Science students do not realize this and waste significant amounts of their valuable college time acquiring expertise in software tools that will do nothing to increase their value to a future employer.

You can easily figure out what software tools are in demand. Read the computer job classifieds. Visit the Real Salary Survey each month and see what skills the people have who are reporting high paying jobs.

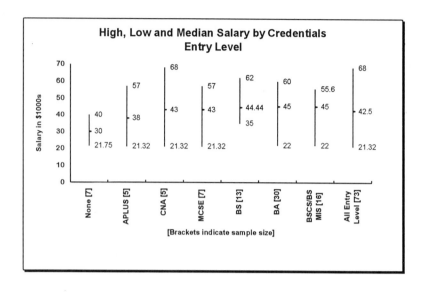

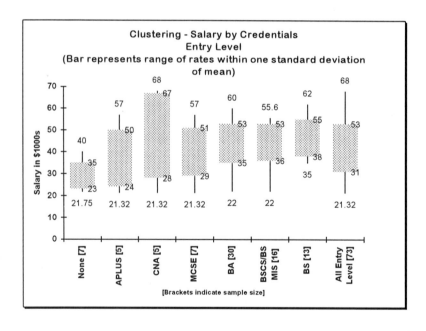

Source: January 2000 Real Salary Survey Report

There's no genius needed here. If you want to be in line for jobs like the ones you see listed, you will need to get experience with the software tools these jobs require—and to work in the same industries that use these kinds of tools.

LISP and Smalltalk may be fascinating from a theoretical standpoint, but be sure that if you master them, you also master the workhorse languages used in industry, like C and C++, and that if possible, you get some experience with a SQL database like Oracle.

Do not expect to get worthwhile career advice from your professors. Few of them are in touch with the needs of the business community. Many professors became computer science teachers because they received degrees in Mathematics during the 1960s and 1970s when the Comp. Sci. department was a branch of the Math department and have read nothing but scholarly journals ever since. Their knowledge of what goes on in the business world tends to be rudimentary and they often express a strange contempt for the work that working computer professionals do on the job, since it is not as interesting to them as their own areas of theoretical research.

You can learn a lot about computers while in college, but you may well have to do a lot of that learning on your own because it is unlikely that your college curriculum, designed by a committee and revised every five or ten years, will have caught up with the technology that is in demand in the workplace now.

Fortunately, it is not hard to get your hands on the software and hardware you need to master these useful computer skills. The chances are you already own a decent computer and have access to the Web. Use your Web access to find the best new books describing the latest development tools as well as the newsgroups and bulletin boards where people discuss the problems they've had with these tools. There will be plenty of other students interested in the same technologies you are, and you can learn from them too. If you get stuck you can probably find someone on your school's staff—perhaps even the people who maintain the school's network, who can help you understand the things you need to know.

Though you might feel that you ought to be learning all the computer technology you need in your classes, this is a serious mistake. Throughout your career you will *always* have to take the initiative to teach yourself the latest software tools if you are to keep your career alive. The person who can jump in and learn something new before it makes its way into curricula and training courses will always be the one who commands the highest salary and the greatest respect.

For four-year degree students the time to start your job search is in your sophomore year, right after you declare your major, because that is the time you should begin looking into summer internship programs. Many companies with large computer installations bring in a great number of college students each summer to work as programmer trainees for periods of two to three months. The work you do in these positions varies. Some trainees do nothing more than run commercial software to generate reports for busy users. But others write programs for new systems, and some do maintenance and enhancements for large production systems. If you do a good job in a summer intern position you are almost certain to be offered a job by the company when you graduate and you are likely to get a better starting salary since you already have a track record within the company.

And this is not all the good news about intern positions. Many companies will hire promising college interns to work on a part-time schedule during the school year. If you are paying your own college costs this can make the difference between living on hot dogs or steak. Furthermore, when you graduate college after having worked for a year under this arrangement you enter the work force as an *experienced* employee, and can demand a corresponding boost in pay anywhere you take a job. Obviously, students who are serious about their future will take advantage of an opportunity like this!

Surprisingly, a great many students don't. I have personally worked alongside college interns filling software development jobs who informed me that they were majoring in other aspects of business and had no interest in pursuing a software development career. They told me that they only took these intern positions to earn money. Where, I wondered, were the Comp. Sci. majors who'd be flocking here next spring to find jobs?

If you plan to try for an intern position you should bring the same discrimination to that job search as you would to the search for a position after graduation, since the intern position can easily turn into one of these. Why waste your energy establishing your reputation in a company you would never want to return to?

Corporate Recruiters at College Interviews

As a four-year student you will probably be hired into your first job as a result of an interview arranged by your college placement office. Typically, corporate recruiters will come to your campus throughout the year to hold interviews. You should start looking at the bulletin boards in the placement office as soon as you know you want a computer-related career in the business world — in fact, even before you decide exactly what kind of computer career you want. Find out what companies regularly interview, and presumably hire, students from your college. You should pay careful attention to their interview announcements, especially what qualifications they require of applicants. You should also pay attention to the kinds of entry-level positions they offer.

Then you should try to talk with older students who have interviewed with these companies. Find out what kinds of questions they were asked and what kinds of jobs they were offered. Talk to people who worked as interns in these companies too. Treat this as the most important research project of your college career, because it is. You will have to stay in your first full time job for at least a year and probably two before you can even think of changing companies. If you don't do this research before you interview, the job you fall into may well represent wasted time you can never get back. Because the most fulfilling careers start off with a job that offers great training coupled with the opportunity to rack up accomplishments, the effort you expend finding the right first job can mean the difference between a lifetime of career satisfaction or burnout in five years.

Once you have chosen the companies you would like to work for, you have only just begun. You have to find the right positions within those companies. This is no simple task. Far too many college students land, almost randomly, in whatever positions recruiters happened to be interviewing for during the week when the student got around to signing up for interviews at the campus placement office. They trust that the same forces that have carried them through high school and college giving them the best of everything because of their good grades and good test scores will give them good jobs. They won't.

Schools are devoted to aiding their students' personal development. Corporations are devoted only to making a profit, and their interest in students is only in how quickly they can contribute to that profit. Recruiters come to college campuses to fill open positions. Some of them are terrific and some of them are dead ends. The recruiters fill them with whomever they find that meets the qualifications set by the hiring managers. To the recruiter there are no "bad jobs." Recruiters hope to fill them all, and they don't save the best ones for the most deserving students.

It is up to you, therefore, to learn to identify what constitutes a "good job". Obviously, and most basically, a "good job" for *you* should be one that leads to the career track you'd like to pursue. This sounds obvious, but a surprising number of people sign up for entry-level jobs that, no matter how well they pay, make it impossible for them to pursue their chosen career paths. Because their goal is merely to fill open positions, not to advance the new hire's career, corporate recruiters will happily place CS graduates who long to be developers in Testing or System Administration entry-level positions that will not give them the programming experience they would need to progress into development jobs. So you will have to be very careful to get all the information you can, not only about any entry-level position that is offered to you, but also about the career paths it will lead to. The second part of this book will provide you with some tools with which to penetrate a recruiter's salesmanship. The most important thing for you to realize now is that you need these tools.

Not All Corporate Recruiters Are Really Recruiters

One word of warning about preliminary interviews you may have with recruiters from out-of-town companies. Many companies will ask management-level people to take an hour or two to interview college students if they happen to be going to another part of the country for business or personal reasons. Often these people will interview people for jobs unrelated to their own fields of expertise. Their job, as far as I can tell, is to make sure that the applicant has a nice suit and can speak English. When their trip is done they relay résumés and brief reports to corporate recruiting offices that take it from there.

If you end up having an interview with one of these, do your best to make a good impression but don't take too seriously anything they might say, positive or negative. When I applied to IBM for my first job in 1980, I had interviews with two IBM managers who were visiting children at a local university. The first manager who came from IBM's Burlington, Vermont, plant took one look at my résumé, grunted that he couldn't imagine a single job at Burlington that I would be qualified for, and spent the rest of the interview complaining to me that the salt on the Vermont roads was destroying his car. The second manager was from Poughkeepsie. He declared that he was very impressed by my humanities background and that several of his best people had backgrounds very like mine. He even asked me to give him a call when I came to Poughkeepsie for a follow up interview so I could meet his wife, since he thought we had a lot in common.

Did I ever get to Poughkeepsie? Only on visits from Burlington where I was subsequently hired. I never even got a Poughkeepsie interview! It turned out that the man with the rusty car was an engineering manager whose job never brought him into contact with the plant's business programmers. Nevertheless, when Human Resources (HR) received the engineer's report they realized that I had business programming skills that another department needed and immediately flew me up for three business programming interviews.

First Jobs for Students with Weak Credentials

If you have only a two-year degree or if you have a four-year degree with a poor grade point average you will have a harder time breaking into salaried computer work. Certain companies simply will not interview you. Even if you do get hired you can expect to be brought in at a considerably lower salary than a four-year grad with a 4.0 GPA. However, if you are realistic and do some research you can get a job that offers you training and future prospects that are just as good as those received by the top ten percent. Indeed, after a few years on the job you may find that you are making the same—or better—salaries than they are.

You chance of getting hired with a weaker academic record hinge greatly on the economic strength of your local economy. If things are booming and people are earning $9.00 per hour flipping burgers at fast food restaurants, the chances are good that your area will have a lot of unfilled computer jobs. In that case, some companies will also be sending out recruiters to interview students at junior colleges. They will probably be from local banks and insurance companies which run yearly training classes in the summer, but you will also see people from local manufacturing firms who have had good experiences hiring people from your school. In a strong market, four-year students with "ho-hum" résumés may also get quality interviews.

However, with weak credentials you cannot afford to be too picky about your first job. If you have a choice between two jobs, evaluate them using the criteria given in the second part of this book, but be reasonable! The time for you to concentrate on getting the perfect job will be in a year or two when you have some experience and no one will be paying attention to your college record. However, though you must be flexible, you must still be very careful to hold out for a job that leads to the career path you are interested in. If you want a software development job, make sure the job you are offered is not a glorified clerical job or one involving a "computer" technology that is used nowhere but in the single company that hires you.

If your local economy is not in great shape you have several alternatives. You can move to a part of the country where conditions are better or you can stay in your current geographical area and be extremely persistent. If you do the latter, plan to spend six months on your job hunt, expect to encounter a lot of rejection, and interview for any entry-level computer job you can get.

Do not go to employment agencies. Respectable recruiters will tell you flat out that legitimate IT placement firms only place people with previous paid experience. The profiteering agencies that prey on people with poor—or no—credentials may make you pay a hefty placement fee. This fee can be $10,000 or more. In return for this fee the agency will send you out to interviews that you could have found for yourself if you had done a very small amount of research. Most likely they will try to talk you into taking a job in an entirely different career area where they have an opening. One friend of mine, straight out of college and desperate for a job, asked an employment agency to find him a job as a programmer or computer operator only to be sent on an interview for a job as a machine tool operator!

What you have working in your favor in a bad market is this: the majority of people who went to school with you and have the same credentials as you will give up fairly quickly. You will be competing with a crowd of job hunters in the spring, but by August or September many people will either have found jobs or have stopped looking. If you have been making regular phone calls to local IT managers and recruiting departments, by now they know who you are and may even be impressed by your persistence. (By regular I mean once a month, calling more frequently may be considered a nuisance!) Sometimes they will interview you for an open position you otherwise wouldn't get to see just to get you off their backs. Most won't of course, but it only takes one.

As an illustration of what you might have to go through, consider the experience of a friend of mine who graduated from a two-year college in the Dallas area just as the Dallas economy was sinking into a deep depression in the early 1980s. That year not a single employer held interviews at his school. The local banks that had traditionally hired people at his level canceled their annual training programs because they were cutting back staff. Undaunted, this young man went to the public library and compiled a list of 204 companies in the area large enough to possibly have an IT department. He then began calling every single one and asking to speak to an IT manager.

This calling resulted in his getting three interviews over a period of five months. One interview was with a manager who had no open positions. One interview actually resulted in a job offer that was withdrawn two days later because the manager who made the offer did not realize that his company would not hire anyone who did not have a four-year degree.

Things were looking pretty bleak for my friend. Four months had passed and he had not even been able to find a job as a computer operator, when a follow-up call to a friendly HR department secretary who had previously remarked that a trainee class would be forming sometime in the future revealed that the class was indeed being formed—but that HR had already selected the people to be interviewed for these new job openings. This intrepid soul reminded the secretary of the many calls he had made, which he documented with the date he had made them and what he had been told each time. As a result, he was grudgingly allowed to join the interviewees for the training class and given a grueling exam, which he passed with flying colors. This time he got the job!

There is more to this story though. A mere ten months after completing this miserable job search, this programmer, who had even been rejected for entry-level jobs tearing printouts off of printers, was recruited by an out-of-town recruiting firm for a programming position in another part of the country. He got paid relocation to the tune of almost $10,000 and a hefty raise in his new job. Why? Because he was now considered to be an *experienced* programmer—and the same managers who would not look at new graduates with indifferent credentials were desperate to hire anyone with paid experience.

This tale may seem a bit extreme, but I know of an ex-typist and an ex-waitress with no qualifications beyond a lot of spunk and a six month certificate program at a for-profit business school who have used similar strategies to break into programming and who are now well on the way to having good careers. Their secret, too, was to be persistent. Each spent about five months pursuing an entry-level job.

When You Have No Academic Credentials at All

The days are long gone when a person with only a high-school degree and an interest in computers could expect to be trained in software development or systems administration by a large corporation. The only way open now to such an individual is a long and increasingly chancy one. If you can manage to get hired into an entry-level help desk job or as a maintenance technician you may, some three or four-years down the line, be sent to the company's in-house programmer training course (though these courses are now rare), or you may be able to finance a degree in Computer Science using the company-supplied education benefit.

However, because so many two-year schools now graduate people with certificates or degrees in IT you will have to compete with them for these poorly paid entry-level positions. Even if you manage to make it into a programming department, you will probably enter with a job title and job class that indicates your lowly origins. This will likely be accompanied by a pathetic salary. Typically you will have a technician job class and there will be several promotions to pass through before you reach the professional job class that the college graduates begin at. This is true even if you are doing the same work that they are.

If you are considering this path, or if you have already started out on it, your best bet is to take courses at your local college or junior college and to plan on finding a new employer as soon as you have attained the degree you need to have to be taken seriously as a college new-hire.

Another difficult career path leads up to programming or systems administration from clerical positions. Many women in traditional "pink collar ghettos" begin working with word processing and database applications in their administrative assistant jobs and discover they have a real knack for working with computers. When they express an interest in pursuing a computer-related career path, managers move them into low status technician-grade jobs in which the worker's prime responsibility is usually to copy files, fill in forms, and update documentation, both on paper and on-line. These are jobs in which they work very hard, since IT departments usually have enormous amounts of this kind of administrative work to be done, but one in which the worker retains a clerical job class and salary. These jobs may, over a very long period of time, lead to becoming a real programmer or administrator but only after years of drudge work that adds nothing to your technical skills. If you develop an interest in computer work and are currently working in a clerical job, do the smart thing: get yourself some college training so that you can qualify for the real entry-level computer jobs.

When You are a "Retread"

"Retreads" is the term I use for people who have good credentials and work experience in some other field entirely unrelated to computer programming. I'm a retread myself. In the past many retreads were school teachers searching for better incomes and trained musicians glad to earn any income at all who were recruited when management found out that studies showed that many musicians had high aptitude for programming.

Nowadays, many retreads are people with degrees in the hard sciences as well as hardware engineers for whom there is no longer any work in the hardware area. Years ago, it was easier for people with backgrounds like these to break into computer jobs and there are still many of them currently working in the industry, but prospective retreads must now compete for entry-level positions both with college computer science graduates both from the United States and from other countries.

If you are a retread and you already have a four-year college degree you can adopt a different job hunt strategy than a person who doesn't, no matter what your degree was in. But your chances of finding work have a lot to do with the strength of your local economy. Job hunting strategies that may work very well in one part of the country where the demand for intelligent programmers is strong will fail miserably in another where demand is weaker.

If you are a retread, you need to determine what minimum credential you must add to your existing degrees and accomplishments to get you into an interview. In some areas attending a junior college and getting an Associate degree in Computer Science will be enough to qualify you for interviews. In others attending a six month training course that results in your getting a recognized vendor certification can give you enough training, coupled with your current four-year degree in something else, to get you started. However, in other parts of the country either of these strategies would be a waste of time.

Before you invest in expensive retraining, talk to HR department recruiters and to managers at local companies and ask them directly what kind of credential they would have to see added to your résumé in order to give you an interview. Talk to people at several companies and pay attention to what they say. When I started looking into what I'd need to do to make the transition to programming, at a time when my sole credential was a Masters Degree in American History, recruiters at the largest insurance company in the city where I lived told me they would recommend that I attend the local state-run two-year technical college and get an Associate degree there because their experience was that the technical college graduates got better, more practical, hands-on training than the graduates of the expensive four-year college I had been considering. My two-year degree cost me a mere $75 per quarter and led directly to a software development job with IBM.

When you talk to people in a position to hire you, you'll find that there is great variation in what credentials impress people in the different regions of the country. When I lived and worked in Dallas, programmers treated training from a trade school called CPI as a joke, classing it with the radio broadcasting and modeling schools that advertise on matchbooks. When I later moved to Hartford, a city with a disproportionate number of programmers in its population because of the IT-intensive nature of the insurance industry, I was astonished to find that a great number of the programmers I worked with, especially those with degrees in other fields, had gotten their training at CPI. You will have to do some research to determine what credential will impress people in a position to hire you in your area.

When You Have No Credentials but Hot Skills

What if you have no academic credential at all and no paid computer work experience but believe that you do have the skills it would take to hold a computer job? In this case, one successful approach might be to put together a demo of your work and use it to convince hiring managers that you have the skills they need. This is most easily accomplished if you are looking for a position doing something like hardware repair, Web site design, or software development on stand-alone computers — or anything else where you can realistically expect to achieve a professional level of work working only on your home system.

You will have to make the initial contacts yourself, as reputable agencies won't usually represent someone who does not have paid experience. But if you have friends who are working in software development environments who know and respect your work, let them know you are looking for a job and ask them to recommend you to their boss so that you get invited to that vital interview.

Before you do this, put some time into making sure that you really do have the skills that the employer would need. Read ads and talk to people who work in the field to find out what set of skills are needed for the kind of entry level job you'd like. For example, if you design Web sites, reading job ads will make it clear that you will need solid skills in either PhotoShop and graphic design or Java programming to qualify for most salaried Web-related jobs. Just knowing how to write HTML pages will probably not be enough to get a job.

When hunting for work on your own there's little point in approaching large corporate employers. They are deluged with applications, so résumés that show no previous paid experience are usually screened out by their HR departments. With good skills and weak credentials you will be much more likely to find a starting position with a smaller company that doesn't have a formal HR department and rigorous HR guidelines. This is the kind of company where you may be able to show off your demo to a manager or impress someone in a position to hire you with what it is that you can do. If you pursue this kind of job hunt, you should also expect to start out at a relatively low salary, no matter what your skills.

Another way to make businesspeople aware of your technical ability is to do volunteer work for civic groups like your Chamber of Commerce, Church, or local Survival Center. This is a great way to meet local business leaders and gives you an opportunity to demonstrate your skills in action rather than just talk about them.

If you have excellent computer skills and no credentials, you may do better taking an entrepreneurial approach to your career. Develop a software application and see if you can sell it as shareware. Offer to develop Web sites or software for small businesses that can't afford the high rates of experienced consultants. I know one woman who without even a High School degree mastered Web site design and built up a flourishing Web site design company that now has enough work to employ three other people.

But keep in mind that no matter what salary you start out at, once you have that essential year or two of paid experience—assuming that your experience involves the use of technologies that are in demand in the marketplace—you will be able to apply for many more jobs, and will find it a lot easier to get interviews.

Do What You Love or Expect to Crash and Burn

Whatever your background or credentials, in the long run there is one final factor that really determines whether you will be able to break into and succeed in a computer job. It is this: Do you love to work with computers? Do you, deep down, find that learning the ins and outs of software programs and debugging them is fun?

I worked with one woman who had a master's degree in advanced mathematics who washed out of programming in two years in spite of an impressive college record. The reason was simple. She hated debugging. When the system she was working on bombed it offended her. She had trouble dealing with disorder, which is the state in which most computer systems exist most of the time. So when a non-programming low-level administrative job offered itself she fled into it without a look back.

There is a lot more of this kind of burnout happening now in the computer field as young people rush into it attracted by the lure of big bucks, instead of a love the work. I worry about high-school students who are pushed toward computers by parents fearful for their economic futures. Many of them would be happier—and more successful—doing other things.

The people who succeed at computer work as a long-term career are the people who love to code and debug, who must hook up the latest device to their own computers no matter what it costs just to see what it does. They are the people who find computer software so interesting that they browse manuals at lunchtime. These people will have to choose their jobs wisely and learn how to function in a business environment dominated by businesspeople whose characteristics are very different from their own. But with good planning and by following the principles set out in this book, people like this can find themselves in the enviable position of doing something they love, and doing it well, while earning the hefty financial and personal rewards that computer work can bring.

CHAPTER 3

Your First Job

A great number of computer science graduates are shocked to discover what it is that "real" computer professionals do all day. This is largely because most college computer science curriculums have been developed by people who have little or no experience using computers in the business world. Because people with Ph.D.s in computer science whose areas of expertise are of interest to businesses can earn so much more working in industry, college curricula are often designed by professors whose focus is on theoretical subjects of limited relevance outside of the academe. The curricula they design reflect their theoretical bent, with heavy emphasis on subjects like database theory or operating system and compiler design.

While courses in which they write their own compilers or operating systems give students a grasp of the underlying structure of the software they will be working with and may be intellectually stimulating, they bear little relationship to what it is that most computer professionals are paid to do in the real world. Unless you go to work for one of a handful of vendor firms it is very unlikely that you will ever write a compiler or an operating system. Business needs computer systems that are easily learned and easily maintained and that means that the vast majority of the companies that hire computer professionals use off-the-shelf operating systems and compilers that they buy from well-known vendors with a history of good product support.

Experienced computer professionals know that when companies do attempt to develop their own systems software, the result is often a nightmare: a poorly documented system where all too often the vital facts needed for ongoing maintenance are stored in the brain of the one or two geniuses who cooked it up. Homemade system software does exist in the IT world, but, as we will discuss later, becoming involved with it can spell real career suicide for the student just out of college.

Business programmers do design databases, but only after having achieved many years of on-the-job training. Again, to ensure that they can be maintained, the databases they design are usually built using off-the-shelf vendor database management systems packages. The theoretical discussions of database design courses bear little relationship to the task before a business database designer. Their task is rarely to design an index structure from scratch. Instead they must take an existing vendor database management system, whose quirks they have already mastered, and use their exhaustive knowledge of the applications that will use their database to organize their data efficiently. The most valuable asset a real-world database designer brings to the job is their experience with other real-world systems, especially the disasters and embarrassments they experienced with them. "Data Integrity" and "Performance" are not just words underlined in a textbook to the experienced programmer who has faced an irate customer whose entire day of transactions has disappeared, or the systems analyst faced with a "daily cycle" that takes two days to complete!

This means there is very little likelihood that the student coming out of college will do most of the things they learned how to do in school. As a new hire, they will not analyze and design major systems. If you are told in an interview that you will be designing major systems software or that you will be designing a database system from scratch you can assume that either you are being lied to in order to attract you to an otherwise awful job or that you are dealing with lunatics.

What you should hope to find yourself doing on your first job(s) in the corporate environment is watching real, as opposed to theoretical, computer systems in action. What you can expect to be given to do are small, clearly defined tasks that will give you the opportunity to wallow in existing programs, slog through manuals, and slowly put together the picture of a large complex business computer system.

Reading Code

In college you learned how to write programs. But when you begin your career as a software developer you are going to have to learn to do something much harder: You are going to learn how to read programs written by other people. It is this skill above all others that will set you apart from your coworkers, because the person who can read and understand existing code is the person who can make changes that don't crash production systems and the person who can read other people's code is the one who gets the reputation for competence, which is the key to all subsequent career moves.

You may be lucky. The system you begin on may have been written in the last five years by enlightened disciples of the latest software development methodologies supported by a management that demanded they take the time to get it right. In that case reading the code that makes up your system will simply be a question of paging through the listings and following the program logic.

If, on the other hand, you start working on a more typical system, what you will find will be quite different.

In this case your normal reaction after your first encounter with production code will probably be fear. The chances are that the stuff you are looking at was written ten years ago by someone who was showing off and who was proud of the fact that no one but themselves could figure out what they were doing. I once had to work with some code where the explanatory comments were written in Italian—in Vermont! I have also seen a program in which the field named "FOUR" was assigned the value "3" somewhere in the program execution logic. Imagine what this does to the simple COBOL statement "ADD FOUR TO COUNT1."

And this is only the beginning. The chances are that the original program has been changed fifteen or twenty times since it was written by people who made no notes anywhere explaining what the changes were supposed to accomplish. If there are comments, they will usually be so cryptic as to be useless anyway. Why, you wonder, in there a special subroutine to execute if the customer number is 43211706? This, dear neophyte, is called hardcoding, and it is what desperate programmers do late at night when a job keeps blowing off at a specific customer record and the programmer can't figure out why. They put in code to ignore the problem record and the program (maybe) continues. But what about this, why is there a special routine that only gets executed in April of a leap year? Good question, and one that you can ignore only if you don't have to make a change that involves that routine!

If you have been thinking of yourself as a "supertechie" programmer, your first brush with real code can be unnerving. The listing is over an inch thick, not a few pages like the ones you wrote in school. The clever shortcuts that were such fun to use when you were writing your own code are incomprehensible when you find them in someone else's. Suddenly you realize that the programmer who eliminated a few lines of typing for themselves has added hours of puzzling for everyone else who will ever have to maintain their code.

There is no shortcut in these cases. You cannot leaf through this stuff and get the gist of it. What you have to do—and this is true for the old-timer as well as the neophyte—is read every single line slowly, jot down all the field values as they get changed, and follow every single subroutine call. And then, slowly, the code will begin to make sense.

This is far from what most new programmers imagine themselves doing at work. It has no glamour to it at all. It is not elegant. But by humbly immersing yourself in the programs that make up the system you have been assigned to, you prepare yourself to walk on water at some future time. Your attention to a detail will bear fruit when you are the only one able to find the solution to some showstopper of a system failure that has stumped your boss. Then you begin to emerge from the crowd.

Magical Manuals

Wedged on a shelf somewhere in your department are some thirty or forty books and manuals, perhaps in institutional metal holders. Chances are they are covered with dust because no one has looked at them in ages. I hope you are not allergic to dust, because if you are serious about your career, the minute you get a free moment you are going to go over to that rack and start reading through every manual you can find that describes a software product you have access to.

A lot of computer professionals waste a lot of time waiting to be sent to courses for things they could learn by reading the manuals that are sitting on a neighbor's desk. Most people don't mind if you borrow their books as long as you return them. So if you see something interesting, borrow it!

And don't be put off if the manual for something you really would like to learn seems incomprehensible and assumes that you know things you don't. Often if you just keep reading you will find paragraphs later on in the same book that illuminate what stumped you earlier. It is not that you are stupid; the books are badly written.

After some time spent soaking up all this random information a funny thing will happen. People will start to come and ask you questions when they get stuck. You won't know the answer right off, but you will have some vague memory of having seen something somewhere that might be useful and you will root around in your pile of books until you come up with the little fact about your software that offers a solution—a solution that the person asking the question could have looked up just as well as you did, but didn't. Pretty soon the word will get out that you know everything. You don't, of course, but you do know how to find things out. Many people never get this far. Once you begin to build up this kind of "guru" reputation you are really on your way!

Avoid Beginners' Mistakes

There are a couple of behaviors that scream out "newbie!" It is natural that you will display some of them, after all you *are* a newbie! But with some foresight you can prevent yourself from making the more flagrant errors that new people are prone to.

In almost every case these errors come from a new person's lack of appreciation of the complexity of the environment that they have entered. Often, too, they occur because the new person, fresh from school, is used to working as a lone individual and not as part of a team and they are not used to thinking about what effect their actions will have on the many other people who are working on the same system as they are.

It is this unawareness that leads new people to edit system files shared by many other programmers and forget to mention it or leads them to move their own untested modules into the department's test system, again without mentioning it. In many "test" environments there are programs that are shared by all programmers currently doing testing—programs that may be considered "test" programs because they are not the actual production programs run to do the company's business but which twenty or thirty programmers use to enable them to build a framework in which to do further testing. If you mess with one of these debugged "test" programs you can easily ruin many other programmers' entire day of testing. Move your own .dll file onto the test server, and Windows starts crashing on everyone's machines. Change a batch module shared by several applications and reports from final "parallel" test runs, which are supposed to have perfect output, can show up with junk all over them. Worse, the programmers who unwittingly use your modification of a testing module often waste a lot of time debugging your code, thinking that the errors they see are coming from their own changes not yours.

Take the time to have your test environment explained to you in detail and when you are in any doubt about whether you can modify something—ASK! Attempting to appear smart by not asking "dumb questions" usually just results in you doing something far dumber— screwing things up for your coworkers.

Another typical mistake that new programmers make is to write tricky code that cannot be understood by ordinary mortals. Seeing an opportunity to use something they picked up in school, they use a little-known technique (the more devious the better) that a teacher or, more likely, a lab assistant showed them. This devious solution solves an immediate problem, and the person rushes it into production without writing an explanation of what they did because they know that they did a great job and assume that no one will ever have to fix their code. Two years later something changes in the system and their tricky code ceases to work. Perhaps they used some undocumented feature that no longer works under the latest release of the operating system. Perhaps they "faked out the system" by doing something tricky to a system control block somewhere that the vendor just changed. Whatever the reason, such displays of brilliance always result in time wasting and frustrating work for other people.

No matter how smart you are, the code you write will always need work someday. Write it so the dumbest person in the world can understand what you did. Believe me, the worst possible experience is having to give an immediate lifesaving fix to tricky code that you simply can't follow, and then realizing that you wrote it yourself a few years back!

There is another common mistake made by brash young program-mers. They comment loudly on the deficiencies of the old software they have been given to maintain. "Look at this!" they crow. "The documen-tation stinks! Talk about spaghetti logic! I could have written this whole routine in six lines! Who wrote this garbage?"

The answer, all too often, is "the current boss." This is especially prone to happen when the new programmer doesn't recognize the boss's maiden name.

Even if the author is not in a position to slow down your career there is never any excuse for insulting the people with whom you work. But beyond that there are often very good reasons behind the writing of what looks like "bad" code. The code in question may have been written in response to hardware or software limitations that have been remedied in intervening years. The code may have been developed before stan-dards that are now commonly taught to all fledgling programmers were even thought of. After all, those standards only could develop after a large enough body of work had been developed and maintained that the need for the standards became apparent.

Finally, the code you are looking at might have been gorgeous when it was first developed but since then has been subjected to a host of en-hancements and fixes applied by harried maintenance programmers who preferred to remain anonymous. The developer whose name is in the documentation at the head of the program is often the only person whose name can be found, even though only slight vestiges of their actual work remain.

The wise programmer will therefore keep their exclamations of dis-gust to themselves and share them only with members of their immedi-ate family. You can be sure that a certain percentage of the code you are writing right now will embarrass you in years to come.

Sometimes our brash programmer doesn't stop at just commenting about old code either. They take it upon themselves to improve it—with-out consulting their boss first. They lavish time on rewriting routines that already work in order to make them more efficient. Since their own sala-ried time is usually worth a whole lot more to the company than the nanoseconds they save, this kind of behavior marks our new program-mer in the eyes of management as someone who is not yet aware of the rules of the business game. Even worse, when improving the program's efficiency our new programmer all too often fails to grasp some obscure function the sloppy code was performing so that the software, at some future time, fails.

Another set of problems occurs because new programmers fail to understand the sanctity that surrounds the company's production sys-tems and the elaborate safeguards that must protect them. Most places have a test environment that consists of libraries and files the programmers can pretty much do what they want with, and a production system that does the company's actual work.

Production is a very big deal. In a factory where each day the line turns out half a million dollars' worth of product, stopping that line for half an hour costs the company over $10,000—or as much as the entry level programmer's salary for three months! If an on-line system that processes customer orders stops processing them for more than a few minutes, hundreds of employees are suddenly being paid to sit around and shoot the bull—and a vice-president is going to want to know why.

Because of the importance of production systems most installations have rigid procedures in place to ensure that any new versions of programs that are moved into production are thoroughly tested. Unfortunately, new programmers often don't understand the need for these procedures and see them only as obstacles keeping them from making their target dates. The rigmarole involved in moving stuff into production *is* irritating. It involves collecting signatures and filling in forms. It is only after a programmer has been called in at two in the morning because the module with their latest change in it halted a production system that many programmers develop a healthy respect for the testing process—especially since it is always some stupid, niggling detail that was forgotten while making a tiny fix that causes the system failure.

Experienced programmers have learned that there is no such thing as a "minor" change. Something as minor as going in at the last moment and changing a comment can cause a program to bomb. Experienced programmers get serious about testing—paranoid even, and are never in a hurry to move anything into production. They would much rather fix problems known to no one but themselves at their workstation in the morning than be called in late at night to fix something that will be reported to the boss.

Who Is the Boss?

On the day you begin your first job, the person who hired you will introduce you to someone they identify as your team leader or maybe your manager. The terms may differ, but their function does not. This person, and no other, is in direct control of your career.

It is very important to understand the team leader's role. Learning the business realities of the environment you have stumbled into is as important as learning all the technical details that go into making you a technical expert. In fact, a cynical person would probably say that if you master the details of maneuvering in the business environment you can probably slack off as regards the technical stuff and still get promoted before anyone else in your trainee group. They might be right.

Businesses are usually organized in a hierarchical fashion with each person reporting to a single superior. Your team leader therefore is the only person who has authority over you. They will be the person who assigns and evaluates your work. They will tell you what specifically they expect you to accomplish and assign deadlines for your work. You will report any accomplishments to them and at the end of a predefined period they will conduct some sort of appraisal, formal or informal, and report its result to their boss. If they say that you are doing a great job the word will be passed on and you may get a raise or a promotion. If they say you stink, nothing you can do or say can undo the damage, no matter how much respect your coworkers have for you.

Obviously your relationship with this individual is of prime importance to your career. If you find yourself in an ambiguous situation, which occurs sometimes, and are not sure who really is your boss, do whatever you possibly can to get a clear answer. I have seen a situation where a person was told to take technical guidance from a so-called "team leader" but was informed that another, less-visible person would be in charge of administrative details, such as vacation time. When the "team leader" got into a clash with the administrative person the programmer did what the "team leader" wanted, only to discover too late that the administrative person was not only their real boss but was preparing to fire them for doing what the team leader, not the administrator, had suggested.

Your boss may be the nicest person in the world, eat lunch with you, and dance around at company parties with a lampshade on his head. Don't drop your guard. Your boss is not your buddy and the main thrust of your relationship with any supervisor must be doing what it takes to receive the highest possible rating from them at appraisal time.

The irony for you in this situation is that the person with this kind of power over you is actually situated at the very lowest administrative level in the management hierarchy. They are not very important in the business scheme of things, even though they are of great importance to you.

To understand this, take a look at the sample organization chart you'll find on the next page. Managers use charts like this to represent their view of the company. Organization charts depict the flow of authority from the top of the organization downward. In the example given, E. Henderson is a programmer working under team leader J. Shmoe on a development team designing, testing, and coding a Widget On-Line Inquiry System. Note how many levels of management separate the team leader from the three highest levels of the corporation, which are the executive levels where most important decision making occurs. Note that on this chart the programmers are the end of the line. Their names don't even appear on the chart in boxes. This is true no matter what their technical level or their salary. In actual practice the names of the programmers in the various departments would not appear at all on the organization charts used by upper management. These names appear only on the charts distributed to technical staffers after a departmental reorganization. You should be sure to get a copy of the organization chart mapping your department and familiarize yourself with your company's management's view of how you fit in.

The team leader who is your direct superior is usually a person who used to have a job like yours who has recently taken the first step toward a management career. They have just moved from a position where their technical skills were of the most importance to one where they are expected to demonstrate leadership and organization ability.

Unfortunately for you, people vary widely in the facility with which they can make this shift. Your team leader may be able to select just the tasks to help you develop your own systems knowledge and make the maximum contribution to the work at hand. Or they may have real difficulty delegating work and may simply try to do, themselves, the work they are supposed to give to you.

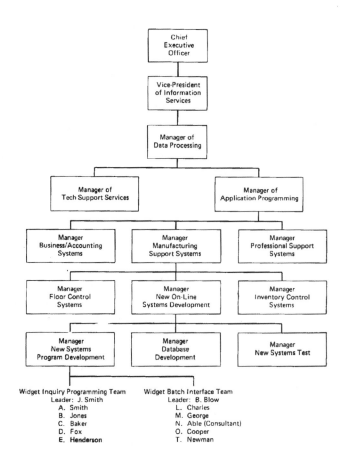

In the worst case a team leader may go so far as to mark on the program listing the very line where a change should be made and write out what the change should be. In a case like this you need to control your emotions and do the best job you possibly can. Your task here is to assure an insecure team leader that you won't totally screw things up for them if they give you some responsibility.

If you have been exclusively a supertechie in college you owe it to yourself now to do some hurry-up reading about management. You need to understand what it is that the people who are in charge of you think they are doing. As you will find out, there is a complex ritual going on around you in the business world, and if you intend to have anything approaching a career you must understand it, no matter how foolish or irrelevant it appears to be. The penalty for ignoring it is career stagnation.

We will talk about management again in the next chapter, but when you are a new hire the most important thing you need to understand about management is that your team leader is your intersection with the company, and your only one.

You will further your career inestimably if, when you encounter problems with your team leader you do *not* do any of the following:

♦ Ignore what they told you to do because it is stupid and do what you think is the correct thing instead

♦ Go to their manager and complain about their behavior

♦ Announce loudly at the lunch table what a turkey they are

In the business world the basic ground rule is that you relate only to your immediate supervisor. You should violate this rule only if you are so desperate that you are prepared to quit.

If you have problems with your team leader there are several things you can do. If the problem is not something major you can sometimes wait it out. Businesses often reorganize and you might find yourself with a new, easier-to-deal-with team leader in a few weeks. If any rumors of change are in the air, wait and see what happens.

If you are really stuck, you should take refuge in memos. Write to your team leader documenting what it is that they have told you to do and then document that you have done it. Make suggestions, politely, in print. Always approach your memo writing in the most positive tone possible—you don't want to be seen as a troublemaker, but you do want to make sure that in case of a conflict you have a paper trail that demonstrates the correctness of your actions or makes it clear that you did whatever you did at their direction despite your better judgement. If you confront a team leader in a polite way with this kind of evidence sometimes you can head off trouble.

If you are not getting enough responsibility, be aggressive in pointing out the good work you have done and present the team leader with a memo stating what you would like to be given for your next assignment. Give them a couple of choices so that they have to give you something you want. Most of all, understand that if you are having problems with them it is often because they are having a hard time doing their job and are probably very anxious. Try to present yourself as someone helping them achieve departmental goals, not as someone just looking out for themselves and you might be able to turn the situation around.

Learn from Old-Timers

Another very important thing that you should do in your first year on the job is get to know as many people as you can. By this I don't mean socially, although that is always nice. What I mean is that you should learn what it is that the people around you know. You will never be able to know everything about an applications system, the software environment, or a company's business. What you can do is figure out who you can ask about what.

Universally you will find when you enter a new company, that certain people will present themselves to you as the experts. Universally too, you will also discover that most of these loudmouths are the very last people to go to when you have real problems to solve.

You must identify who it is in the systems area that really understands the business part of your application. This person can tell you which individual to go to in the user group when you need a business issue clarified. Next, find the person who is the Walking Manual—the person who knows all the little-known features of the software your company has installed. Then find the "oldest living programmer." This is the person who was there twenty years ago—or perhaps, if you're in Silicon Valley, one year ago—when the very first program was written, who knows the complete history of the system. Often they can explain the seemingly unbelievably stupid things in your system by telling you the political situations that swirled around a project's developmental phase.

Be friendly, humble and nonexploitative to these people. If you treat them as valued resources and bother them only when you really cannot find an answer on your own you will be able to get answers in tricky situations that stymie other programmers, because you will know who to go to for help.

Be Careful Who You Hang Out With

Another rule-of-thumb to keep in mind when you enter a new environment is that it's a good idea to avoid associating yourself with any particular group of people when you enter a new job situation. You simply cannot tell until you have been in a company for awhile what is going on all around you. Eat lunch with different groups of people every day until you have a clearer picture of what is going on. If you identify yourself too strongly with any one group you may later discover that you have unwittingly taken some kind of political position in your department that could limit your career growth.

Do all this, and your first year should be an exciting worthwhile time. By its end you should feel confident in dealing with the technical details of your environment and you should have begun to see the business issues you will have to confront as your career develops. You probably will have changed a few of your original ideas about what you would enjoy doing in the business world, and it is likely that you will have several future possibilities roughed out for career development. If you are lucky you will even have been able to pull off some technical feat that has given you a local reputation, and managers will soon be striving to get you on their teams because of what a good worker you are. Now it's time to look at the divergent career pathways that will begin to open up for you at the end of your first year on the job.

CHAPTER 4

Corporate Career Paths

In this chapter we will look at the career paths experienced people can choose from and examine both their perils and possibilities—paying particular attention to the challenge of staying technical in a business-ruled world.

By the end of your first year of working as a salaried computer professional you should have begun to figure out the rudiments of what is going on around you. You will have gotten your bearings and perhaps begun to make a name for yourself. Now it is time to start thinking about which of the many different IT career paths available to you would give you the most pleasure. The sooner you do this the better. Unfortunately, those who do not actively plan their career paths will have career paths foisted on them—career paths that rarely serve their own best interests.

That is because, in computer work unlike most other professional careers, the forces of specialization kick in within weeks after you take your first job. A doctor may try out four or five specialties during the internship year before declaring for a specific specialty. A CPA may specialize in an entirely different branch of accounting than the one they encountered in a first job. But potential employers begin to treat a computer professional as a certain kind of specialist based on the work they do in their very first year or two of salaried employment, and with every passing week it gets harder and harder for computer professionals to redefine themselves away from that specialization. So it is vital that as soon as you have gotten your bearings on your very first job you start deciding what direction you want your career to take and what kind of specialist you really want to be. Then, when that decision is made, you will have to take active and aggressive steps to ensure that you steer your career in that direction.

A SUCCESSFUL ATTITUDE

"Change the mental attitude from 'work for this employer' to 'work for yourself with the employer as your main customer.'

"It sounds cliché in these times, but it's so true. It's just a mental adjustment, and from that, one's total outlook (as well as job performance) goes to the better."

Don't Let Management Plan Your Career!

The most dangerous illusion that people working in large organizations fall into is the belief that, if they work hard and do a good job with what they have been assigned to do, the company will reward them by giving them the assignments that are the best for developing their long-term careers.

Many employees, misled by the trappings of performance reviews, especially the sections where the employees list their career goals, assume that their employer is dedicated to actively trying to help them attain these goals. As a result, they allow their managers to do their career planning for them. It doesn't work. The company will see that you get the occasional congratulatory plaque, the appropriate rewards banquet, and whatever unfilled job it has available at the moment you are not needed on your current project. Relying on the company for career development is entrusting your future to random chance. The company satisfies its own short term needs not your long-term ones.

To let a lower level manager steer you to a new job can be career suicide. That is because the company's best use for you is to have you continue doing what you have already done well. But if you do this you will not enlarge your "bag of tricks" or enhance your skill set in a way that opens more options for your future. At worst you can become so specialized in some obscure area of value only to your company that at some future time when the company abandons that technology or application you will be labeled "dead wood" and eliminated in the next round of downsizing.

The truth is that the only person in the corporate environment who is really interested in helping you develop a long-term career is yourself. The sooner you accept this and take on the responsibility, the sooner your career will progress.

You can, however, utilize the fiction that the company projects of wanting to build your career to your own advantage. Your first step must be to work hard and work smart until you have established the kind of reputation that causes you to stick out from the crowd of people at your level. Until you have established a reputation for competency — or brilliance — any career-building strategy is likely to backfire.

Once you have established your reputation you must constantly agitate in a tactful but determined way, asking for specific opportunities you have decided you need. You must be able to demonstrate that it would be to the ultimate advantage of the company to give you the jobs or the training that you are requesting. You must also do as much self-training as possible to show how well invested the company's education dollars will be in you. You must take pains to project a feeling of corporate loyalty and not make snide remarks in departmental meetings. If, like a lot of bright people, you project the feeling that you are too good for where you are working no one is likely to give you training that would be your ticket out!

Finally, when you are due a new assignment let management know what you would like to move into long enough before the change is made so they can take your wishes into account. Management is often very responsive to well-thought-out requests for assignments because they are unusual. Most workers are confused about what they want and only ask vaguely for "something more interesting" to do. By having a clear idea of the direction you want to go you are making things easy for your managers, as long as you have a realistic idea of your abilities.

You do have to understand the organization you work for and the principles it operates on. No one is going to move you into management six months after you enter the company as a college new hire. Neither are they going to send you to a Unix kernel class when you have only served one year maintaining a couple of CGI scripts. What you have to do is identify the series of logical steps that leads from the job you have to the job you want, steps that you identify by studying the careers of people in your organization who are doing the things you would like to be doing. Then you can suggest a viable move to management which they can let you make, particularly if you have served the company well and they would like to reward you.

Now let's turn to the career paths open to you if you stay a salaried corporate employee

Business Application Expert

In IT the term "application" is used to describe the business area that the computer system supports. Examples of applications areas are insurance, banking, e-commerce, and real estate. An application programmer is one who writes software to support the business needs of the company they work for, for example software that maintains an order database for an e-tailer or that calculates agent commissions for an insurance company. Most new-hire programmers start out in jobs that involve applications support so the career path that leads to becoming an expert applications programmer is virtually a career "default."

An experienced applications expert would be a programmer who has worked with a specific application or a family of applications for enough years that they have mastered both a mass of business-related trivia as well as the specifics of the software products with which their business applications are built. For example, a programmer who began working in a pensions administration environment and who wanted to become a pensions application specialist would gradually, through working on different portions of several pensions systems, learn how pension contributions are credited to different investment funds, how pension withdrawals are made from these same funds, how tax law changes affect pension transactions, how investments earnings are accounted for, and how pension administrators prefer to keep their records. After a few years this person would be able to hold an intelligent conversation with a manager from the pension administration departments on topics like legislative changes to 401K plans, Roth vs. conventional IRA's, the accounting requirements of SEP and SIMPLE plans, or the reasons behind the company's current document retention standards. On the technical side, the applications expert would know what programs in the company's system were involved with each of the above functions and would be affected by changes in legislation and would have mastered the ins and outs of the languages and databases used to develop these programs and be aware of any technical limitations in the system which would require future programming efforts to correct.

When the company decided to revamp the computer systems used by the pension administration areas, it would be this person who would be given the job of developing the specifications for the new system. Their task would be to take their knowledge about the business aspects of pension administration and their ability to understand the users' description of the new features they need and design a new set of programs, using the department's chosen set of software tools, that could provide these new features at a cost the users could afford.

Though this kind of person would need to have a solid understanding of the technical aspects of the system, it is likely they would have only a middling interest in technical matters. Decisions requiring a greater depth of technical expertise would probably be made in conjunction with consultants expert in the chosen technology or with people from a company technical support or system administration department who would review the application expert's plans and specifications. Successful applications experts have a very clear idea of the limits of their own technical knowledge and have built up a strong relationship with people in the more bits and bytes areas of the company who usually have a compensating lack of interest in business concerns.

At first glance this sounds like a great job. Here we finally get to design systems from scratch. This is a very visible job and should lead to some kind of recognition for the applications expert.

Limitations on Applications Programming

The problem is that companies very infrequently develop systems that call for the technical expert's vast experience. Most of the time applications areas confine themselves to making modest changes in existing systems that respond to small changes in the way that the company does business. A major development project is a very expensive and highly risky undertaking for management. Many development projects waste thousands of corporate dollars before being rejected as infeasible. Many more development projects languish for awhile and then are canceled when upper management changes direction. So in many companies there just aren't all that many opportunities to do really exciting work at the applications level.

Thus, for the large number of people who would like to stay applications programmers, corporate life can become very drab. The long-term applications programmer can expect to work for years on the same systems, making a change here and a change there, installing a vendor package, or copying their system in order to create a new clone system. After a while they will know most of what there is to know about the system and the feeling of excitement that comes from learning new things will be gone.

The other problem that the application expert faces is simply the fact that no matter how good they are at their job, if a new system does actually get designed, no matter how brilliantly they design it, the person within the organization who will get the lion's share of the credit for the success of the project is the project's manager—not the system designer. Businesspeople generally assume that the programmers did as good a job as they did because of the excellent quality of the management that they had! Thus when the project "goes live" and the corporate bigwigs assemble at the awards banquet the hard-working applications expert often is chagrined to hear the corporate vice-resident attribute the success of the project to "Bob and Sally" who are second- and third-level managers, rarely to the person whose intellectual child the system was.

Applications experts who do distinguish themselves on a project are usually rewarded by being invited into the lowest rung of management. If they do not take this "promotion" they face the risk of being viewed by their own management as being sadly lacking in ambition, deadheads who just want to stay "in a rut" doing the same old thing and not improving themselves—i.e., leaving programming to become a manager.

After a couple of years of bucking this system most application experts allow themselves to be washed into the lower administrative levels of the company. Often they move in and out of low-level management and staff positions.

I have met only a few people who were strong enough to stay applications experts and still keep their career momentum growing. The key for these people seems to have been a combination of spectacular programming skills— the kind that simply cannot be faked, and an ability to pick projects that are highly visible and likely to succeed. These successful applications experts also seem to have outgoing personalities of the kind that made them extremely popular people on a personal level— the kind of people who remember the first names of all their coworker's children. Finally, and not surprisingly, these people, while not wanting to go into management themselves, usually understood what it was that their managers did and were able to interact with managers in a businesslike way to get what they wanted. I suspect that part of these people's success derives from the fact that it is very clear to anyone in management that these people could easily succeed in management if they wanted to and that their decision to stay in technical roles was not a reflection of some inadequacy or failure.

There are many other people who are applications experts in less happy situations who change jobs every few years looking for some place where they can recover the excitement. Others have simply accepted salary levels that have topped out and a comfortable job that they know how to do and can do well. These people are happy with their role in their companies, content to see younger people steam by on their way up the corporate ladder, and satisfied with their cost of living salary increases. If you can accept these things and draw a feeling of satisfaction from being a solid applications programmer then this might be a reasonable career path for you to follow.

Technical Administration

There are many kinds of technical administrators. By definition, systems, database, and network administrators are the people who take care of the software and hardware environment that application programmers use to develop user applications.

There are two different kinds of systems programmers or systems administrators. One group is made up of people who usually started out as computer operators or technical support staff, usually with no college training. On mainframes they became experts in things like JCL and disk pack management and on PCs they installed operating systems and software, cleared out viruses, hooked new computers to the network, and attempted to make sure everyone was running the same releases of the company's chosen software tools. Eventually if they showed promise at this, their employers sent them to training schools to learn how to install and configure vendor software products and how to apply the fixes that the vendors sent out. In the past, by the time a person coming from the computer operations area had put in enough years to demonstrate their worthiness for administrator training they were long-term employees and not likely to move around to other companies. However, the strong demand for Unix system administrators caused by the expansion of the Web in the late 1990s has given that group a lot more mobility and higher salaries than other systems administration specialists.

The other kind of systems administrator or systems programmer is more of an IT aristocrat. Typically they have gone from being an applications programmer using hardware and software tools to being the person who troubleshoots that hardware and software for other applications programmers when they are at their wits' end. The people who solve CICS problems for IBM mainframes fall into this category as do people who can restore PCs after Windows has trashed its drivers or registry, database specialists and many network administrators.

The highly successful administrator can become an expert in subjects like building computer networks, defining database schema and queries, or evaluating software packages for purchase by the company. Some become experts in evaluating hardware options too. Yet others get training in software tuning, the fine art of improving system performance. However, what tech support systems programmers or administrators do not do is develop or code programs. Most of their life is spent dealing exclusively with vendor software or hardware.

This can be a gratifying career path for a technically oriented person. These positions command great respect. The salaries paid to database administrators (DBAs) are often higher than those for applications programmers at what are supposed to be the same job classes. For example, The Real Salary Survey showed that in the last half of 1999 the median DBA earned $70,000 a year in contrast to Senior Programmers' $65,000 and that DBA salaries clustered in the range between $52,000 and $98,000 while Senior Programmers' clustered between $52,000 and $86,000. While median annual salaries were lower for System Administrators at $58,000, some system administrators report salaries that reach into the low $100,000 range.

Pitfalls of Technical Administration Career Paths

The main problem with this career path is that it is so hard to break into. The training that high end administrators receive, which enables them to support popular networks, databases, and software packages, may increase their value on the job market tremendously, so employers rarely give people this kind of training until they have put in a lot of years demonstrating loyalty to the company.

At the same time since there are many different kinds of tech support units in a company, requiring widely different skill levels, some so-called administrator jobs may turn out to be near-clerical dead ends that require little technical expertise and give you no new, marketable skills. An example of this kind of job might be work on a help desk answering user questions about off-the-shelf software products.

Other administration jobs involve nothing more than increasing the red tape that applications areas have to deal with — for example configuring and supervising access to the company's production servers. In these types of jobs the prevailing attitude can often be that the administrator's job is to defend "our stuff"—the system—from all those darn programmers and users who keep messing it up. This attitude is not rare. After all, if applications programmers wouldn't keep adding their software to the system it might just stay stable!

The major problem all technical administrators face is that, even more than applications programmers, their career viability is tied to the software and hardware they support. If it goes under, they may find it impossible to get the hand-on, on-the-job experience it takes to sell themselves as administrators using a different technology. Novell network administrators, for example, whose career prospects looked solid five years ago, are now scrambling for jobs where they can get experience with NT or Unix-based server technologies. Certified experts who configure Cisco routers currently command high salaries, but like mainframe network hardware specialists, they could find themselves unemployable if a new technology supercedes that of Cisco in the router marketplace. Unfortunately, once you are pigeonholed as one kind of administrator, it may be impossible to find a job that gives you training on a new platform. And when the technology leaves you behind, you can't expect your employer to retrain you even if you have done excellent work for the company in the past. In today's cut-throat business climate an executive in another city whose company has just acquired yours and who knows–and cares—nothing about your history of company loyalty is likely to decide that it is easier to fire you and hire someone who comes in with ready-made skills.

In a similar vein, if you do decide to become a technical administrator you should be very careful that the expertise you acquire is the kind of expertise that is marketable outside your present company. Keep current with articles in the trade press. By knowing what trends are occurring in the software and hardware world you will have some idea whether the software and hardware you're mastering is the software and hardware that will be in demand in the future.

Software Product Developer

Another career path for the technical programmer is product-oriented software development. Here you work for companies whose product is software rather than for businesses that use software to support business operations in another industry. This niche is growing exponentially as increasing numbers of businesses prefer to buy vendor software rather than develop their own in-house.

Many vendor software companies will still require that you have a strong background in an application area since their products must solve some business problem of their customer base. Vendor software development may also require that you have stronger C++ or Java skills than you would need in a corporate setting. While there should be opportunities to evolve into both architecture and management roles in a software vendor company, you may run into a lot less pressure in this environment to go into management since there are likely to be a lot fewer management positions and a greater consciousness of the importance of having technically strong developers on staff.

There is much more glamour to these vendor development jobs than there is in traditional IT development. After getting year or two of experience behind you in a larger development shop you might be very attractive to a smaller vendor firm or start-up, since these companies may not have the time or resources to train college new-hires. However, before you rush to join one of these you need to be aware of their pitfalls.

Pitfalls of Start-ups and Vendor Software Firms

The biggest one is that many vendor companies are so small that their finances are precarious. They may have bet the company on the success of a new handheld device or a particular network or operating system or they may have one large client who supplies ninety percent of their income, leaving open the possibility of disaster if the client moves on. This means that employees of these kinds of small companies can come to work one day and find that the company has gone out of business or that the company has been acquired by an out of town company whose first act is to move it to another state—minus the development staff.

Many software companies are start-ups founded by people with little or no experience in the software business who are merely hoping that by jumping on the bandwagon they can attract obscene amounts of investor money for some "can't fail" scheme. These people may have unrealistic ideas of what developers can do and impose impossible schedules on them. They may also make you, the developer, the scapegoat when their improbable schemes fail. Start-ups are also famous for 90-hour work weeks and for hiring only under-30 singles who can be trusted not to have anything else in their lives—like children—that would interfere with a non-stop work schedule.

Programmers are often lured to work at start-ups with promises of stock options, though most experienced programmers view these deals with a jaundiced eye. Very few "pre-IPO" companies make it to the IPO, and even in those that do, because the stock prices of thinly traded new companies often decline precipitously after the IPO, and because employees are barred from selling their stock until months after the IPO, only a small percentage of programmers who are offered stock options make any money off of those options. So if you are attracted to working for a start-up software company, scrutinize the past histories of the company's executives for signs that they actually know something about software development and make sure that their past experience suggests that they can run a successful business.

HOW BAD CAN IT GET?

"I took a development job at a 'start-up' that was going to revolutionize the use of email. It seemed OK at first, but I had nothing to do for three weeks. I was then contacted by another company that was more established, post-IPO, and infinitely more 'exciting'. When I interviewed I saw that almost everyone was under thirty, lotsa the guys had dyed blonde hair, there were attractive women, people wore shorts to work, there were no cubes and everyone wanted to be cutting edge. It sounded great. I was offered a Sr. Software Engineer position in the new Media and Entertainment Dept. for more money and 3000 shares, so I took it.

"When I arrived for work I had no place to sit for 1 week and nothing to do other than read documents and download and evaluate software that I may or may not use (no one was sure) - generally tried to keep myself busy for three more weeks. More and more people kept getting hired and there was no place for them - 20 people a week at least for no discernable reason.

"The Media and Entertainment Dept. was fully staffed with Information Architects, Designers, Front End Developers, Engineers and a few undefined management people who looked good at meetings with show-bizzy clients. Unfortunately, there was no work, no project had been landed.

"A project was finally found six weeks after I arrived. It was a disaster from another department. It was a true Death March project that was months behind schedule, over budget with clueless developers. The general manager called us all together, apologized for the situation - blamed it all on mismanagement - and told us we would be expected to work overtime and weekends to finish the project.

"So, the project slips and slips for three months. The Media and Entertainment Dept. is dissolved a week ago and 20 people have no idea what is going to happen to them. In the meantime, the stock is split and everyone's vest date is pushed back three months so now everyone has to stay 15 months instead of a year to see any of their options come to fruition.

"I've found yet another job for more money but I'm not going for stock options. I pray that the company is not run by ex-TV magnates, HTML coders, graphics designers and UNIX hackers who insist on rewriting application servers because they know so much Java...

How to Use your IT Apprenticeship to Prepare for a Strong Technical Career

No matter what technically oriented career path you choose, there are a couple of fundamental strategies you will need to pursue if you are to become successful. You will need to:

- Build your technical skills using tools in strong demand
- Build visibility within the company
- Understand management's role and its goals

Any company with a large investment in computer systems is forced to keep a few good technical people around who can solve the problems that, left untended, can bring those computer systems to a complete stop. No matter how many management directives demand that head count be kept low and staff be cut back there will always be a need for truly good technical people until the day they close up the building for the last time and everyone goes home.

Technical skill cannot be faked. You cannot bullshit software into working right. A manager may overstate their results. A salesperson may slide around the truth, but a computer professional brought in to solve a computer problem has to find its source or the problem remains. Because of this if you want to be valuable to a company as a technical person you have to be a very good one. It is possible to build a career without learning anything more than what you picked up in your first-year training program. But to build a strong technical career you must learn as much as you can about the systems of the company you work for. At the same time you must strive to keep your technical skills general enough so that if your company should hit bad times or if it should merge with another company and cause your job to be eliminated you could find a similar job in another company. You do this by making sure that your résumé always includes experience with a few of the software products that are industry standards for software development, database management, and, increasingly, client-server communication.

The next thing you must pay attention to in the formative years of your career is building visibility within the companies you work for. It is not enough simply to accomplish wonders — you must make sure that the people who run things know that you have accomplished them. If you solve a pesky problem, particularly one that other people have encountered before, write up a short, clear memo describing the problem and the solution and email it around your department, making sure that it goes to your manager. If you see a potential problem emerging, it is often a good idea to write up a memo describing the problem and suggesting solutions to management. For example one person I know noticed that a huge mainframe-based insurance policy database was filling up more rapidly than had been anticipated, wrote a memo pinpointing the exact week when all available disk space would be full, and then suggested a simple way of staging older, less useful information off of the database. By doing things like this you help management appreciate the work that you do and ensure that it will be rewarded.

Finally, just because you have decided to be a "techie" doesn't mean that you don't have to understand management. In the corporate world managers control the flow of resources. They get to pick what jobs you are assigned and even decide what kind of computer you get on your desk. As long as you are in the business world you must understand what managers think about and what fears drive them. You must be able to show them your worth in their own terms.

One programmer I knew who was truly a "supertechie," with awe-inspiring mastery of assembly language programming and operating system logic, found himself receiving consistently mediocre performance reviews. One manager finally explained that as he was now a senior-level person he was supposed to be providing "leadership". Management didn't realize that this individual had personally solved all of the technical show-stopping problems of not only their own but several other departments for the past several years because it had never occurred to him to mention it. All management saw was his gray locks bent over program listings in his office or a bunch of people looking like they were having a gabfest in that office. The solution this programmer found for getting better performance appraisals and improved opportunities within his company was to define what he was already doing—showing newer people how to approach and solve difficult debugging problems in a complex environment—as providing "technical leadership." By adding up the number of times a month that he had taken a newer person through this process, he was able to show in the quantifiable terms that management loves best that he had indeed been leading ten or twelve people very effectively.

But before he could do this, this person had to understand the value system of the people writing his appraisals, who, unfortunately, having very sketchy technical skills of their own, did not have enough technical knowledge to appreciate the value of the service he was providing to their project. Most importantly, the solution for this programmer was not to deny that the most valuable thing he could contribute was "leadership". That is the way that managers think and no technical person will ever change that. The programmer just had to demonstrate that "leadership" could take a new form!

If you can build up your skills, let management know what you've done for them lately, and communicate with management on their, not your, terms, then you can eventually fill the role of "Guru." As such you will be treated with considerable respect and earn a reasonable livelihood with much better job security than many of the managers, whom you will see come and go. When people come in to be interviewed for jobs, fresh from college you will often be trotted out and exhibited proudly as proof that in your company there really is a technical career path that works. And, if it doesn't, you will always be able to find a job somewhere else.

Going into Management

Most of us became technical people because working with hardware and software was something that interested us and we were pleased to discover that our skills were valued in the marketplace. It therefore comes as an unpleasant surprise to discover, after a few years of earning our livings as techies, that many of the people we work for see no better way to reward us for the good technical work we've done than to make sure we never get to do it again!

The reality in many, if not all, companies is that there are very strong forces pushing people who demonstrate intelligence and competence away from technical work and into management. Most programmers come into the work force vaguely aware that management is a career option open to them but determined not to take it, convinced that they would not be happy in an environment of memos, budgets, and meetings. Many of these people a few years later reluctantly join the herd competing for entry-level management jobs, convinced that there is no other way to get their career—and income—moving again and kicking themselves for not having directed their efforts toward management earlier in their careers.

Becoming a manager is not really the only viable career path open to ambitious technical people in the corporate world. It is merely the simplest and most lucrative! But for most technical people, going into management is a terrible mistake. In the pages that follow we will look at what kind of career you can expect in IT management and examine some of the pitfalls that going into management brings. But before we do that, it is worth taking some time to look at the reason why there is and will always be a fundamental conflict between competent technical people and the businesspeople who manage them, because it is this conflict that makes going into management so problematic for the competent technical person.

Why Management Hates Competent Techies

In every business I have ever worked in no matter how much lip service was paid to the importance of technical people, the managers got the nice offices, the managers got the big salaries, and the managers got most of the corporate perks. In business it is management that gets to give out the rewards, and not surprisingly, the skills that management rewards most highly are precisely those that management itself has—and those are definitely not technical skills. No amount of railing and protesting is going to change this. It is something that all technical people must come to grips with in the business world.

Because confronting the diverging management/technical paths is usually the most traumatic event in the career of a computer professional, you need to understand just why it is that business does not value technical people for what they do but instead tries to force them to leave their technical skills behind if they want to advance. To do this we need to examine the role that technical people play in a business as seen not by these technical people themselves but by the businesspeople that pay their salaries.

The following analysis might seem a little jaundiced to a person unfamiliar with the way that businesses manage their technical operations, but I assure you that any working computer professional has seen these patterns repeated every place they have worked. A 1988 survey of *Computerworld* readers found that a whopping one out of three cited "ineffective or poor management" as the most frustrating aspect of their job, putting this factor way ahead of any other cause of complaint! Based on what I've read on on-line bulletin boards since then, in the intervening years this percentage has risen substantially.

The fundamental truth that anyone who ventures into a corporate environment needs to understand is that all rewards in the corporate world stem from the degree to which you are helping the company make a quick buck. Companies are evaluated quarterly on their ability to make a profit. The more instrumental you are, personally, in making that profit, the better you will be rewarded.

Here we encounter the two features of this system that work against high quality technical people and keep them from in receiving their just rewards. The first is that the whole computer operation in every company that isn't a software vendor company is just a chunk of overhead that does not contribute directly to profits.

The second—and this applies even more strongly in software vendor companies—is that there are no rewards in business for any but short-term successes. Quarterly profits are all that count, and managers are graded almost entirely upon how successfully they meet their deadlines. What they meet those deadlines *with* is of far less consequence. So there is no benefit for managers in putting time and effort into achieving such long-term goals as high quality system design, bug-free implementation, and easily maintained code. Meeting the next deadline with something—*anything*— that works is all they will get rewarded for.

Computer Support is Overhead

This fact should be engraved in large gold letters over the doorways of all IT offices: Computer support is overhead expense. Except for the relatively small number of companies that make their profits selling computer hardware, software, and programming services, the effort spent configuring and programming computers is not directly contributing to the profitability of the corporation.

The company makes its money from sales. Customer write checks to the XYZ Corporation in return for widgets, or widget cleaning, or insurance for their existing widgets. They may even pay for advice on how to best use their widgets. But they do not directly pay for the computer systems that the XYZ Corporation uses to track its widget production, design new widgets, estimate widget costs, pay its staff, or send out invoices. The company could go right on selling widgets without even having a computer system if it had to. It has bought those systems in the hope that by doing so it could cut down on its other overhead costs, usually salaries, and be able to keep more of the widget sales dollar as profit.

Because computer support is overhead all good managers want to keep it as controlled as possible. The problem, unfortunately, is that computer systems costs are uncontrollable.

The management that blithely decides to bring in a system that is supposed to make things easier usually finds itself several years down the line supporting an ever-growing IT budget, forced to constantly upgrade its hardware, and worst of all, dependent on a steady stream of quirky, unbusinesslike computer programmers and administrators who quit whenever they are offered indecently better salaries by competitors, have little interest in widgets, and are the only people who can keep the darn systems working. So, from a senior management perspective, computers and all the people associated with them are a hard-to-manage pain in the neck.

Let's look now at the programming life cycle from the perspective of management. Most of the major decisions that lead to the development of new computer systems in large companies are made by nontechnical upper management types who don't want to go overboard on costly computer systems but are swayed by the press releases that they read in the business press and the blandishments of very effective vendor salespeople. They read glowing descriptions of their competitors' new systems and don't want to be left behind—not realizing that the articles don't mention the spiraling costs and misplaced efforts that often underlie the system being touted.

Salespeople from hardware, software, and management consulting firms assure the nervous executive that although their new system has high start-up costs, in the long run costs will come down. Once the new system is installed, the computer, aided by a couple of lowly operatives, will be able to do the work previously done by legions of better-paid staff who can now be laid off. Computers don't get pensions and computers don't unionize. The appeal is irresistible.

Often salespeople will go out of their way to assure hesitant executives that they will not be dependent on programmers. Murmuring buzzwords like "a total e-commerce solution" and "enterprise-wide resource planning" the salesperson bears tales of a wonderful future in which computers will program themselves, conversing with the (executive) user like well-raised children.

Meanwhile it is true that the company will need to have a few programmers around, but the salespeople assure them that is only until the system is installed. Ah, that's a wonderful word, "installed" suggesting as it does the kind of stability usually associated with plumbing fixtures.

Senior managers make all the major decisions about the new system and then, belatedly, bring in the lower-level grunts who are going to have to write the software that gets the system to do what the various hardware and software salespeople told the executives it could do. (As a footnote to all this, in a vendor environment a typical "in" joke is "How can you tell when a salesperson isn't lying?" The answer is, "Their lips aren't moving.")

Salespeople will always promise that computer systems will do whatever it is that the customer wants. If the system cannot currently accommodate the requirement, the salesperson announces that the *next* release of the product they are selling has just that feature — and then writes frenzied letters back to the company's development department demanding that the feature be integrated into the next release — usually without ever consulting with the vendor development people who have to pull it off.

Yet in spite of the fact that senior management rarely gives the grunt-level technical people real input into selection of the hardware and platform or into the high-level design process, a surprising number of competent IT teams are able to deliver what it is that management ordered. After an impressive effort the new system is put in place and goes live.

It is as this point that upper management expects to be able to cut down on technical staff and start realizing the cost savings that the computer system was brought in to achieve. But is it also now that management discovers the extent to which, like the heroin user who believes it is safe to try only a single hit, they have become addicts.

Why a Computer System Is Not Like a Bathtub

The problem that management faces is that an installed computer system is a lot more complex than an installed bathtub.

Your average bathtub is designed to do one thing. Once installed it does that one thing until, perhaps, your investment portfolio does well enough that you can afford to pull it out and replace it with a Jacuzzi.

No one shows up one morning and tells you that the building code has changed and all bathtubs now have to have built-in can openers. Nor does the average homeowner expect their bathtub to easily convert into a swimming pool big enough to fit all the neighborhood kids.

Like the bathtub, a newly installed computer system also exhibits a certain rigidity. Although its rigidity is not evident to the naked eye, the components of a software system are welded together in a very specific way to perform the very specific functions that the original designers expected the system to perform.

The problem is that the owner of the computer system is constantly demanding that changes be made to the system that were never foreseen by the original designers—changes that correspond functionally to adding a built-in can opener to your tub. These changes are not always voluntary, either. Government regulations and legal requirements can suddenly change and force a business to add that new function to the system.

Finally, to return to our swimming pool analogy, as businesses grow their original systems become inadequate for their needs but they often resist throwing out existing systems that work because of the prohibitive cost of starting from scratch to produce the larger, completely redesigned systems that would accommodate their needs.

As a result, many large corporations—and virtually all major software houses—have the entire neighborhood squeezed into their bathtubs by now. Many manufacturing and insurance systems running today were originally designed in the late 1950s or early 1960s and have been run through a series of conversions from one generation of computer to another. Programs designed to function in computers that had less capacity than today's handheld computer now run on multimillion dollar networks—but they do it with logic and design that would not even be appropriate for a desk top system.

In 1986 I saw one IBM mainframe system, perhaps still running right now, in which subroutines were called every time it was necessary to add or subtract a decimal number. Why? Because the second-generation computer the code was originally developed on did not have the decimal instruction set that all mainframes since the mid-1960s have had.

I also observed 1980s mainframe programs which laboriously spooled their own print files because the early system on which they were developed only could print one file at a time. The fact that these programs ran on an MVS/XA computer that could write out thousands of files at once was irrelevant. The code was converted but never rewritten.

The need to prepare for Y2K caused management, belatedly and at huge expense, to pay programmers to locate, eliminate, or rewrite many of the most embarrassing examples of this kind of software persistence. But ironically, the same forces that made mainframe software such a nightmare in the mid-1980s—a generation after mainframe programming became significant in industry—now ensures that software developed for the PC—which is now almost a generation old itself—will follow the same course.

For proof of this, you have to look no further than the Windows operating systems that still include vestiges of code designed for the 8-bit processor memory model used by the earliest release of MS-DOS. Given the size of industry's current investment in its existing code, which is far larger than anything seen in the 1980s, it is likely that the millions of lines of C, C++, or Visual Basic code developed in the late 1980s and early 1990s will be running, somewhere, on some platform, for many years to come.

The reason that systems designed to be bathtubs end up being tortured into swimming pools, is, of course, to keep development costs down. It is always cheaper to add something new to an existing system than to design a new one from scratch. But this is where technology exacts a price for management's short-term thinking. The long-term price that management pays for the refusal to spend money on its installed systems is that the systems eventually become so confusing and difficult to maintain that they resemble Rube Goldberg machines. The bathtub not only has a built-in can opener, it turns on the furnace and pitches baseballs. Unfortunately when a system this complex gets joggled only the slightest bit, the baseballs slam into the furnace door, open the latch and flames can engulf the whole operation! Eventually these elderly systems require the most assiduous programmer attention. These systems are also the hardest to recruit programmers to, since very few competent people yearn to do maintenance in what is perceived to be a dead-end situation.

How the Dream of a Programmer-Free System Leads to Ruin

So the truth that upper management never wants to learn is that a computer system is never entirely finished. When your business changes, your computer systems must change too. There is no easy way around it. And changing a computer system correctly is an expensive proposition requiring skilled people, especially programmers—the very same programmers that the executive hoped would fade away once their system was installed.

The hope that programmers can be eliminated has been behind many temporarily successful programming products introduced over past decades, but what managers don't often see is that there is a trade-off. Today you can get by without programmers a lot better than you could fifteen years ago by using off-the-shelf software, but you then have to work within the confines of your programmer-replacement software. This means that your systems won't always work exactly the way that you would like them to, which introduces a whole new level of frustration.

The desperate attempt to eliminate programmers has led to some of the most expensive debacles I've observed in industry. One strategy that was fashionable for a time was so-called "parameterized programming." The idea here was that since program elements are known to be prone to change you put any item that could possibly change, like report lines or formulas, into tables kept in files, which could be edited, instead of in the programs themselves. Then, this theory argued, you wouldn't need programmers to make your changes, just low-level—and low-paid—operatives to fix up your tables.

The problem was that by time you got all your tables set up to handle the complexity of a real, live system your tables were so confusing that it took a highly skilled programmer to figure out which table to tweak to achieve a desired change. In one debacle at a major insurance company that adopted this approach a parameterized program that was supposed to be programmable by clerk-level people eventually required the services of seventeen outside contract consultants each billing somewhere around $40 per hour to straighten it out.

Another programmer-eliminating approach upper management reads about in magazines and adopts, to its sorrow, is getting an outside vendor to do its systems work. Lured by the idea of fixed costs, executives decide to buy a vendor package to computerize some function. The usual sequel to this is that three or four years later the original package, after absorbing an incredible amount of in-house time, is revealed as incapable of providing some subset of the functions that simply have to be performed by the system. In-house people are ordered to "fix up the package," and eventually the package becomes the unrecognizable kernel of a huge system developed in-house—a system that has had its design stage fatally crippled by having to build on the foundation of the albatross package.

One last programmer-eliminating strategy, which has become far more frequent during the 1990s Decade of Mergers, is to acquire a company under the blithe assumption that the acquired company's IT systems can be quickly modified to provide for both companies once the merger is complete. The difficulty of converting from one system to another is always underestimated, and the result is usually highly visible failure. Clients don't get their bills, stores don't get their products, salespeople don't get their commissions, or bank customers get locked out of their ATMs for weeks while the merged companies put out press release after press release asking for "patience while we improve our computer systems."

Part of the problem here is that the people who have the set of skills that characterize upper management are precisely those least likely to be able to understand the realities of dealing with computer systems. Executives generally pride themselves on seeing the big picture and not getting hung up in details. Unfortunately a computer system is the ultimate cluster of details. Executives need to be flexible and always able to change course. Computer systems are rigid.

It would help a lot if executives could learn more about the nature of computer programming so that they could understand that if some process their business carries out is dependent on a complex computer system there is no painless way that that process can change quickly and inexpensively. But don't hold your breath. It hasn't happened over the past fifty years and there is no sign that it will start now.

Shooting the Messenger who Brings the Bad News

There is yet another reason upper management has come to develop an aversion for technical staffers—they always bring bad news. Managers who put a poorly designed, badly tested system in place "on schedule" receive immediate awards for having met their targets. No one looks at the system's next ten years of miserable performance in relation to those initial rewards. Usually the managers responsible for a system are rotated away from the system after it goes live and given new development projects to work on. Since most of the problems in a poorly designed system do not show up until you stress it or attempt to modify it, the person who encourages slipshod work is almost never connected with the damage their policies cause.

Indeed, managers who attempt to develop systems by rigorously applying the principles of good software design are usually viewed by their bosses as being obstructionists. Why do they need a year for their projects when other managers get their whole systems in place in only three months? The growth of the Internet and the pressure to deliver instant dot.coms to investors has made this even more true today than it was a decade ago. Few investors are interested in anything that can't be developed in three or at most six months.

As a result, any intelligent person who has any hopes of rising in management realizes very soon that they must produce something, anything, that can possibly be interpreted as satisfying the system requirements as soon as possible and as cheaply as possible. If the system eats money for the rest of its life it is not coming out of their budget. But the technical staffers always try to spoil things, insisting that things have to be done "right!"

Typically, when a major change is needed, upper management takes the "broad view" of the situation and makes what it considers to be the brilliant business decisions needed to implement the change. Since no one with detailed knowledge of the computer system involved participates in high-level management colloquies—remember, techies aren't welcome because they get too hung up in details—it is only weeks or months later that the unfortunate programmer assigned the task gets to evaluate the change at the highly detailed level at which the change must be implemented. It is then their unpleasant task more often than not to explain that the task will take far more resources in terms of money and time than the company can afford.

As an example of this, one group I worked with was handed the assignment of rewriting about 120,000 lines of outstandingly devious operating system type assembly language code in six months. Management understood correctly that if the code was rewritten in a high-level language it would be easier to maintain, but had no idea of the amount of effort needed to convert that amount of highly complex code. Three levels of management passed down the order rewrite the system without demur. None of them had ever read or written a line of code in their lives. The four programmers who were assigned the task were left with the unappetizing job of announcing that it could not be done. To start with, no one around had the foggiest idea of what those 120,000 lines of code did. There was no documentation and the code was poorly commented. It would take time just to analyze the programs' current functions. Besides that, of the four programmers assigned the task only one had any experience working with assembly language code. The rest were COBOL programmers.

When told there was a problem, management offered to increase the size of the team. The programmers had to explain that the situation was analogous to thinking that if one pregnant woman could produce a baby in nine months then nine women should be able to produce a baby in one.

The high point of this project for me was my interview with a high-level manager who listened to my explanation of the technical problems involved and then exclaimed in exasperation, "You programmers! You always want everything to be perfect. In management we have to learn to compromise!"

But, as any programmer knows, you can't compromise with code. Anything not coded correctly will fail and the software will not do what it is supposed to do. Management typically cannot understand why if a certain situation occurs only one percent of the time the programmer must include processing for that situation and test it as thoroughly as the code for the situation that occurs ninety-nine percent of the time.

So as a computer professional your job will be to destroy management's schedules and bollix up their planning. You will have to tell them that they have to spend far more money than they want just to keep their operations afloat. You will be rigorously excluded from the decision-making process but your career will rise or fall based on the wisdom of those management decisions.

Is it any wonder that after a few years of dealing with this, many technical people reach a state of utter frustration?

A large number of technically strong people enter management in the hope that by doing so they can exert control over the way that the technical side of things is managed. "I was tired of having jerks tell me what to do." is the typical explanation from one techie turned manager. Unfortunately in order to remain in management the manager must shift into the short-term result mode and play the game as it is played. If they don't meet their deadlines, they don't stay employed. If they don't give the investors the slick demo of the system that no one has had time to architect, someone else will. And if they don't get their product into the market, first, they will never catch up with the company that does, no matter how buggy its product might be. So all too often within a few months the once-competent technical person appears, through a weird alchemy, to have been transformed into the jerk they used to loathe.

I have no easy answers for how to improve the situation. It goes way beyond any individual and is rooted in the basic assumptions with which American business operates. The best you can do is be aware of the inevitability of the conflict so that you can avoid being chopped up in the meat grinder represented by this conflict at its worst.

With that in mind, let's turn to a more practical discussion of what moving into IT management entails.

What Do IT Managers Do?

Typically your first managerial role will be that of team leader. Team leaders are expected to function as part technical person and part administrator. The amount of each role given team leaders varies widely from company to company. Usually team leaders have responsibility for setting up schedules. They tell management how long a specific task will take to accomplish and if they are to get any further in management they must be correct! The team leaders' other responsibility is to dole out the work that their team has been assigned. They assign tasks to each technical person in their group, keep tabs on how staff are proceeding with the tasks, and assist them in getting help when they get stuck. A good team leader does not necessarily help by solving technical problems, but becomes a resource directory instead, pointing the technical person to other individuals within the technical organization who can help him.

In most cases team leaders are also responsible for giving the technical people under their direction periodic evaluations. These evaluations are like a report card and in most organizations bear a direct relationship to the size of the staffer's next raise. Team leaders are also responsible for getting additional special recognition for their team members such as bonuses and awards. Usually, but not always, the team leader's managerial role stops short of controlling a budget.

Departmental Managers

Most team leaders remain at the team leader level for a year of two. If they distinguish themselves they may go on to the next level of management—if a position opens up. It is at this level that they are usually given a small budget to control. If you've been paying attention you should notice that we have just hit *money*. The control over money, not people is what characterizes real management. The departmental IT manager who has control of a chunk of corporate dollars is now, for the first time, really a manager, albeit at the lowest level.

These managers usually have two major responsibilities: to interface with similar levels of management in the departments that are the users of the department's services and to control the production of the work that they and the user group managers decide should be undertaken. For example, such a manager might have responsibility for the IT side of a function such as an accounts receivable system. They would meet constantly with the accounting department managers at their level who manage the clerks who handle outstanding accounts. These accounting managers would present the IT departmental manager with lists of problems that their subordinates need to have solved. These will range from the trivial—a strange message appeared on an input screen for example, to the important—the balances are wrong on Thursday's batch run totals. They will also periodically come up with requests for new system functions: wouldn't it be nice if there was a way to display the summary results from the batch run on-line the next day.

The departmental IT manager takes valid requests to their team leaders and asks them to determine what is causing the problems the users are experiencing and to estimate how long it will take to fix the problems. If new functions are requested they will go to the team leaders and ask them to estimate how much work will be needed to provide the new function.

At a later meeting the manager will report back to the user managers what it will take to service their requests in terms of company resources, time, and money. Remember, the IT manager's whole department is usually an overhead expense to these same operational areas that make up their user group!

If the user managers give the go-ahead, the manager then tries to juggle the existing budget for programmers and hardware resources to accommodate the users' requests. This means moving people out of lower priority tasks or hiring new people. It is this level of manager who will usually interview you and make the salary offer when you are interviewed by a company, although once you are hired it is not this manager but their subordinate, the team leader, who will control your career from thence forward.

If managers cannot accomplish what has been requested with their current resources they must prioritize the work requests they have been given and compromise with the user group to accomplish whatever tasks they consider to be the most important or else they must go to their own management, at yet a higher level, and make a very good case for increasing their budget to allow them to hire more people.

When a department is working on a project that is all new development, the departmental manager's role is not all that different. The only difference is that they must do much more negotiating with user group's managers on the subject of what can and cannot be delivered, and when, and they face a more complex task in drawing up schedules and following them, since the development environment is much more unpredictable than the more stable enhancement/maintenance environment.

Functional Managers

If you make it to the rank of departmental manager, you should expect to stay at this departmental level of management for three to five years — or possibly forever. Past this level there are fewer and fewer managerial levels open and the competition is more intense. The next higher level of manager is usually a functional, rather than departmental level. These managers are in charge of the managers of a group of related departments. Their job is to relate to the user area functional managers, to set major priorities for the whole function, and most important, to control the money which will become the various departments' budgets.

This level of management concerns itself with what are called "policy issues." At this point we are steaming away at a furious rate from details and entering the realm of buzzwords and management fads. Managers at this level are the ones who hold meetings to announce that from now on all programmers will make "quality reengineering" their watchword. They are the ones, too, who get excited about programmer productivity aids. Often too they send managers and programmers to expensive seminars on effective systems design. Less often do they allow the managers beneath them to submit schedules that reflect what they learned in those seminars.

In many companies this level of management spends a lot of time rearranging the departments under their control, performing the corporate rite of reorganization. Rarely does a person at this level have any technical knowledge. In many cases it has been so many years since a person at this level did any technical work of any type that their knowledge of the current technology comes only from talking with people who use it, not from using it themselves. I once had to teach a functional manager at IBM how to log on at a terminal. When he had been a programmer, all program development had been done by keypunching cards.

Unfortunately, this kind of manager is the lowest level of IT professional who ever gets to talk with corporate vice-presidents and the other executives who make the major policy decisions affecting IT.

Top Management

Beyond this level there may be one or more levels of management that control all IT functions, including computer operations and system support. The actual reporting structure at this level in the hierarchy varies widely. In some companies the IT management eventually reports to a user area manager, for example a manager in charge of all accounting functions. In others IT management is a separate organization up to the vice-presidential level. Eventually you reach the end of the IT leg of the organization chart. For an IT manager to cross out of the IT management chain and into the broader corporate management world is quite difficult in most organizations. If you intend to enter IT management you should realize that the chances are not very good that you will ever be vice president of anything other than IT. At best you may make it to Chief Information Officer (CIO), though tenure in CIO positions is often brief and ends traumatically. You will almost never be considered for a CEO slot.

This, again, is because IT is usually overhead. The real movers and shakers in business tend to come from the revenue-producing areas, which are sales and, increasingly, finance. Companies reward best those who are given credit for making the most money for them, and all that most IT managers can do is cost money, or at best save money. Only in those industries most dependent on computer systems such as vendor software, Web commerce, banking and financial services is there any hint that this might be changing, as computer systems become more and more what the company is actually selling.

If you are entering IT management under the impression that you are on a fast track to the executive suite I would suggest that you save your pennies and invest in an MBA from one of the nation's three or four top business schools. Doing it by coming up the IT management ladder is definitely doing it the hard way.

And don't be misled by articles in the business press touting the "Data Processing" background of high profile VIP's like Robert Crandall, who was the CEO of American Airlines, who moved into his leadership role after being vice-president of Data Processing at TWA. If you look at his résumé you will see that his "DP" background included an MBA from the prestigious Wharton School, one of the nation's top business graduate schools, not years spent as a programmer. John Reed, who was the chairman of Citicorp and another executive with IT credentials, received an engineering degree from MIT, but again, this was supplemented by a degree in Industrial Management from MIT's Sloan School of Management. The very few programmers, like Oracle's Larry Ellison, who have become company presidents have generally done so by starting their own companies, not by rising through the ranks. And most of these ex-programmer executives, unlike Ellison, find themselves edged out of the companies they have founded, when venture capitalists with substantial stakes in the company or stockholders demand that the company be headed by "professional" management as the company matures.

IT management will be satisfying to you if you can accept its inherently limited scope and if you enjoy the combination of administrating and politicking. I always feel like laughing when new hires announce that they want to go into management because they "like working with people." Managers don't work with people, they work with money. They don't socialize, they control. Far better to say you would like to go into management because you like working with lists and schedules! You need to understand the game of business to succeed in management and you need to understand real leadership, which entails getting people to give you their best stuff in exchange for the least possible return.

The manager that the company will reward for being the best is rarely the one people like working for the best. The final judgement on your managerial worth will always be made not on how happy your workers are but on how much you could get done by your department for the least amount of money. As long as your employees don't quit in a group you will often be rewarded for the kind of "people skills" that earn you dislike from those below you.

If you are seriously interested in a management career read everything you can get your hands on about business and management and learn to play within the rules of the business game.

And here is one last piece of advice for the new computer professional: Don't make any major pronouncements you might later regret. If you make the point repeatedly that you would rather eat a live mouse than enter management, the chances are good that the opportunity will pass you by. Try to remember that people change as they grow older. The management functions that appear stodgy and dull at age 22 often have a certain appeal at 35. The politicking that offends you in your youth may exert a certain fascination as you enter middle age. And most important, the challenge of keeping technically current that lends excitement to a young career may become an exhausting burden to the older person who has mastered several technologies only to see them become obsolete. If you are going to remain in the corporate world you should never rule out the managerial alternative as a future possibility.

Management's Big Pitfall

Any logical person who examines a hierarchical organizational chart can see that as you go up the chart there are fewer and fewer boxes. Managers are expected to move up the management ladder, but there are decreasing numbers of slots for them to go to. If only one of the twenty-five departmental managers in a company can make it to IT Manager, what happens to the rest?

The answer is, they get fired, and when they do they find it very difficult to find another job that offers the same kind of salary and prestige. And it is not necessary to fail as a manager to lose your job. When two companies merge, middle management positions are often eliminated in one of them, often quite suddenly. A sudden downturn in the economy can result in projects being canceled to save money. When projects are canceled project management is an unnecessary frill. Technical people caught in such situations usually have little difficulty finding new jobs, but middle-level managers who have lost their technical skills are valuable primarily for their knowledge of their particular company and the way that it does business. Such people, particularly if they are over forty, can find the job search process a harrowing one.

The so-called golden parachutes you read about are not given out at the levels of management that most IT managers attain. At best you might get a few months severance pay, but this is little when you consider the years left in which you need to support yourself.

So when planning a career in management you cannot assume that you will be one of the lucky few who make it to the top. The wise thing to do would be to always have a contingency plan in the back of your mind to cover what you would do if you needed a new job. Keep up your contacts with people outside your company. Try to anticipate the kinds of business situations that might lead to your company cutting back drastically on staff and, if you see one coming, try to get a new job somewhere else before it hits. Finally, as a last resort, consider entrepreneurial alternatives that would use your business knowledge and contacts.

You should never let yourself be lulled into complacency when you are filling a managerial job. You must always maintain a realistic view of the true value of your managerial services to the company as it pursues a profit. All too often companies flush with success reward employees by giving them fundamentally unnecessary management-level jobs, inserting level after level of supervision between the people making the decisions about what should be done and the people doing the work. When cost cutting becomes imperative these people's salaries are the logical place to begin cutting—and that is exactly what most firms do. During the recession of the late 1980s, in a Hartford area company, upper management went so far as to send one group of managers an ultimatum: Go back to work as programmers—doing something the company really needs done—or get fired. The affected managers were horrified and at least one quit. But nobody who had worked under these individuals was surprised, nor, may I add, did the departments run any the less smoothly without them.

Using your IT Apprenticeship to Position Yourself for Management

If you've decided you want to pursue a career that will lead you up the management ladder you will have to be very careful to craft the best possible apprenticeship for yourself during the first five years of your IT career. You need to select jobs in those years that will do the following:

◆ Teach you the business fundamentals of the portion of your company's IT shop that is going to be the most active in the next decade

◆ Give you visibility to management

◆ Give you the grounding in technical matters that will let you make wise management decisions in the future

If you want to get somewhere in management, you simply have to be where the action is. Determining where that might be is no simple task, and getting yourself a job there can be even harder. There is definitely a certain amount of luck involved, but if you are to succeed in business you need to be able to make your own luck. You must do a lot of research about the operations of a company before you take your first and subsequent jobs to find out whether you are joining an area that expects to see a lot of future development team formation and will therefore need more managers, or whether you are coming into an older, more established area where opportunities to make a real mark will be harder to come by.

This is particularly hard to gauge because often the areas where there are the most opportunities for major growth are those where the budget is axed first if belt tightening occurs. The new and innovative can be dispensed with, but the old established systems must be maintained.

Once you have found your job you must do two things. You must do the best possible job with any work you are assigned, no matter how seemingly menial, and you must begin thinking like a businessperson.

No matter what your ultimate career goals are, you have been hired to be a technical person. You will have to establish your competence as a technical person before anyone is going to give you an opportunity to do more. But the way you will hasten your advancement into business is by showing that in all situations you are aware of the business implications of everything you do. This means simply that you must realize you are a business resource and start out by managing *yourself* effectively. If you have a choice between doing something that is technically challenging or doing something that will save the company money, you must choose the money-saving option. This may sound obvious, but too many programmers operate as if they were visiting scholars on loan from a university rather than people hired to make money for a company. You can really stand out of the crowd if you show that you remember what the company thinks you are there for.

Besides working hard, you must do something equally important— you must let management know just how hard you have been working.

This is called gaining visibility and is a very subtle thing to achieve. The basic truth is it is simply not enough to do a job, you must make sure that the people with the power to reward you know what a good job you did. The much-maligned business memo is often an invaluable tool to help you in this. Managers complain that the biggest obstacle faced by technical people who want to get into management is poor communications skills. Get started early working on this, writing memos and documentation and sending out project summaries and monthly status reports whenever you can justify it. And try to get some feedback from your managers on the stuff you send. How would they suggest you improve it? It is not so much *what* you say but the fact that you are saying something — demonstrating your communications skills and your awareness of the group nature of the situation you find yourself in — that makes an impression on your bosses and shows that you are a contender for a leadership position.

Take advantage of any change you get to address groups too. Teach classes if you are offered the opportunity. Never miss a chance to give a presentation at a meeting, and when you do, take the time to do a professional job with your charts and graphs.

Remember too that visibility is a two-edged sword. If your project hits a snag, your visibility is not going to go away. But your ability to function in a strong and confident manner despite a negative situation may, in the long run, win you more respect than anything else you do.

You must take initiative, but remember this does not, repeat, *does not*, mean doing other people's work — the sure mark of someone who does not understand the rules of the business game. Taking initiative means finding things that are currently nobody's work and doing them in your spare time. By identifying a problem and solving it without ever causing your manager to have to add it to a schedule you will begin to stand out as a self-starter, and managers will want to have you on their teams, especially if you tactfully and modestly announce what you've done in a tasteful memo.

Don't think that because you want to be a manager you don't need to become a good technician. You don't want to be thought of by management as a head-in-the-clouds technical person but you want to be sure you know your stuff. So many of the managers you will be competing with are technically weak that you will be able to accomplish things they can't and avoid debacles simply by having a good enough grasp of technology to make use of what your subordinates tell you. The most effective managers in technical areas are those who know how to use their people's technical knowledge in combination with their own strong business perspective. Rhetoric about team spirit won't get the job done on schedule unless you have a good grasp of the obstacles that you are likely to encounter along the way.

Finally, if you come into a new job situation with hopes of becoming a manager, be very careful how you treat your coworkers. In the period when you are working to become a team leader you will be very dependent on the help of the people you work with to get things done. If people view you as a self-seeking opportunist you may find that help is hard to find when you need it. People don't rush to rescue people they loathe.

Many would-be leaders tend to copy the management styles of the successful managers they see around them. There is nothing wrong with this but don't forget you can learn just as much by watching the failures of those who don't make it, observing the reasons behind their failures, and taking them to heart so you can avoid their fatal mistakes.

Benefits of a Corporate Apprenticeship for Those Planning Careers Outside of the Corporate World

A corporate apprenticeship can contribute a lot to your subsequent career, even if you intend to strike out in a more entrepreneurial direction, for example, into developing your own software products or running your own consulting business. The major benefit, of course, is that you learn a lot about computers. But beyond that you should pick up the following:

♦ Knowledge of how a business operates

♦ Contacts within the corporate community

♦ Knowledge of the needs of the business community, which can lead you to base a successful business on filling those needs

If you are like many technical people, you have always felt convinced that you would end up with your own business because you have such great ideas, but you don't see yourself as a business type. A few years of working in a profitable, well run company can teach you a lot about how to think like a successful businessperson. When you encounter marketing people, production staff, and financial professionals and see the responsibilities they must take on, you begin to get a feel for what you will deal with in any business of your own, even though yours will be on a much smaller scale.

You will gain respect for the problems you can encounter in each of these areas. You should also begin to see people who have a knack for getting people to give their best and conversely, people who can create interpersonal havoc with their management style. All this is real-world experience and it may prove far more valuable to you as a fledgling entrepreneur than any business school coursework. Should you start a business of your own you will need to perform most of the functions that the larger companies do, the only difference being that you will have to be a lot better at it than they are, since your margin for error will be a lot slimmer.

If you are planning to take off in an entrepreneurial direction you will need more than experience. Chances are that you will need business contacts. If you are selling something to business you will need to know who has the authority to buy what you have on the market. If you have paid attention while working in a couple of companies you should know who these people are. Keep aware of who does what in the companies you work for. Make sure that middle management knows you by name if at all possible. When you leave a job, do it carefully, and don't use leaving as an opportunity to blow off steam and let management know what you think of their lousy way of doing business. If you want to sell services or software your current managers—and some coworkers—will be your future customers. Many of those who enter as trainees when you do will be entering management just around the time you will be beginning to get your business off the ground.

Your apprenticeship period is also the time when you are most likely to meet people you could partner with when you go out on your own, as well as people who you could hire when your company's needs expand.

So no matter how confining you might find the corporate world as a potential entrepreneur, tell yourself you are prospecting for customers. Establish your reputation for competence and your IT apprenticeship may build a very strong base for an entrepreneurial future.

Finally, if you are alert during your corporate apprenticeship you should start seeing all sorts of niches in the corporate world where services or products you could provide might fit in. Corporations are the best customers to have because they have lots of money to spend and they tend to think in big numbers. Keep your eyes open for the ways some of that money could be spent on things that you could sell.

CHAPTER 5

Contract Consulting

Some people are cut out for the corporate life. They enjoy the security of knowing that their paychecks will arrive regularly. They are proud of the products the XYZ Corp. produces and proud to have something to do with producing them. They are joiners and feel good about being part of a large powerful company. They enjoy the people they work with, too, and feel confident that their efforts will be rewarded fairly.

Other people are different. After four or five years of working in a corporate environment they want something else. The predictability of their paycheck is irksome because, while it is always there, it is always the same amount and they know it will not make them rich. Maybe the rigidity and the bureaucracy of large companies gets to them. They find their creativity stifled and are frustrated by a system in which it seems mediocrity, not originality, is rewarded. Maybe it's just the fact that no one ever laughs at their best jokes. Whatever the reason, there comes a time for many people when they decide they want something new and for many experienced computer professionals, that something new turns out to be a switch to contract computer consulting.

Contract computer consulting, which we will be abbreviating to "contracting" here, is an odd blend of entrepreneurship and employee-ship. Contractors have a lot more control over their earnings, assignments, and career development than do salaried corporate employees yet they still work for corporate employers doing jobs very similar to those done by regular employees. Some contractors work on a salary basis and are paid the same as regular employees, but others, who are willing to take on more risk and know how to negotiate the best deals, can earn impressive incomes. The median hourly rate reported to the Real Rate Survey in 1999 by contractors paid on an hourly basis was $65 per hour, a rate that could conceivably generate an annual income of $130,000 or more, while the *highest* rates reported by contractors to the Real Rate Survey were above $150 per hour—rates that in ideal conditions might generate an annual income as high as $300,000.

What makes this all the more interesting is that despite these impressive earnings, in most cases the jobs these contractors fill are identical to those of employees paid far less. Some contractors work for a single client for many years. Others manage client employees or take on high-level project architecture tasks.

In the pages that follow, we'll look into what is involved in computer contracting, what it takes to get started in it, and how to protect yourself from its most obvious pitfalls should contract consulting be the career path you choose.

Most "Consultants" Are Temps

Although the term "consultant" conjures up the image of a wise adviser sharing wisdom with admiring recipients, most so-called consultants in no way consult. The term "consultant" in the IT world has come, more and more, to be an upscale synonym for temporary help. Almost all consultant positions that are advertised, both internally within companies and externally in the newspaper or by employment agencies, are positions that call for people to do exactly what they would do as full-time corporate employees but to do it for a limited time. The reason that these people are called "contractors" is that each temporary job is defined by a legal contract, signed by the person doing the work, which sets out the job's length, rate of pay, and other pertinent conditions.

During the 1990s, as a cost cutting measure, many companies downsized most of their salaried IT staff only to replace them with consultants. This trend reached a peak as companies prepared for Y2K. At the height of the consultant boom it was not unusual to encounter entire IT departments staffed only by contractors. Though rapidly rising contract rates in the year 2000 convinced many employers of the wisdom of going back to using a full-time-employee-only hiring strategy, most large companies still employ far more contract consultants than their stated hiring goals would suggest. This is particularly true when projects involve cutting-edge technologies.

Advantages of Using Contract Workers to Employers

Hiring consultants prevents a company that faces fluctuating headcount needs from having to lay off workers and having to deal with the ill will that such layoffs can generate. It allows them to dispense with having to train employees and it lets them bypass all the restrictions that the Human Resources (HR) department might impose on them that would make them have to treat employees fairly. Contractors can be hired and fired at will and with no lengthy formal justification process, they receive no performance reviews, and they do not need company picnics to motivate them. Best of all, contract consultants get no benefits—no company paid health insurance, disability insurance, or pension contributions—which in itself can represent a huge cost saving to employers.

Another benefit of hiring contractors is that, if paid enough, they will often take jobs in areas that regular employees would shun as dead-end or low status. A surprising number of highly paid contract consultants can be found doing the most boring kinds of work on aging systems so that the company can offer its regular employees more challenging assignments.

"Consulting Firms" and Salaried Contractors

As more and more large IT employers replaced their salaried staff with highly paid contractors in the late 1980s, the business of providing these temporary staffers became an extremely profitable one. Name brand consulting firms routinely billed clients rates of $225 per hour for the services of their personnel—though of course, the personnel themselves never saw more than a very small fraction of this billing dollar.

But the potential of making this kind of profit soon attracted companies from a wide variety of other industries. These included employment agencies like Kelly and Manpower that traditionally specialized in placing typists and warehouse workers, major accounting firms like Arthur Andersen, and even hardware vendors like IBM and GE. Suddenly all of these companies reinvented themselves as "Enterprise Solution Providers" offering IT Consulting Services.

Most of these "consulting" companies prefer to sell their corporate customers the services of their own salaried employees rather than hiring true consultants who would work each assignment on a contract basis. And though their clients may pay very high hourly rates for their "consultant's"services, these consulting firms treat their "consultant" employees no differently than any other salaried employee. They receive a salary that is usually close to the median for salaried employees with their level of skills and experience and they receive standard company benefits, periodic raises and salary reviews.

You will frequently be recruited into this kind of "consulting" job early on in your career, since many of the name brand consulting firms are notorious for having senior partners *sell* projects while college new hires perform the actual work. When demand is strong, these companies will also recruit experienced computer personnel with two to five years of experience. The pitch that these companies use to recruit more experienced employees usually appeals to people who are bored with their career but not willing to give up the security of a permanent job. Typically these companies promise that as their employee you will get intensive education in new software and will work on exciting state of the art projects. The salaries these firms pay may be a little higher than the salary you received as a regular corporate employee but not by much. The recruiters stress that they offer benefit packages and job security, promising potential "consultants" that if they are unable to find them contract work they will have paid time off while "on the bench."

Needless to say, these companies are not in business for their health and few people ever get paid while lolling on the beach.

Most employee consultants that I have encountered work at least full time and often a lot of overtime. If the company cannot find them work that they can bill out at $225 an hour they will usually drop their rates and bid less until they can place the employee somewhere, since anything over about $40 an hour represents profit to the company.

Occasionally these kinds of consulting firms staffed with full time salaried "consultants" specialize in creating project teams. They work like this: The company is brought in to bid on a specific project, competing against similar firms. The company asking for bids will provide the consulting firms with some kind of specification package describing the job they want done. The consulting firm then gives its experienced systems analysts the job of estimating the project in terms of how it should be done and how much time and effort will be required to complete it. Based on these estimates the company submits a bid offering either to do the job for a fixed amount or else offering to do it in a specific way but billing for time and materials. If they are awarded the contract the consulting firm then assembles a team made up of experienced systems analysts with project management experience and other programmers with the specific skills needed for the project and sets them to work on the job. If the customer changes his specifications or requests more function the price of the project must be renegotiated.

Small companies and mom and pop consultant groups rarely get to bid on these projects, since the larger companies can devote full time sales forces to lining them up. Programmers working on a project team like this might get good experience in learning how to effectively estimate and manage projects, since a company working under such arrangements has the strongest possible incentive to estimate correctly — if they are wrong they may have to eat the difference. Sometimes, however, this kind of contract leads the consulting firm to subject its employees to sweatshop conditions; unending overtime and intimidation tactics have been known to occur in this kind of situation, particularly when the company is employing salaried personnel.

Some of these consulting companies represent valid corporate career paths and do provide their employees with excellent training and exposure. The very best companies offer the potential to become a part-ner in the company at some future time with the possibility of an income well in excess of $100,000 a year. But these are the exception. Most con-sulting firms are quite different. They are called "body shops" in the trade because their forte is supplying warm bodies at cut-rate prices to desperate employers.

Body Shops

Though they like to portray themselves in advertisements as "consulting firms" in fact body shops are really nothing more than temporary em-ployment agencies. Their permanent staff have little or no knowledge of IT or software development. Their only function is to find an open con-tract position and fill it. Their recruiters, whose own career histories usu-ally include nothing more than telemarketing-type sales work, are notorious in the industry for sleazy ethics and shyster behavior. Though these companies will try to portray themselves as the peers of companies like the Big Five and IBM, they are frequently fly-by-night operations that do nothing but match contractors with open positions. In return for their matchmaking services they keep anywhere from thirty to eighty percent of every dollar the client pays for the contractor's work for the length of the contract. You will find these companies everywhere. They advertise in the newspaper and clog Web job boards.

Contractors who Work Direct

Many experienced contractors who have built up relationships with cli-ent companies work without any middleman. They find their own con-tracts, negotiate these contracts themselves, and bill the client directly. Though most of these contractors still function as temporary workers, a very small number of them eventually evolve their businesses to where they are true entrepreneurial consultants rather than temporary workers.

Evaluating Consulting Firms

If you are thinking of working for a consulting firm talk to several people who have worked for that firm for a few years and find out what kind of assignments and working conditions they have experienced. You can also find out a lot about a consulting firm's reputation by posting a query on the Realrates.com BBS or on other Web consulting discussion groups.

If promises of job security, benefits, education, and interesting work tempt you to take a salaried—rather than hourly rate—consulting firm job, try to find out how long people actually work for this company. Do they lay people off quickly when the business cycle enters one of its con-tractions? Do they send people out on projects that sound interesting to you? What education have they provided their employees in the previous year and what did the employees have to do to get it? If work runs out in your local area, will the company fire you if you don't take any contract they present you, including those involving the most dead-end technology and located two or three hours away? Finally, check out the average number of years of experience of their so-called consultants, and beware of those firms who are peddling people with brief work histories or whose employees are mostly foreigners brought in on H1-B "guest worker" visas whose visa terms make them for all practical purposes captives of the consulting firm. These are often the firms that are the most unscrupulous to deal with.

You will have to judge any opportunity with a consulting firm carefully. You must, as usual, be highly skeptical of any claims made by those who hire you. You should also try to track down people who have worked for the firms, even more so than when looking at other kinds of employers since the potential for abuse is greater. Nevertheless, positions with dynamic consulting firms run by ethical, intelligent data processing professionals can offer a welcome change from working at a single corporate employer.

The Many Confusing Statuses of Computer Contractors

If you decide to become a contractor you will discover that there is a great deal of confusion in the marketplace about your actual status on the job. Contractors doing the identical work on a project may work as regular salaried employees of consulting firms or they may work instead as a special kind of W-2 employee who is paid on an hourly rate basis — for actual hours worked — getting no benefits but earning much higher dollars per hour. Yet other contractors may fill the very same contract positions working as self-employed independent contractors (ICs), whose earnings are reported to the IRS on 1099 forms at the end of the year, or, in yet other cases, they may fill them while working as employees of their own corporations.

This is because lobbyists for a couple of large body shops talked Congress into including some obscure wording into the Tax Reform Act of 1986 that made it far more difficult for programmers, systems analysts, and engineers to qualify for the self-employed "independent contractor" status which would let computer professionals be treated as true contractors. In response to these lobbyists, Congress toughened the standards by which a programmer or engineer was judged to be a contractor and raised the threat of major tax penalties for employers who did not withhold taxes and social security from the pay of computer "contractors" that the IRS reclassified as employees.

The portion of the Tax Reform Act of 1986 that did this was called *Paragraph 1706*. Up until the passage of Paragraph 1706 programmers and engineers were exempted from having to fulfill all the conditions of the common law definition of independent contractor because of an earlier law, called Section 530 of the Revenue Act of 1978, which provided a so called "safe harbor" relieving technical contractors from having to fulfill these conditions. As a result, before the 1986 Tax Reform almost all computer contractors worked as sole-proprietors or incorporated small businesses.

To modify this, Paragraph 1706 of the Tax Reform Act of 1986 stated merely that Section 530 "shall not apply in the case of an individual who, pursuant to an arrangement between the taxpayer and another person, provides services for such other person as an engineer, designer, drafter, computer programmer, systems analyst or other similarly skilled worker engaged in a similar line of work." Needless to say given the clarity of this language, no one, including the legal departments of most client companies and consulting firms has ever agreed on what the law really meant or even to whom it applied. Particularly questionable was whether the paragraph applied to *all* contractors, including those who found work with clients on their own. or only to those who worked through *third party firms* — i.e. consulting firms.

However, the common law definition of an employee as interpreted by the IRS says that an employee is a person who works at the premises of his employer, for an hourly rather than a project rate, can be fired by the employer at will, has his work directed by the employer, has his tools furnished by the employer, and runs no personal risk of losing money on an assignment, among other factors. This renders very iffy the claims to independence of computer contractors who work on site forty hours a week for a single client, doing what that client's managers direct them to do, using the client's equipment — sometimes for years at a time.

As a result of this, many client companies will not deal with self employed computer contractors for fear of encountering tax penalties and insist that the "contractors" they hire be salaried employees of consulting firms. However, experienced consultants with in-demand skills who wanted to earn the best return for these risky, short term temporary stints put pressure on consulting firms to establish a special class of employee for them — one that retains a more entrepreneurial flavor.

The result is that there are now *two* different types of consulting firm employees. One is the regular salaried employee who is paid a normal employee-style annual salary with benefits and who expects to work for the consulting firm for the foreseeable future, and the second is the "hourly rate employee."

Hourly Rate Contractors

Hourly rate contractors are a special group of employees who take jobs that are intended to last only for a limited period. The length and conditions of their employment on these temporary jobs are defined by legal contracts very similar to those used by true independent contractors. These contractors usually receive no benefits and are paid an hourly rate for actual hours worked. This hourly rate is a percentage of the hourly rate the consulting firm bills the client for their services. The rate the contractor receives is usually much higher than the amount they would receive for each hour worked as a regular salaried employee. But they are being paid a premium because they face unemployment as soon as the client has no more need for their services.

Though most body shops will try to talk you into working for them as a salaried employee, most savvy contractors refuse to take the jobs these companies offer on any basis except as hourly rate contractors — and they negotiate fiercely to make sure that the rate they are paid is at least sixty-five percent of the amount that the client is paying the consulting firm for that same hour of work. These contractors are not taken in by the argument that company employees get job security or valuable benefits that hourly personnel don't, because they know that body shops will lay anyone off as soon as the work runs out and they prefer to buy their own benefits with their much higher hourly rate earnings.

Since they are legally employees rather than self-employed business owners, hourly rate contractors have taxes withheld from their paychecks and cannot deduct their business expenses or contribute to a Keogh or SEP small business pension plan. Nor can they deduct the cost of self-paid health insurance as they could were they true independent contractors. But contractors paid on an hourly basis earn a lot more for their work than do regular employees and unlike true contractors, they covered by all federal and state labor laws and can qualify for unemployment compensation.

To make the picture even more confusing, in some cities many companies still allow computer contractors to work for them as sole proprietors, especially if the contractors can show that they are working for more than one client at a time and have significant investments in their own business. In other regions corporations will hire only independent contractors who are incorporated and thus, legally, the employees of their own corporation. Which status employers will demand contract workers adopt often varies from city to city. So if you decide to become a contractor, you will need to do some research about the conditions that prevail in your region before you can determine what the best status would be for you. This topic — and many others relating to how to succeed at computer contracting — is discussed in much greater detail in my book, *Answers for Computer Contractors*.

Drawbacks of Contracting

The major problem with contracting is that it is a very unpredictable way to make a living. Despite claims that salaried consulting work offers job security, salaried consulting firm employees are likely to be fired as soon as the company cannot find them another client. If you choose work from contract to contract on an hourly rate basis you may earn more on each job you work, but you won't be hired at all if consulting firms can fill an open contract with a cheaper, lower-paid salaried contractor or H-1B visa holder.

Furthermore, you are utterly at the mercy of your client and the consulting firm, either of which may fire you at any time. And although your contract specifies an appealingly high hourly rate, all kinds of factors can limit the number of hours you actually work. For starters, you don't get paid on company holidays. Getting sick becomes painfully expensive when you are losing upwards of $600 a day for each day of the flu. The hour or two that you are accustomed to taking as an employee to drop in at your kid's school play or to see the doctor suddenly costs you a bundle. So when you try to estimate your earnings from a contract you must plan for these inevitable unpaid hours.

Because you may very well find yourself with several unpaid days every month—or without any work at all—if your financial situation is such that you must have a certain amount of cash coming in each month and you have no cushion of savings to tide you over, contracting should probably be your last resort. It is best to try contracting only if you have six months worth of living expenses stashed away or are faced with no other better job alternatives. And don't fool yourself that you are covered because you have been offered a six-month-long contract. Contracts written for any length of time can disappear in a moment leaving you with no recourse and no visible means of support.

Some companies will let you keep more of your billing dollar if you wait for your pay until the client company pays the consulting firm. This can be an excellent way to add another $5 or $10 an hour to your check. However if you go this route be aware that you may not receive a check for several months after you submit your invoice. Companies are often agonizingly slow to pay and the consulting firm is not going to antagonize a customer by hounding them if they are assured that the company eventually will pay, as most do. Again, don't take this route if you could find yourself in economic distress from missing a paycheck.

Health Insurance

If you have a spouse who has a job that provides good health benefits you don't have to worry about providing your own health insurance. But if you are supporting yourself or are the family's main breadwinner, health insurance becomes a major issue when you are an unbenefitted contractor. The extra pay you earn as a contractor can comfortably cover paying your own health benefits, but this will represent a major line item on your personal budget. If you work as a hourly rate employee consultant you can't qualify for small business insurance plans either so you may have to pay extremely high individual rates to get coverage.

There is a potential land mine here, however, of which you should be aware. If you apply for individual health insurance—or for group health insurance when you were not previously covered for eighteen months by a group insurance plan—you might be horrified to discover that you can be rejected if anyone in your family has anything in their medical history which suggests anything less than perfect health. Insurers may ask you to pay for doctors' examinations to determine the extent of your family members' problems and then reject you when the doctors make their reports. The only insurance open to you then can be ruinously expensive—or unattainable.

A federal law, the Consolidated Omnibus Budget Reconciliation Act (COBRA) of 1986, requires employers of more than twenty employees to offer former employees continued insurance coverage under the company health plan as long as the former employee pays the premium. In addition, some state laws force your previous employer to allow you to remain on the company plan as a self-paying member for a longer period than does the federal law. This group insurance may also cover benefits that the individual plans offered by the same organizations do not, like prescription drug reimbursement. But it is often extremely expensive.

Another important law to keep in mind is the Kennedy-Kassebaum Insurance Portability Act, which mandates that you cannot be turned down for group insurance as long as you have been covered by a group plan during the past eighteen months. This law is of great help to anyone whose family members have a history of illness of any kind. However, you can jeopardize your eligibility for group coverage if you don't maintain membership in a group plan after you leave a job that included company-sponsored group health insurance.

So obviously, before you leave a salaried job that provides health insurance coverage you must be sure to find out what your insurance options will be when you quit. A single uncovered health emergency with its hundreds of thousands of dollars of hospital and doctor bills could be a life-shattering disaster. Remember that no state or federal assistance programs help people who have modest assets. You could lose your home if someone in the family came down with a sudden serious illness or had an uncovered accident. This is not an area in which you can afford to be sloppy.

Some consulting firms will let hourly employees join their plans by subtracting a fixed amount from each dollar you earn for the premiums. This is a good deal for you only if you have no other alternatives since as soon as you leave the plan your insurance will terminate.

Disability Insurance

If you are a contractor you should also consider buying disability insurance, because you will stop getting paid the day that an illness or accident makes you unable work. Unfortunately, once you have a health history of any kind you cannot purchase this kind of coverage. So, consult with a capable insurance salesperson while you are still healthy and find a plan that has the least restrictive payout conditions. On a contractor's income you can afford it. Why leave yourself open to disaster?

Contracts Evaporate without Warning

A major problem with contracting is your fundamental helplessness when dealing with both the consulting firm and the client firm where you do your work. Although you sign an ornate contract that specifies a term during which you are supposed to work, as far as you, the contractor, are concerned this contract is a piece of junk. If you break it you can find yourself enmeshed in acrimonious disputes with the consulting firm and may have your wages denied or even face a lawsuit. But all consulting firm contracts and most direct client firm contracts are written in such a way that the client company you are contracted to work for can dump you at any time without penalty and there is nothing you can do about it.

Many a shocked contractor has thought that if the client terminated the contract before the specified term ended they were owed some compensation, possibly the full amount of the contract. Absolutely not. Business needs change and projects get canceled. No client company would sign a consulting firm contract that bound them to pay you no matter what their needs. If the project you are hired for gets the ax, you can be on the street with five minutes' notice. Worse, if you encounter a personality conflict on the job, you can also be canned instantly with no recourse to the usual procedures that companies have in place to prevent vindictive firings.

Even if your contract might technically enable you to go to court when you are the victim of abuse, the company can always claim that you were not doing a satisfactory job. Most consultant contracts are worded so that "unsatisfactory performance" is grounds for immediate termination. And no matter what your legal rights, are you really ready to pay a lawyer to take on a multimillion-dollar corporation? Who needs that kind of hassle?

You can't expect the consulting firm that is legally your employer to act in your best interest either. If a client employee lodges a malicious complaint against you and the client firm throws you out without even considering your side of the story, the consulting firm is not going to jeopardize the future business it could do with that client company to stick up for a single contractor, even if they know that the charge is not true.

This is not a trivial problem. A large number of the projects that are forced to hire contractors are projects that are in trouble. As a contractor you have no clue as to what political forces are operating but you may find yourself at the very center of them. In a project that is failing to meet its dates or has insurmountable technical problems it is not unusual for management to seek scapegoats to blame for the disaster. Blaming the contractor can be the perfect short-term solution in this case, and you might find yourself fired for no better reason than that a manager needed to show his boss that he was taking aggressive steps to "solve" the project's problems.

Even in a project that is not a complete disaster consultants can find themselves the target of unreasonable abuse. Disgruntled employees often focus on the contractor's high pay rate and try to shoot the contractor down, loudly pointing out to their management and coworkers the contractor's errors. If you are unfortunate enough to make the kind of mistake that results in a dolly-load of paper being delivered to your output drop—as has happened to us all—or if you move something into production that bombs on its first run—which also happens—this kind of employee will make an issue out of it. If management considers the complainer important enough to pacify, out the door you may go, no matter what the quality of the rest of your work.

What this means is that as a contractor you must exercise incredible care in your relationships with everyone you work with. You cannot survive more than one or two complaints about your work since there is no review procedure as there would be for a full-time employee. Even if you are blameless and a star performer you must never assume that your contract will run the length of the time that it is written for, since you can be terminated any time management decides its time for some visible cost cutting.

The Threat of Technical Obsolescence

Beyond these drawbacks there is another issue you need to take a hard look at before jumping into contracting. Though many people have a glamorous picture of contract consulting, the reality is that probably eighty percent of the contracting jobs that you turn up will involve doing work which would cause you to quit had you been given it as part of a regular, full-time job.

Consultants get to do the most boring parts of any project since most companies prefer to give the interesting stuff to good employees so that they will be motivated to stay with the company. So as a contractor—no matter how well-paid—you may end up doing a lot of drudge work: brute coding off of other people's detailed specifications, setting up reports, and creating test data. This frees up the regular employees to do the fun stuff.

The fact that you have impressive experience—much better experience than the people running the project do, means nothing. Clients hire overqualified contractors to do simple tasks because they thus guarantee themselves that the work will be done perfectly. This can result in situations like one I've seen where a consultant who had written articles about CICS internals published in the trade press spent several months on a project doing nothing more than typing in the text for help screens.

This can be very frustrating if you are used to being a team leader or having your opinions taken seriously when design issues come up. You will have to watch the employees getting the interesting work while you deal with boring junk. You rarely will be asked to do any true knowledge work unless you work as a contractor in the same department for several years.

Closely related to this problem is that if you remain a contractor for a long time your skills may atrophy. This is because you will almost always be hired to work with only those software tools that you have used on past assignments. You will rarely get any formal training in new tools or techniques. Even if you pay for your own training it may be very hard to find a contract where you can use new skills, since clients usually demand that you have previous paid experience with a technology before they will hire you to use it as a contractor. So after a few years of contracting you may find that you are not getting exposure to the latest tools technologies and eventually your niche may dry up all together.

Problems Getting Paid

If you are used to dealing with large corporate employers that are bound by complex federally enforced labor laws you might find it a shock to discover that a small consulting firm may try to get away with not paying you for work you have done. It doesn't happen a lot, but it does happen, and most working contractors can tell you a few war stories. Your money may be held back because of a dispute with the consulting firm if your consulting firm interprets your contract to mean one thing and you disagree. If you quit a contract abruptly, you may have real difficulty collecting your last few weeks' earnings. Other reasons a firm may hold your checks might be if you take another contract at the same client company with a different consulting firm, or if the consulting firm itself goes out of business. In cases like this you might have unequivocal legal right on your side, but it can be a huge hassle recovering the money due to you.

If the amount is not large you may be able to recover it in small claims court. Look into what the dollar limits are in your state. If the amount owed is more than a few thousand dollars you are looking at serious litigation to recover it. It is also worth contacting the state bureau of labor if you are working as any kind of employee.

Your best protection against this kind of problem is to know whom you are dealing with when you enter into a relationship with a consulting firm. Be very suspicious of out-of-town consulting firms with no local reputations. Talk to contractors who have been in the business for awhile and ask them explicit questions about any firm you are considering. But even this may not be enough. After a harrowing brush with one outfit, I found that all my buddies knew about that company's unethical practices, but no one said a word when I began my relationship with them, because, as one friend told me "I thought, maybe my problems with them was just me." So I didn't hear the horror tales until I had had my own experience.

The Contract Itself

As an employee contractor working through a consulting firm, the only legal relationship you have is with the consulting firm who is your legal employer — you have *no* legal contract with the client for whom you will actually be working. This means that you must be very careful to examine the actual contract before you sign it and to modify or eliminate any clause with which you are not comfortable. Make sure that you understand everything you are signing. Don't rely on any verbal assurances you are given that contradict what is written on the paper. If there is a difference, insist that the assurance be written into the text of the contract. If you get into a conflict, only this written contract document will have standing in court. There is nothing that says that you can't add terms or cross them out. In particular, be very careful to limit the scope of the consulting company's exclusivity clause.

Exclusivity Clauses

Exclusivity clauses are little bombshells buried in most contracts supplied by consulting firms that bind you to working for the same consulting firm in future contracts, either at the company where the consulting firm is placing you or, sometimes, even at other companies. Try to limit the scope of any exclusivity clause to the single department or the division that you are will be working for. Otherwise, if you have a falling-out with the consulting firm you might find yourself unable to work at a customer site where you are very much in demand. You might also have to turn down contracts at that company offered by other firms which would have given you a better rate. Since your goal, if possible, is to work directly for clients without any middleman, the shorter the time period that an exclusivity clause is in effect, the sooner you can work directly for a satisfied client without the consulting firm taking their cut. One year is standard. You should also exclude from the scope of an exclusivity clause, in writing, the names of any managers or departments you have previously established links with that might yield future contracts.

Technically, these exclusivity clauses are probably illegal in many states they are written in, since they contradict right-to-work laws. However, the amount of legal hassle you have to go through to defend yourself in court is not worth it. There are a few truly rotten companies that prosecute cases involving this issue through court after court and appeal after appeal — even though they continue to lose.

In negotiating the contract make sure that there is some way you can get out of the specified term. As an employee you always have the right to quit with notice. Even when you work as in independent, most clients will accept your leaving if you give a few weeks' notice. Make sure that this is in writing so that there is no conflict if you have to leave. Otherwise the consulting firm or client may withhold your last check.

Finally, be very careful when the question of signing an extension of the original contract comes up. Make sure that the original contract does not somehow specify that you must extend the contract at the original rate. You should be able to negotiate for more money when a six-month or year-long contract ends.

BEST CAREER MOVE

"Generic database development experience led to Lotus Notes experience. After gaining Lotus Notes development expertise (2+ yrs), I started contracting for a fifty percent initial jump in pay. A year later, that increased by another seventy percent.

"It's wonderfully freeing. I'm an on-site contractor (1.25 years and counting) so I'm accepted as one of the team, but I'm less affected by office politics. It's nice to be able to leave work at work. Plus, I only work forty hours per week!"

Benefits of Contracting

Having just painted a rather bleak picture of consulting I would like to remark that it is the way I made my living for years. With all the possible pitfalls, it offers some unbeatable advantages.

Primary, of course, is a sense of freedom. Many of the contractors I know who have been in the business for ten years or more admit they couldn't work any other way. As a contractor, you do not have to take seriously a whole set of things "real" employees do. You do not have to pretend to be loyal to the company. You don't have to get involved in the struggle to get ahead in the company. You don't have to feel bad when dumber people get promoted since you are not playing that game, and finally, if you are an hourly rate contractor and have done your homework, you have the tremendous consolation in every situation of knowing that you are getting paid as much as just about anyone you meet—often more than the managers giving you your assignments.

Being a contractor lets you distance yourself from the business mentality and concentrate on the technical work you love. You also don't have to pretend that you are never going to leave the company. If a recruiter calls with a great job offer and leaves a phone number, it's okay. Everyone knows you are only there temporarily. If you are trying to get a business of your own off the ground you can contract for half the year and work on your own business the rest of the time and still make enough money to pay your bills.

Contracting offers people who would like to spend time with their young children a realistic alternative to year-round day care. While you will probably have to work full forty-hour weeks while you are contracting, you can get by working a lot fewer of those weeks. It is easier to leave an infant or small child with someone else when you know that work will last for only ten or twelve weeks. When the contract is done you can spend undivided time at home with your child, with the security of knowing that you have put a nice chunk of money in the bank and kept your skills — and long term career — alive.

Consulting Versus Working Part-time

Having worked both as a year-round, part-time employee and as a short-term contract consultant while my children were little I would say that being a contractor has several advantages.

First of all, it is a lot easier to find short consulting jobs than it is to find part-time positions. In fact, it is almost impossible to get a high paying part-time IT position unless it is with a company where you have worked full-time for a long time and rendered yourself indispensable. In contrast, very short-term contracts of three months and under are frequently available. You may find it easier to get these extremely short contracts since most contractors don't like them since they prefer the relative security of longer contracts.

Second of all, you are given far more respect as a full-time, short-term consultant than as a part-timer. Businesspeople do not generally like to deal with part-time workers. They fear, rightly, that you won't be there when something important comes up, and wrongly, that you won't work as hard as full-time employees. In truth, part-timers often work harder than full-time employees, not taking the leisurely lunches and long telephone breaks that full-time workers feel entitled to. But businesses probably *really* don't like to use part-timers because they think it demoralizes full-time staff to see others going home early. Whatever the reason, as a part-time worker you will find you have to deal with a lot of unspoken resentment that is not an issue when you work as a short-term consultant.

Finally, there is one overriding advantage to being a short-term contractor. Money. When I worked as a part-timer my bosses acted as if they were doing me a tremendous favor by letting me work at all, and I, out of gratitude, was expected to sacrifice most of the benefits and much of the pay I would have received had I been full-time in the same job. I was paid an hourly salary that was exactly what my old job paid on an hourly basis without benefits. Though I got paid for holidays that fell on my working days I did not get sick days or any health or other insurance benefits even though I worked over twenty hours a week. This is a typical part-time arrangement.

I felt very lucky to be able to work under this arrangement until I had my second child and discovered that I would net about $75 a week for three full days' work after paying taxes and day care charges for two children. That was when I discovered that I could get twice my old hourly rate if I worked, instead, as a contractor. Though I still didn't get paid holidays, I made more money working eleven weeks as a contractor than I had made working six and one-half months as a part-timer—and I only had to pay for eleven weeks of full time day care as opposed to the twenty-eight weeks of full time care I paid for when I worked part-time! With infant/toddler day care running at $250 a week or more per child, you can see that short-term consulting makes terrific sense economically as well as emotionally for the mothers of young children.

Incidentally, after working short-term contracts and establishing a reputation you may find clients who are willing to let you work as a part-time contractor or who will let you work from your home office. This is the best possible arrangement if you want to have time off during the week for your outside interests and still make high consultant rates.

Further Benefits of Contracting

Contracting allows you to travel while earning your keep. I have heard from many contractors who have taken contract assignments around the U.S. and the world. Many non-U.S. citizens have been able to get visas to work in the United States by coming in as contractors too. You might even be able to work in foreign countries with limited language skills since English is used by many international companies as the company language. Even if you work in your own country, as a contractor, you can schedule lengthy trips abroad during two or three months each year when you are between assignments.

Contracting also offers you the opportunity to see local companies as a "tourist." You can work short stints in area companies and get a better idea of what they feel like and what kinds of opportunities they offer. If you would like to be a corporate employee but don't have a feeling for what work you would be happiest doing or what local company you would most enjoy, working short stints as a contractor will give you experience that can help you make up your mind. It will also let you build up a good reputation at several companies, which will make it much easier to get the kind of full-time job there that you would want. It is not unheard of for contractors who have worked extensively at client companies to eventually be hired directly into their managements, at very nice salaries too.

Contracting also exposes you to a lot of situations that sharpen up your systems analysis and development skills — not because you do a lot of systems analysis, mind you, but because you see a lot of poorly-managed projects which have gotten in trouble, resulting in the need for you, the contractor, to be brought in! Since you see a lot of crisis situations you will learn a great deal about how *not* to manage a project, which, should you incline towards management later in your career, can be of tremendous use to you.

The final benefit of consulting is that if you are persistent and handle yourself well after a few years you can build up a client base of your own. This may enable you to dispense with the services of the consulting firms and start making some serious money working directly for clients. If you can build up this kind of consulting practice you can make an enormous income, be treated as an independent businessperson, and perhaps even end up employing others and building a very satisfying career for yourself.

What do Contractors Get Paid?

Contractors new to contracting are often shocked to discover on the job that other contractors with much weaker skills are getting paid far more than they are. This is because many consulting firms take advantage of newbie contractors and offer them far less than the amount they could have negotiated for if they had made an effort to familiarize themselves with the rates and salaries being paid for their skills in their local market before approaching the consulting firm. In addition, contractors who accept annual salaries similar to those of regular IT employees, in the mistaken belief that salaried contracting offers more job security than hourly rate contracting, often earn far less than their peers who work similar contracts on an hourly rate basis.

The chart on the next page shows some actual rates and salaries paid to contractors with different skill sets in different cities in 1999. This data comes from the Real Rate Survey and the Real Salary Survey.

What Experience do you Need to Begin Contract Consulting?

If you are a salaried computer professional who has been considering going the contractor route you have probably wondered what qualifications you need to break in. You probably also wonder how to get started. The answer to this is, "It depends."

The demand for contracting services is extremely cyclical. It rises to peaks as it did in the mid 1980s and late 1990s but these peaks in demand are followed by collapse in the contracting market as happened during early 1990s and, it appears likely, the early 2000s.

Sample Contract Rates

TECHNOLOGY	CITY	ST	INDUSTRY	RATE
Cobol/Idms/Mvs	Seattle	WA	Aerospace	$50
Tandem	New Castle	DE	Banking	$10
Visual Foxpro & Ms Sql7.0/Nt	Fremont	CA	Comp Hardware	$70
Html/Photoshop/Fireworks/Perl	Atlanta	GA	Education	$29
Netware/NT	Houston	TX	Banking	$50
Filemaker, HTML, CDML, Mac/PC	San Francisco	CA	Real Estate	$45
Windows NT/Exchange Rollout	Los Angeles	CA	Health Care	$55
Hp-Ux	Milwaukee	WI	Health Care	$60
Oracle DBA	New York	NY	Financial	$100
Technical Support	Houston	TX	Comp Hardware	$25
Shell/Solaris/Sybase	Palo Alto	CA	Comp Hardware	$69
Java	Hartford	CT	E-Commerce	$55
Asp/Css/Html/Sql	Chicago	IL	Web Site Design	$60
Vc++/Windows/Financial	West Palm Beach	FL	Software	$42
95/98/Nt Web Sap	Brea	CA	E-Commerce	$30
Peoplesoft	Pittsburgh	PA	Retail	$83
Db2 Dba Mvs 0s/390	Dallas	TX	Automotive	$64
Lotus Notes/Domino	Houston	TX	Banking	$40
Vb/Win Nt/Sql	Lisle	IL	Software	$57
Oracle, Unix, Development	San Jose	CA	Telecom	$85
Asp/Sql Server/Vb	Irving	TX	E-Commerce	$58
Sas/Unix/Mvs/Vax	Collegeville	PA	Pharmaceutical	$54
Oracle	Richmond	VA	Financial	$60
AS/400 And Mainframe MVS	Lenexa	KS	Telecom	$25

Sample Contracting Salaries

TECHNOLOGY	CITY	ST	INDUSTRY	SALARY
C++, Java	San Diego	CA	Financial	$150,000
Configuration Management	San Diego	CA	Financial	$150,000
Lotus Notes Development	Chicago	IL	Consulting	$44,000
Windows95	Poughkeepsie	NY	Consulting	$37,500
Rpg/As/400/Bpcs	Atlanta	GA	Consulting	$73,000
Windows NT	Salt Lake City	UT	Networking	$50,000
Telecommuincations Networks	Leesburg	VA	Consulting	$99,000
Data Warehouse	Chicago	IL	Consulting	$65,000
Oracle Developer/Designer	Tampa	FL	Software	$84,000
Siebel	Boston	MA	Consulting	$45,000
Cobol/Cics Mainframe	Springfield	IL.	Consulting	$67,000
Project Management	Overland Park	KS	Telecom	$51,000
Novell Netware	Columbus	OH	Other	$49,920
Sas/C/Unix/Pc/Mvs/Html	Madison	WI	Education	$45,000
Infrastructure (NT, IPSEC, NDS)	Chicago	IL	Consulting	$99,000
Java, Nt, Vb6, Internet	New York	NY	E-commerce	$120,000
Sap / Plant Maintenance	Chicago	IL	Consulting	$100,000
Oracle,Perl/Cgi;Unix,Nt;Dw	Washington	DC	Consulting	$70,000
E-Commerce And ERP Systems	Boca Raton	FL	Consulting	$105,875
Sap Applications Consultant	New Orleans	LA	Utility	$72,000
Software Development	Phoenix	AZ	Software	$62,000
Progress 4GL RDBMS	Atlanta	GA	Food	$160,000
Information Security	Trenton	NJ	Financial	$70,000
Peoplesoft Technical		GA	Consulting	$120,000
Network Consultant For Firm	Houston	TX	Financial	$47,000

So the amount of experience you will need to break in is directly related to the strength of the demand for technical people that exists in your geographical region. When business is painfully short-handed you may be able to work a solid contractor year—about eight months of full time work—with only two or three years of solid experience. But at times when there is less demand or in regions where there are fewer computer jobs, whether it is because there are fewer large computer installations around or because of a business slump, you might need seven or eight years' experience to break in, and that experience might have to be with specific software that is in great demand.

One indicator of the strength of the contracting market is the number of advertisements for contractors or "consultants" in the paper. These are usually very specific as to what skill levels and software experience are in demand. Be aware however that five contractor ads requesting Java/Visual C++ doesn't mean that there are five Java/Visual C++ positions open, just that the five consulting firms are all trying to fill the one opening that a client has for that skill set. Watch the papers for a couple of months to get some idea of how steady the demand for contractors seems to be in your region.

If you are looking at out-of-town ads that promise huge salaries or rates be aware that these high salaries often reflect skyrocketing costs of living, particularly in places like New York, Boston, and Silicon Valley. You might get what seems like a very generous rate and still not be able to find a place to live. A February 11, 2000 article in the Washington Post reported that people earning $50,000 a year at technical jobs in Silicon valley were turning up in homeless shelters, unable to afford the extortionate rents in the regional housing market.

The kind of work you have been doing also will have a lot to do with whether or not you can break into contracting. Most of the demand for contractors is for software developers and applications programmers with backgrounds that include coding in languages like C++, Visual Basic, and Java, and using popular databases like Oracle and e-commerce-related Web development software, though there is still a small amount of contract work for people who are specialists in older platforms like IBM MVS mainframes and AS/400s. If you have extremely specialized technical skills, for example writing device drivers, you may be overqualified for the majority of the contract positions that come up. Your rate will be higher than average when you can find contracts calling for this kind of highly specialized work but you might have to wait a long time to find one, or you might have to take contracts involving work that is less technical.

If you are interested in trying contracting there is nothing wrong in contacting a few consulting firms and then waiting to see if they call with anything you would be interested in. No matter how interested they seem in your résumé it is only when they send you on interviews that you know you have a future in contracting.

You may encounter a Catch-22 situation when you first decide to consult. Many consulting firms have clauses in their contracts with clients that forbid them to recruit the client firm's employees. If you work with a company that hires contractors from local consulting firms you may find that none of the more reputable local consulting firms can hire you! Your only hope then is to sign on with a company that does not do business with your current employer. But sometimes the reason they don't do business with your employer is because of a previous history of unethical conduct.

In making the decision to become a contractor you should always weigh your ability to take on additional risk with the benefits of your current situation. Perhaps the best time to begin contracting is when you are at a major turning point and find yourself between jobs. Perhaps you have come back to the work force after having taken some time off to spend time with your children. Perhaps you have just moved to a new city. Or you may have just been fired from your last job. In this situation you might consider giving consulting a try before you turn to looking for a full-time job.

In any case, don't ever quit a decent full-time employee situation until your first consulting contract has been *signed* and you are sure that you could survive financially if it should fall through the next week.

But having prepared for the worst possible case the chances are that you won't encounter it. Many contractors work year-long contracts at extremely high hourly rates for year after year, getting hefty raises with each new contract. As their example shows, contracting can be a wonderful way to make a living as long as you keep your eyes open.

Approaching Consulting Firms

If you do begin dealing with consulting firms, you should go through all the steps we will describe in Chapter 7 "Job Hunt Basics" for dealing safely with Job Placement firms. In addition, make sure that the consulting firm's sales reps are intelligent people with some understanding of technical issues who are capable of interpreting and representing your skills to a potential client. You deserve the best, because with the consulting firm taking thirty to forty percent of your billing rate — or more — you are certainly going to be paying for it!

Besides taking the usual precautions, you must make it very clear that the consulting firm recruiter should never send out your résumé to a client before checking with you first and getting your explicit permission to submit you. This avoids having two firms send your résumé to the same place, a situation in which you will be disqualified from getting the contract.

You should demand to see the consulting firm's version of your résumé before it is sent out too, since many consulting firms insist on rewriting your résumé in their own format. Second-rate consulting firms will often hopelessly garble your qualifications on the résumé, ensuring that you will never get contract.

Foreign Consultants Working in the United States

There has been such a strong demand for contract consultants in the United States over the past several years that many of the larger United States consulting firms have taken to importing foreigners, particularly programmers from the U.K. and nations in the British Commonwealth like India and Australia. These programmers are familiar with the software environments used in the United States and, of course, speak English. Many foreign consulting firms have opened United States offices, trying to break into this market. In 1998 Congress created a special — and highly controversial — visa for college educated professional workers, the H-1B visa, which in 1999 allowed some 119,000 foreign workers into the US to fill positions which industry claims it cannot fill with native professionals.

Foreign contractors can have wonderful experiences working in the United States if they know what they are getting into. Unfortunately, many of them do not. Many consultants brought from abroad by these companies tell stories of having been told lies about the conditions they would find in the United States and being subjected to brutal sweatshop conditions once they find themselves far from home and completely in the power of the consulting firms who sponsored them for their visas. You'll find more discussion of the plight of H-1B workers in Chapter 13, "Corporate Culture" when we discuss the "sweat shop" environment.

Other foreign consultants I've encountered have run into problems with consulting firms that play games with their immigration status. Some consulting firms have promised the consultants that they will sponsor them for their "green card," the permanent visa that allows an immigrant to apply for United States citizenship, when the firm actually had no intention of doing so. You should be aware that getting a green card is quite difficult. Consultants who have counted on getting permanent status have sometimes been shocked when it fell through and they were forced to hurriedly sell cars and furniture, acquired in the expectation of a long-term stay, at a great financial loss. Don't make plans based on having permanent status until your permits are in your hand.

The other major problem foreign consultants encounter is that they are totally unprepared for the cost of living in the United States. Several English consultants I met with in Connecticut told me that they were assured by agencies that it would be quite cheap to live there. The rates they were being paid were generous compared to what they had been getting in England, however they were about half what United States contractors were being paid for the same work and barely allowed the contractors to pay the outrageous rents common in that part of the country.

By far the greatest number of abuses reported to our Realrates.com bulletin board center on the rates and salaries that these companies pay their foreign hires. It is not unheard of for foreign contractors to discover that they are being paid twenty percent or less of the amount the consulting firm is billing their client for their labor.

So if you are a foreign contractor, try to talk with people who have worked in the area you intend to visit before you sign up and do some serious research to determine how much money you will really need. Check out the many thousands of consulting rate reports posted on Realrates.com. Most of all, find out what the prevailing rate structure is in your prospective area by talking to people who have worked there if that is at all possible. You can often find other IT professionals who will give you good advice about a consulting firm, employer, or the cost of living in various cities by posting a message on a Web bulletin board like ours at Realrates.com or in a consulting or programming-oriented newsgroup. You can also search the deja.com Usenet database or a search engine like Google.com for other people's reports of experience with specific companies.

Finally, if you are coming to the United States as a contract programmer don't let anyone tell you that you won't need a car—unless you plan to work in New York or Boston. In the vast majority of American cities public transportation is either nonexistent or limited to the inner-city area. You may not even be able to get to work without a car, let alone go out at night or visit local attractions. Make sure the rate or salary you are getting allows you to afford a good, used car and that you can qualify for a license!

Using your IT Apprenticeship to Position Yourself for Contracting

If you would like to be contractor you should make sure that the jobs you take in your first years expose you to as many as possible of the popular software products used for software development and database management. You need to have about three years of solid experience in what you claim as your specialty, however, any additional software you are familiar with should definitely be featured in your résumé since often a week's exposure to an obscure software product that a client has a requirement for can get you the job.

Avoid working with homemade system software or oddball niche applications. If you don't have easily recognized software skills you will find it difficult, if not impossible, to qualify for contract work. Clients are emphatic when it comes to paying for contractor skills: Your résumé must list exactly the skills they want, and usually what they want is the mainstream stuff. The only exception is when clients need help on projects that involve their own nonstandard software or homemade code. In that case they will usually look for candidates with the most congruent experience and offer them training.

Be realistic about your talent too. As a contractor you are going to be thrown into some challenging situations and will have to become productive in two or three weeks. If you can't honestly say that you are a better programmer or technical administrator than seventy-five percent of the people you have worked with, you probably ought to avoid going into contracting. If you find during your apprenticeship period that you are better at dealing with the administrative parts of your job than the technical side, you might just make a fool of yourself as a contractor.

Analyze how long it takes you to catch on in a new assignment during your apprenticeship period. If you hate having to learn a whole new system you will hate contracting, since you need to learn a new system every time you start a new contract. If, however, you find that the first six weeks of the job when everything is new is the part of the job you enjoy most and that you feel bored in the same position after a year, contracting might be just what you need to keep the juices flowing.

Use your apprenticeship period to pick up transferable software skills and test yourself to see if you could handle the requirements of contracting. And don't underestimate the contacts you can make in the apprenticeship period! The best kind of contracting is the kind you do directly for a client, but most contractors are forced to use middlemen because it is too hard for them to locate a manager who needs a contractor the very week that they are looking for a new job. If you build up a truly sterling reputation in a large company you can build a good relationship with the managers there and keep current on the development projects that are being planned so that once you become a contractor you can schedule yourself in on potential projects. Managers would much prefer to use a known performer rather than a stranger, so any effort you spend building up relationships with managers during your apprenticeship years can be worth a great deal to you as a consultant.

CHAPTER 6

When to Change Jobs

You know it is time to go job hunting when you reach your senior year in college. The same is true when you've just been fired. But during the rest of your career you will often face uncertainty over whether or not to start looking for a new job. Job hopping—changing jobs frequently whenever a better opportunity offers—has long been a tradition in the computer field. But to truly improve your career you must change jobs at the *right* time—and in the right way.

In most professions it is assumed that after you get your first job you will work for the same firm for a period ranging from three to seven years. The person who changes jobs more frequently is often viewed as having something wrong with them that manifests in this inability to hold a job. In contrast, in the computer field, especially during boom times, it has long been common for the most talented individuals to change jobs as often as once a year, earning a hefty raise each time and adding valuable new skills to their résumés.

Job hopping has its place, and you need to understand what that place is to use it most effectively. Changing jobs too often can damage your career. Short-termers don't get offered company sponsored training in the latest and hottest technologies since they haven't built a reputation within the company. Short-termers also may not have time to build up a network of peers who have seen them work and respect their abilities—peers who, as their careers unfold, can connect them with the very best kinds of jobs.

On the other hand, if you stay in a comfortable slot too long you may be building a local reputation for competence and loyalty but you may also be doing the same kinds of work over and over again and letting your skills atrophy.

But while this may seem obvious, the problem is that when you are in the middle of an actual job it is often hard to know what category it falls in — growth opportunity or invitation to stagnation.

What Job Hopping Can Do for You

Job hopping can, pure and simple, lead to dramatic leaps in your salary early in your career, especially if you started out at a salary toward the lower end of the range. This is due to the fact that, while almost no one except large corporations with sophisticated education organizations wants to take on neophyte programmers, there are hosts of companies yearning to hire programmers with one or more years of experience.

The companies that provide training to neophyte programmers are often those that pay relatively low starting salaries. Often they are financial service companies, banks or insurance companies that must employ hundreds or even thousands of programmers to sustain their operations. Because their corporate guidelines limit how large a raise any employee can be given, these companies can only offer their best trainees raises in the ten percent range. This sounds like a good percentage, but ten percent of a starting salary of $35,000 is only $3,500, which brings the employee's salary only up to $38,500. Companies that don't pay for expensive trainee classes lure away the experienced employees who have been trained by these low-paying companies by offering them raises of another ten thousand dollars or more. They find this cheaper than paying trainees a salary while they sit in costly classes or covering the additional time it takes these newbies to become productive in the workplace!

Companies that need smaller staffs of bright and highly skilled specialists usually start their college hires with the 4.0 grade point averages at much higher salaries than do the cast-of-thousands industries, so if you start out working for one of these, changing jobs, while it may give you some kind of raise, is not likely to give you anywhere near as significant a pay boost as people get who work in larger and more bureaucratic organizations — and by leaving a quality employer too quickly you may be losing out on valuable training opportunities. But for the person whose credentials are marginal at the beginning of their career, job hopping early in that career is about the only way to close the salary gap with their more credentialed peers.

Job hopping can lead to dramatic salary growth in the first four or five years of a career. However once your salary reaches a level significantly higher than the median salary for your specialty — which is currently in the middle $60,000s for most IT jobs — this is no longer true. The reason is that you have become too expensive for most of the jobs that are available. You will need to have mastered a technical skill that is in great demand to be able to continue improving yourself through job changes once you have reached this salary level.

The other benefit of changing companies early in your career is that you get a chance to broaden your experience. Many people who stay in the same job for five years don't have five years of experience, they have one year of experience repeated five times. When you change jobs you increase your chances of seeing new techniques and learning different kinds of software and applications. No two companies are the same, even though they might have similar applications running in what are supposed to be the same software environment. You won't realize the extent to which companies have distinct personalities until you have worked in more than one.

Job hoppers usually get a wider experience with different software environments too, which can be useful if you plan to be a consultant in the future. However don't be in too great a hurry to change jobs just to pick up some particular technology you have been yearning to learn. Placement firm ads often use teasers like "Learn Oracle" or "Get into a fast-growing e-commerce environment" as a come-on to get people to answer the ad. If you take their bait, you may find that the job they offer really involves working with the same old dead-end technology you're currently working with. Why should a company train you in something valuable with which you have no previous experience when they could train proven in-house staff first?

Sometimes changing jobs is the only way out of an impossible situation. When you find yourself stymied because of personality conflicts with your management which are not going to go away, or when you are convinced that you will never be allowed to move into any area in the company that you don't loathe, there is no reason to stay in a hated job. Because of the prevalence of job hopping among computer professionals no negative motive will be attributed to you if you change jobs every two years or so. Just be careful that in the interview, when you are asked why you changed jobs so frequently, your answer doesn't suggest to a potential employer that you can't get along with anyone at work!

Another legitimate reason for job hopping may be that your spouse has been offered an attractive job in another part of the country which means that the whole family must either move or live with a difficult commuting relationship. Now that couples with two professional jobs have become the norm, many couples face the dilemma of whether or not the second spouse should automatically make the move and many do not. But if you have been on the fence for a while about your current job, leaving because of a spouse's transfer can often be an easy way of making your exit—though you will need to be careful when interviewing with your next employer that you reassure them that you won't be leaving *them* as soon as your spouse is offered yet another transfer.

How Job Hopping Can Hurt You

If your only reason for changing jobs is that you are discontented in your present job you need to be aware of the sad truth that the majority of open jobs in most companies that are filled from outside the company are those that no one currently working in the company wants. The only exception to this is when a company is bringing in a new technology that no current employees are familiar with and wants to bring in a person experienced with that technology to get things going.

While it is true that many companies are looking for people with one or two years' experience to fill what are for them entry-level slots, a lot more companies are looking to fill the job slots vacated by people with the same experience level as you who fled them as intolerable. You will have to do a lot of research to find out why a company is offering you the great deal it is, and often paying an agency a fee of up to thirty percent of your annual salary to get you.

WORST CAREER MISTAKE

"....staying too long in a job. I spent seven years at a place and didn't develop my skills very much after the first two. It was comfortable so I stayed...when it was time to move on I was terrified...but I have learned more in the past three years than I did in the previous ten.

"Keep your skill set up to date ... never relax anywhere and assume that the company will look out for your interests. Manage your own career."

You need to be skeptical about anything you are told by a hiring manager. It is not uncommon for desperate managers to lie to interviewees about jobs they are trying to fill. They have deadlines to meet and need bodies to sit in front of their workstations. A common ploy of such managers is to tell you that their company is going to be moving to a Unix-based server technology or that it is going to be developing a new system in Java. Hiring managers know that these are products a lot of programmers would like to get experience with. What such managers do not mention is that, although the company will be working with this new, cutting edge software, you will be nowhere near it.

Companies find themselves with a desperate need to maintain the old boring production systems which most ambitious programmers regard as the lowest kind of assignment, and it is these kinds of jobs that usually call forth the greatest use of imagination from hiring managers. Other ploys hiring managers use to attract people to dead end jobs include telling you that you will be a team leader—which sounds great until you discover that your department of ten people has four team leaders—or promising to train you in database administration, which translates into letting you set up new user accounts or do other clerical level "administration" tasks.

Ideally you should have been developing a network of friends in different companies in the period before you consider job hopping so that you can talk to them and build up a realistic picture of the IT shop in a company you are considering. You can usually find out where the sweatshops, slums, and disaster areas are, and conversely, locate the departments with the reputation for turning out the people who go on to leadership roles or get the technical training that leads to real technical growth. Often the best jobs are those offered by someone who has worked with you before and knows and respects your skills.

As a footnote here I urge you never to take a job with a company that asks you sign a contract that makes you liable for employment agency fees should you decide to quit. This sounds like an obvious statement, but in the 1980s one major employer of programmers in the United States, a blue chip company no less, recruited programmers with press gang tactics. Programmers would come to work for this company assured of career opportunities that were pure fantasy on the part of hiring managers, only to find themselves facing law suits for thousands of dollars when they tried to leave the company before the contract period was over. In the 2000s immigrants from other countries are most likely to be victimized by these sorts of schemes and must exercise great care when evaluating the jobs offered to them by companies willing to sponsor them for visas because their immigrant visas make them near-captives of the employer who sponsors them. Many unscrupulous employers staff their workforce with immigrants because their reputations are so poor that citizens won't work for them. Likewise you should never sign anything that makes you liable for relocation expenses.

While the most obvious problem with job-hopping is that it might land you in a position much worse than the one you left, there are other problems with it too. If you are a competent "star performer" in your current company you must be prepared for the fact that the minute you leave your old job behind you have left your old reputation behind as well. You will have to prove your competence all over again. Typically most of us have to live with the reputation we acquire during our first six weeks on the job. You will have to put out your very best effort in those starting weeks if you want to win again the respect that you already enjoyed at your previous job. And there is always the possibility that bad luck will intervene, making it much harder to prove yourself a second time.

There is an up side to this too. When I changed jobs several times and reestablished my reputation most of those times, I gained confidence that my reputation was something real and not a fluke. But there are some jobs out there—and most people encounter at least one in their careers, where nobody can look good. If office politics are out of control, or you have an antiquated system that has no documentation running on an unstable network, you are going to have to walk on water just to keep from drowning. If your reputation as the local guru is important to you, keep this in mind before changing jobs.

Another fact to consider before changing jobs is that when you change jobs your new company owes you nothing. The good work you did somewhere else is irrelevant, and you must expect to wait at least a year before you can ask for any education or other special treatment. Nor will you be able to take off those three weeks you'd been planning for that river rafting trip in Chile—your vacation credits are gone, unless you explicitly bargained for them before accepting the offer. So if you have grown accustomed to taking long lunches, the occasional day off, and still receiving great performance reviews you should think twice before giving up your current job. Similarly if you have children, you can count on their coming down with the chicken pox one week after you start your new job giving you a reputation for being undependable—as mine did.

How Often Should you Change Jobs?

If you are starting in your first job, the chances are that you will have to spend at least a year there before you consider changing. If economic times are tight you might have to wait two years before you make a switch. In tight economies recruiters cannot place people who do not have at least two years of experience, so, in this situation, you will be able to change jobs only if you do the footwork yourself.

When you are looking for a job that is not your first the rules are a little different. By now you are an experienced person with the proven ability to get a new job. You should spend a solid amount of time in your new position and thoroughly exhaust all opportunities for advancement in your new company before leaving. But if you discover that your job hopping has landed you in a terrible job, if you have fallen prey to dishonest managers and imaginary promises, you should not, as many people do, feel compelled to wait out an entire year before leaving the position. Wait three months and see if your initial feelings of hating your new job or finding it a dead end persist. If they do, go out and get yourself a new job. This time ask penetrating questions at the interview and be honest with interviewing managers about why you want to leave your current position. If you were lied to, politely mention it to the interviewer. If nothing else, it will keep them from following the same strategy with you. If you really have found yourself in a dead-end job that does not make use of your current skills a manager who needs those skills should not balk at hiring you before you serve out your year.

CHAPTER 7

Job Hunt Basics

In the previous chapters we've examined the environment in which you'll find computer jobs and the steps you'll have to take to keep your career moving as you go from job to job. Now it's time to learn the mechanics of how you actually go about landing these jobs.

We'll start out by showing you how to prepare for your job hunt, then we'll explore where you'll find open computer jobs and how to get yourself into an interview. Finally we'll examine how you can evaluate any job opportunity you find to make sure it really is the dream job you were hoping for and, if it is, how to make sure that you are offered the highest salary possible.

Why People Hate Job Hunting

Most people spend a lot more time and energy looking for a new car than they do looking for a new job.

There are good reasons for this. Most of us look for a new job in a state of anxiety, especially if we are unemployed. If we have no current source of income this tends to obscure any other career goals we ought to have. Most of us take the first job that offers us a salary within the range we have decided we must have.

Many people loathe being interviewed. They hate the feeling of being put under the microscope and examined for flaws. I know of people who have stayed for years in jobs they hated just because they were phobic about the interview process. This is not helped by the fact that some interviewers really do try to trip people up at the interview or grill them with trick technical questions, sometimes memorized from textbooks, which bear little relationship to the job the applicant is applying for.

Finally if you already have a job, the chances are that the forces of inertia will work to keep you there. It is a lot easier to show up the same place every morning, grab a bagel, schmooze with your work buddies, and do some predictable task than it is to deal with the sleazy salespeople, intimidating interviewers, and uncertainty that comes with hunting for a new job. Many people work in jobs that they know are doing nothing for their careers because of this seductive ease.

Then too, many people feel helpless in the job-hunting situation. They don't feel in control and they don't really know how to go about getting the job they want. So they job hunt when they must, leaving to chance the position they end up with.

Job-hunting *is* stressful. But so is the inevitable result of *not* jobbing hunting. If you ignore it until too late you may find yourself looking for a new job in the worst possible situation—when you are unemployed. And if you wait until then, you will be under the kind of financial pressure that makes it unlikely you'll be able to pick and choose from the jobs available, and, at the same time, you will have the least appeal to a potential employer.

The best time to start your job hunt is *when you don't need a job*! That way you are at your most attractive to potential employers and have the time to pick and choose among the opportunities you uncover. If you have to job hunt in a crisis, do what you have to do to get a new job, but don't let your job hunt end there. Stay in touch with the job market, keep your résumé current, and always know where you could go next if anything should happen to your current job.

Prepare Your Résumé

Before you begin your job hunt you will need to write up a résumé. Anyone who has a job to offer will need to see it, so get it into final form before you start making contacts so that you can respond immediately when you find someone who expresses interest.

You can learn about generic résumé fundamentals from the many books on the market or use résumé writing software. Here we will take a more detailed look at some computer job-specific résumé issues.

Emphasize Technology

If you've been paying any attention to what you've read in the rest of this book, you've probably figured out by now that your résumé will need to prominently feature the in-demand software tools with which you have experience. Many computer professionals have found it useful to include a separate section in their résumé that lists "Software Experience" or "Software and Hardware Experience." This section may be nothing more than a list of the products with which you have worked, sorted by categories like Operating Systems, Development Languages, Databases, and

System Tools. By providing a section like this you make it easy for a person scanning your résumé to decide whether it is worth reading the denser paragraphs that describe what you have actually done with these software products.

It is also important that somewhere in your résumé, perhaps in your description of past jobs, you indicate in what capacity you used the software and what your role on the project was. The extent to which you emphasize this role is dependent on how impressive it was. If you were a low echelon coding grunt doing nothing but editing sub-routines you will not linger on your project role the way that you would if you had been responsible for designing a large system on your own or creating the project specification.

In general the best approach is to emphasize whatever is impressive and leave ambiguous those issues that might keep you from ever getting to an interview. If you can get face-to-face with a manager and demonstrate your intelligence and enthusiasm, you might be able to get over the hurdle of mediocre experience, but if your résumé screams "mediocre experience" you are not likely to get into that interview.

Remember too that your résumé will go through dimwitted gatekeepers before anyone with technical expertise gets to see it, so don't get too complex when describing your jobs. Make sure that you've written the résumé in such a way that an HR clerk or technically ignorant recruiter can make the match between your skills and experience and what their job order is asking for.

AVOID THIS!

"Then Charles, the recruiter, calls your manager up and asks if there are any openings. When your manager says 'No, we aren't looking for people now,' Charles says, 'Well what about Dave's job? I know he's looking.'"

Use Protection

You might want to craft several different versions of your résumé, each one targeted to a different type of reader. At a minimum you will want to have one résumé for sending to unknown employment agencies and placement firms, especially those you find on the Web, and another that you send directly to potential employers. That is because recruiters at sleazy agencies are notorious for spamming job hunters and because they are capable of using the contact information they find on your résumé *not* to place you but to call up your current manager and try to sell them someone to replace you. To protect yourself from having this happen, the résumé you send to an unknown placement firm should include no email address or phone number that can't withstand heavy spamming. Many job hunters use an on-line voicemail/email service like uReach.com or OneBox.com where they are given a new phone number that rolls over to a voicemail box they can check via the Web as well as an email address and mailbox that they use only for their job hunt.

The résumé you send an unknown firm should never give names and phone numbers or any other specifics that identify your current job. Some job hunters go so far as to identify their current employer obliquely, for example, they describe their current job only as "Lead Developer, e-Commerce Division of Major Telecommunications Company," and only reveal the name of the company, the project, and their manager after the placement firm recruiter comes up with an actual interview that interests them.

In contrast, the résumé you prepare for a company that is a potential employer would reveal the name of your current employer as well as the name of your current project or department. But it is still a good idea not to include the names of managers or of personal references. You never know into whose hands your résumé might fall. Some companies have been known to sell the information they get from job hunters to recruiting firms who will call your references and try to sell them jobs — or technical personnel. If your references get hassled too often they may ask you to stop using them, so you should never give out your references' names until you are in an actual job interview.

Keep it Short

When writing your résumé, avoid the temptation to describe your career in detail. Few readers will be interested in any but your last two or three jobs. Even fewer will be willing to read more than two pages. Highlight the specific information you want to get across — "I did this and I know how to do that" — and be done with it.

Don't put in personal information like your hobbies or civic group activities unless they relate specifically to the job you are applying for. You don't know enough about the person who will be screening your résumé to know whether your activities in the Young Libertarians Club will make you more attractive or cause your résumé to land in the trash. By the same token, if you have changed careers, don't linger on the details of what you did before you got into computers. Include only information that is relevant to your current job hunt and leave readers wanting to know more.

If you have gotten details about a company and a specific job from friends who work there and if you know who the managers are who are hiring for that job, it is often worth rewriting your résumé to emphasize the ways in which you would be a perfect match for that particular job. However, you usually do not know exactly what job you are applying for, which is why it is a good idea not to get too specific on the résumé.

You don't want to appear over-qualified—especially if you are overemphasizing your experience—and you don't want to inadvertently say something that will decrease your appeal to the person hiring for an unknown position.

Remember, the résumé is not the place to explain everything. The time to go into detail is when you are face to face with someone who is in a position to hire you, who has enough experience themselves to understand the details of your career history.

Common Résumé Problems and How to Solve Them

Age

Age discrimination is illegal, but it is very prevalent in the computer field and because it is extremely hard to prove that your résumé was thrown out because you were too old rather than because "your skills were not a good match." If you are over forty you will have to relate to it.

There are several reasons why companies don't want to hire older workers into full time salaried jobs. One has to do with the cost of insurance. The presence of older workers significantly increases the price of the insurance benefits that companies provide all workers. Another reason might be the erroneous belief—held usually by people in their twenties and thirties—that people in their forties and fifties have brains that are slowly turning to mush. Then too, if managers in a company are all twenty-somethings, they may feel uncomfortable at the thought of bossing around people old enough to be their parents.

Rumors abound of developers in Silicon Valley who get face-lifts to keep themselves in contention for new jobs. Hopefully you won't have to go that far. But if you are over forty it is probably wise to obscure this as much as possible when crafting your résumé. Only list the jobs you have held in the past five to ten years. Only give the specific dates of your degrees if you went back to school within the past ten years, otherwise just list the degree and the name of institution that granted it. Your goal is not to pretend you are newly hatched—just to make sure that your skills are judged for what they are. By not signaling age in your résumé, by the time the twenty-somethings figure out how old you really are, you'll have gotten a chance to do a face-to-face interview where you can tech-talk them and reassure them that your wizardry will be compatible with their youthful genius.

Gaps

If your résumé includes a period of months without work or a job that terminated suspiciously abruptly the simplest way to deal with it is to describe all the jobs on your résumé in the following format "Sr. System Administrator, Megacorp, 1997-1998" without giving the months involved. Recruiters may suspect that this format is covering something up but they won't know for sure, and you are more likely to get an interview by obscuring the gap than if you make it more obvious.

But what do you do if you had a longer period of unemployment in the recent past? Perhaps you were severely ill and don't want to reveal this before you've had a chance to stress more positive parts of your history. Or perhaps the economy slowed and you could not find a job.

One solution for this is to describe yourself during that period as having been "Self-employed." Keep your description of your "self-employment to a sentence or two" and then get back to describing your salaried jobs. Wording like this suggests that you were attempting to get your start-up off the ground rather than hooked up to life support or trudging to the unemployment office. Because many computer professionals have worked as contractors throughout the past decade or have actually attempted to start entrepreneurial businesses that failed, a stint of self-described "self-employment" will not disqualify you for consideration for salaried jobs if you have the right skills.

Out-of-Date Technology

A résumé that describes nothing but experience with out-of-date technologies is the most difficult to fix. The only real solution is to *get some training in newer technology*. Whining about the situation won't help. Teach yourself a new language, take classes, develop small projects for local charities using your new tools and if nothing else will do it, look for jobs using the older technology that will at least put you into an environment where you can get a little bit of paid experience with something new.

Once you have taken these steps you should be able to put at least one recent job on your résumé that includes some current skills. When you do this, de-emphasize the earlier jobs and when you do describe them, describe them in terms of the leadership and design roles you took on those projects instead of lingering on the technology you used. You should also emphasize your knowledge of the business side of the systems you worked for. Strong management skills and industry-specific business knowledge coupled with some saleable technical skills can make you an attractive candidate for a certain type of job.

In fact, your experience working with obsolete technologies has undoubtedly taught you a lot, and the kind of person you really want to work for will understand that your years with older technology were far from "wasted." But you have to get through the twenty-something gatekeepers (most of whom have computer skills barely strong enough to read their email) before you will be able to sell your experience and wisdom to someone in a position to hire you.

DE-EMPHASIZING OUTDATED EXPERIENCE

"I have ten years of Cobol experience. I have retrained and gotten Java certification. My theory is that even the mention of 'mainframe' or 'Cobol', puts a person on the wrong side of the barbwire fence. You get labeled as part of the 'old' crowd that is too stupid to learn new things.

"Originally, I had a résumé that showed about six years of Cobol experience. I got very few responses. Then I changed my résumé and totally stripped it of this experience, removed all references to mainframe work.

"My résumé looks like I am 'twenty- something', and my two to three years of experience is more like business analyst and entry level programmer in stuff that nobody recognizes as mainframe (stuff like DYL 280). But my résumé is still truthful, I just look less technical and like I did simple stuff. I have had recruiters ask me if I used to program in Cobol, and I say 'No!'

"I am getting a much better response with my 'twenty something barely ever programmed résumé.' I have gotten more phone interviews and more technical interviews. And nobody ever asks what I did before the dates on my résumé.

"My relatives have normal professions (like civil engineering and social work) where they don't hide their experience and their education when they look for work, and when I tell them what is going on here in the IT field, they can barely imagine it."

Why You Might Not Get A Job by Answering an Ad

Every Sunday techies who are burning out on their current jobs turn to that ego booster, the IT classifieds in the Sunday "Help Wanted" section of their newspaper. It is heartwarming to see all those ads begging for people with your job skills and offering salaries better than what you are currently receiving. The ads are usually divided into two groups. Some are placed by HR departments of the actual company you would work for while others are placed by recruiters at job placement firms, either employment agencies or "IT staffing firms" — companies that used to call themselves consulting firms until the market for consultants started to dry up.

If you venture to answer an ad placed by a HR department, even one that seems to describe your skill set exactly, the result can often be a polite form letter claiming that your résumé will be kept on file for future requirements. This usually means that it has been tossed in the trash. This happens because many corporate HR staffers are out of their depth when it comes to evaluating the résumés of technical personnel.

Here's why. When a position opens up the HR recruiter usually asks the hiring manager for a form that lists the specific experience that is required for the position. This works well when recruiting clerical employees since it is easy to determine if someone can type sixty-five words per minute. Unfortunately it is much harder to quantify on a short form all the different kinds of experience that a technical candidate should possess. Once they have the form, HR people tend to look for a one-to-one correspondence between the items listed on the résumés they receive and on the job requisition form. They do not have the technical knowledge to understand that an item listed on the applicant's résumé indicates that the applicant has the experience the manager needs if it looks different from what they see on the requisition. Thus a person who lists "Perl" and "CGI Scripts" on their résumé might never make it to the interview for a job where the requisition asked for "Perl" and "HTML" since the HR clerk won't see "HTML" on the résumé—even though any technical person knows that a Perl programmer familiar with CGI scripting would know the necessary HTML. In a similar vein, a system administrator who only cites "Solaris" on their résumé may not get an opportunity to interview for a job where the form asked for "Unix."

Because this happens so frequently, IT managers have learned that they are unlikely to find the candidates they need through the HR department. They may allow HR to flail around for a polite period but then they go to outside job placement firms, staffed by people they believe are better qualified to match requested skills with available applicants. Sometimes the HR department itself realizes that it is out of its depth and hands the job order directly to the IT placement firms with whom they have negotiated deals. During a job search of my own years ago, the HR recruiter at a small insurance company I contacted during the job hunt expressed surprise that a programmer would actually call her directly and immediately referred me to the job placement firm her company used to find programmers.

What Job Placement Agency Recruiters Really Are

While recruiters from job placement firms that have established relationships with the companies you are interested in can usually get your résumé past the trash can, to use them effectively you must realize that most recruiters are not what they attempt to present themselves to you as being. Recruiters try to appear to be "career counselors." They will interview you and ask many questions about your career goals and long-term plans in an attempt to build your confidence that they are helping you and looking out for your best interests. However, recruiters are *not* career counselors. They do not receive a single penny from you for their career advice. They are salespeople, and they make their money, tons of it, by placing you in a job—any job—that is open, any job where the hiring manager can be persuaded to accept you and you can be persuaded to go.

When a job placement firm recruiter places you, they get paid a percentage of your yearly salary or some other hefty amount by the hiring company. Most professionals know this. What they don't often know is how *large* a percentage the job placement firm gets: Current percentages range from twenty to thirty-five percent with thirty percent being very common. That means if you get placed in a $60,000-a-year job the job placement firm is earning something like $18,000, which is then subdivided between the owners of the headhunting company and the salesperson who made the placement. With many experienced professionals earning salaries of $75,000 to $150,000, fees of $25,000 or more for a single placement are not unheard of.

A placement firm that places you in a "temp-to-perm" job, one where you start out as a contractor and then convert to being an employee, will probably be getting thirty-five percent of every dollar the client is paying though some placement firm take as much as fifty percent or more of what the employer is paying for your work!

With money like that at stake, it should be clear what the real dynamic is between you and any job placement recruiter. Despite the pose that they are helping you advance your career, to the placement firm recruiter you are merely some merchandise they might be able to sell. They get paid by the customer, the firms buying their services, not by you, and they have no motivation at all to look out for your best interests.

Many recruiters claim that they have a pipeline to the best jobs that are never advertised. This is not usually true. If you carefully follow the ads you will notice that often all the recruiters in town are describing the same few jobs that are open that week—often those that were advertised by the hiring company in a display ad placed by their HR department a few weeks back.

Other job placement firms run ads every week that are nothing more than a long list of desirable skills. You will realize after a few weeks that these ads—or the corresponding Web Job Board listings—do not describe real job openings. They are just come-ons designed to get you to call their office and add you to their database of contacts since a major problem recruiters have is attracting people—product—that they can sell to their customers. Sometimes these sleazy firms' real reason for posting ads that attract technical staffers is to pump them for information about their current employers and the names of their current and previous managers so that the recruiter can add these managers to their cold calling lists.

Less-reputable firms engage in all sorts of creative maneuvers to get their hands on programming flesh. A 1985 *Infosystems* magazine article told of recruiters calling up managers and pretending to be watch repairmen, claiming to have lost the last name of a programmer who dropped off a watch to be repaired, just to get the names of programmers in the department so that they could call them later and offer them new jobs. With the advent of Internet-based job hunting, many companies now place ads on Internet job boards that list juicy but phony jobs to build up a database of email addresses. They then spam the programmers themselves or sell their names to others.

Out of curiosity I once answered an ad for a position as a job placement recruiter with a sleazy local firm. The owner explained what my job would be: In return for seventy percent of the fee the company would get when I made a placement they would give me a desk to use and a script which they claimed had almost magical powers to persuade. I would memorize the script and then start calling everyone in the internal phone directories of local companies who might possibly be a programmer. If I managed to find a programmer among the typists, actuaries, and maintenance supervisors I'd bothered, I would launch into the script offering the programmer a shot at a much bigger salary and suggesting that I had inside information on a position for someone with skills just like theirs. If they took the bait, then my work would really begin. I would have to coax their résumé out of them and then scurry around pestering managers until I found one who had an open position and was desperate enough to interview my victim for a job. The owner told me I could expect that this routine might bring in one or two prospects per one hundred calls, if that. I would also be expected to work on any likely prospects to extract from them the names of their friends and coworkers.

While this kind of sleazy behavior was the exception rather than the rule in the IT placement business in the 1980s, because of the huge amounts of money to be made in today's business climate, by now it is standard operating procedure.

Beware of Plunging Cleavage

A new wrinkle that has crept into the placement business over the past few years is that many firms, realizing that their target placement is a young male whose technical skills are greater than his social skills, now hire female recruiters clad in seductive attire who employ techniques more appropriate to the "oldest profession" to dazzle prospective hires into accepting jobs that are otherwise unattractive. These saleswomen may feign breathy ignorance, but experienced computer professionals warn you to be aware that they are rarely as dumb as they appear. These pros suggest that you "enjoy the scenery" and treat them as you would any other salesperson. Others argue that any company that would use a seduction strategy to sell you a job is one that you can safely write off.

Whatever you do, don't get lured into thinking that the salesperson has a personal interest in you and let that blunt your resolve when it is time to negotiate.

That placement personnel can carry on this way and stay in business is a sign of how hard it is for managers to locate qualified, experienced personnel. As irritating as managers might find these people, they must maintain an uneasy alliance with them because when they do need to hire IT professionals the job placement firm recruiters are often their only source.

Who Works with Job Placement Firms?

Slightly over one third of the computer employees who reported their salaries to the Real Salary Survey reported using either a job placement firm or a consulting firm to find their current job. And our data show that despite the high fees they charge, job placement firms tend to find people jobs that pay *better* than the jobs people find on their own. Our Real Salary Survey data show that the median salary for jobs found by Job Placement agencies was $70,000 which was $12,000 higher than the median salary of the jobs that job hunters found on their own. However, the explanation for this differential may be not that agencies find better jobs you can't find on your own, but merely that, because of the fees they charge, agencies can *only* place the more experienced professionals who naturally earn higher salaries.

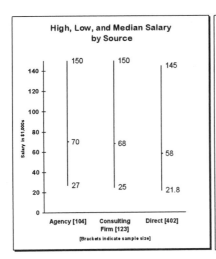

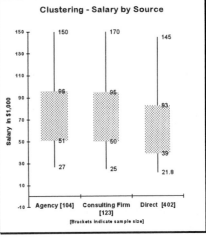

WEB COMPUTER JOB BOARDS

www.careermosaic.com
Career Mosaic

www.ceweekly.wa.com
Contract Employment Weekly Job Board

www.computerjobs.com
The Computer Jobs Store

www.computerwork.com
Job Board & Résumé Bank

www.dice.com
DICE Job Board

www.itcareers.com
Computerworld IT Job Search

www.monster.com
Monster Board

How to work with Job Placement Firms

There may be benefits to using a job placement firm, if you have experience and very current, in-demand skills. But you must be very careful to find a decent job placement firm to work with. Though there are depressing numbers of slimeballs in the IT placement business, there are also in each market a few reputable firms run by people with a lot of experience in the IT field and a solid base of contacts among local managers. Often these companies place only IT people. If you choose a reputable firm that has been in business in your community for a long time, the chances are that they *can* place you in a job you might not have known about or might not have been able to get an interview for on your own.

The important thing to remember is that a job placement firm can only place you in a job that calls for someone with the skills you already have. A company is not going to pay a job placement firm to provide an unqualified person or a person, whatever their credentials, who requires expensive training. They can usually find lots of people who don't have the specialized skills they want on their own. The premium paid to the job placement firm is for finding a person ready-made for the position.

Contacting Recruiters

If you haven't already done so, before beginning your job search, your first step should be to set up a special job hunting phone number for voicemail and email address. Never give your real phone number or email to an unknown recruiter!

You can post your résumé online on one of the many Web job sites, preferably those that specialize in computer jobs, but if you do this you can expect to get literally hundreds of emails, mostly from fly-by-nights who will ignore everything you wrote on that résumé. You will be offered opportunities hundreds or even thousands of miles away from your home by people looking for "Cobalt" programmers and worse.

It is usually better, if you do visit Web job boards, to do some serious searching of their job listings before you contact anyone. As you look through the postings you will start seeing some that sound real and others that look more like the "we need all skills" ads that are clearly just attempts to build résumé banks. You should also spend some time talking with other people in your specialty, either locally or on-line, about which firms to avoid. There are some that are notorious and you don't want to deal with them.

After browsing the Web postings and looking through classified ads you will be ready to start responding to the most interesting ads you've found. When dealing with HR or agency recruiters it is best to phone rather than use email—few recruiters are as comfortable with messaging as they are with the phone. If you are contacting agencies, be prepared to face a lot of obstruction. In your first contact most recruiters will try to extract the most information possible from you—especially your salary requirements—without telling you anything about any open positions they might have available or what their own credentials might be. Instead of divulging anything on the phone they will often try to force you to come in for a face-to-face interview–where they have you are on *their* turf and you can be more easily manipulated. While it is legitimate for a recruiter to ask to meet you before sending you out on an interview, do your best to determine that they really do have an interview available before wasting time with a face-to-face interview. If you can afford to be choosy, make it a point only to follow up on contacts with recruiters who are willing to give you some useful information on the phone.

Screening Recruiters

To screen a new recruiter either on the phone or in person try to get answers to the following questions:

♦ **Is this a firm that specializes only in placing people in IT?** This is extremely important. Agencies that really specialize in clerical or unskilled staffing have jumped into IT placement because the money is so good. Frequently they go so far as to change their names so that you won't recognize them as the temporary warehouse worker placement company they were a few years ago. Often the recruiters in these places are extremely ignorant about the IT world. If you use one of these they are likely to send out a garbled résumé that will hide from prospective managers any skills you might actually have.

♦ **What is the background of the person interviewing you?** You want someone who can understand your technical skills and who is capable of interpreting and presenting your résumé to potential employers in the best light possible.

♦ **How much does the recruiter know about your current job?** Do they know the names of the managers you currently work for? Do they know what your department does without your telling them? If they don't, you have to wonder what use they will be in finding managers and jobs elsewhere. A good recruiter should show you that they have some familiarity with both your company's IT operations and that of other companies in which you are interested. They should be able to suggest several places that you haven't heard of which might have interesting work for you. And, most importantly, do *not* let them use the interview simply as an opportunity to grill you for the names of your past managers and the details of your job so they can plump up their list of contacts!

♦ **Do they ask you to sign anything before you interview?** If a recruiter insists that you sign any kind of pre-employment contract, politely refuse to do so. There is never a reason for a professional to sign a pre-employment agreement with an agency. The more reputable firms will operate only by your word. The sole form you can sign before being hired is a nondisclosure agreement—and that is only when you are about to go out and interview with a firm that requires it.

♦ **How long has the firm been in business?** Employment agencies pop up like mushrooms after a rain. If you deal with one that has not been around for a while, you have no way of checking on their performance or ethics. Be aware, too, that in some job placement firms each recruiter is working entirely on their own. This means that if they quit the company—or are fired—your file leaves with them. If a recruiter you have been working with does leave, it is very unlikely that their replacement will tell you where they went, since they will be interested only in selling you to make their own commission. In that case you are back to square zero.

♦ **Does the recruiter suggest inappropriate jobs to you at the interview?** If they do. it is a sign that they are just shooting in the dark and don't know much about the IT marketplace.

♦ **Does the recruiter play bait and switch with money?** If you were attracted to the recruiter by a job posting or ad that mentioned an unusually high salary be alert for signs that the real salary for the job will be much lower. Some of these are subtle conversational attempts to convince you that your experience isn't as valuable as you think it is, or being told that the job in the ad is already filled but there is another that pays less which is still available.

After you've made initial contact, go back to your peers and check with them about the new company. Has anyone you know used this firm and been happy with the results? Post your query on Web bulletin boards frequented by people with skills similar to your own. You'll hear an earful.

Treat a job placement firm with the same circumspection you would use with a car salesperson. Let them describe what they have to sell but ask a lot of questions. Don't rush out to interview the moment they call you with a "terrific position." Try to get as much information as possible on the phone. If they won't or can't give it to you it might be the tip off that you would be wasting time going to the interview.

If you do go to an interview and find that the job placement firm has seriously misrepresented the job to you, tell the interviewing manager that you don't want to waste their time and then leave. Have nothing more to do with this recruiter. Your time is too valuable to waste, and you don't need to raise questions at your current job about your long lunches.

Finally, if you get through the job interview and are considering a position, avoid any lengthy conversation with the recruiter until you have made your mind up about whether you want the job or not. Remember that the recruiter is a salesperson and will get paid only if you take the job. Naturally then it is in their own best interest to convince you to take any job where the manager has made you an offer, no matter how little it might suit your own career goals. Recruiters who have stayed in business for any period of time have succeeded because they are good at what they do. They are likely to be persuasive salespeople and that persuasion will be directed at getting you to take the job and earn them their commission. So before exposing yourself to their blandishments, consider the different factors discussed in these pages, talk the offer over with your family and a few good friends, and make your own decision. Don't open yourself up to a recruiter's hard sell before you know exactly what you want to do unless you really want to be talked into taking the job.

Alternatives to Using Job Placement firms.

There are several alternatives to using a job placement firm to find your next job. Let's look at some of them now.

Network with Acquaintances

The very best way to find a new job is to use your contacts with friends who have technical skills similar to your own. They can alert you to where new projects are opening up and what companies are the best to work for. Let your friends know that you are interested in hearing about any job openings their companies might have. The very best interview is one with a manager who has already gotten a glowing recommendation for you from someone who knows you well or has worked with you in the past.

Temp-to-perm

Consulting firms will often try to sell you new jobs under a "temp-to-perm" or "temp-to-hire" arrangement. Under this arrangement you work for three months as a contractor. Then, if the client likes you, they convert you to a salaried employee. This gives the employer a chance to see if you can do the work while they retain the freedom to fire you at any time.

Sometimes these arrangements start out by paying you a contractor's rate, with the understanding that if you are hired permanently your pay will drop to an employee's salary. Sometimes temp-to-perm contracts start out only paying you an hourly rate based on the salary you would have as an employee rather than a true contract rate. This is an even worse deal for you, since the point of earning a higher rate for a short term contract is that the higher rate is supposed to compensate you for the risk you are taking of being unemployed in the future and for your lack of benefits.

When you are looking for a permanent job, you should treat a temp-to-perm contract just like any other three-month contract and take it only if you would be happy if it terminated without turning into a salaried job. Demand the same rate you'd ask for any short-term work. Be prepared on most temp-to-perm jobs to put in a lot of unpaid overtime. Experienced computer professionals have found that unscrupulous companies use the lure of permanent employment to talk people into working their brains out for lower than usual rates, while having no real intention of offering the contractor a permanent job.

If tempted to take one of these deals, it's worth remembering that if you do well on *any* short-term contract job many clients will invite you to become a permanent employee even if you haven't signed a temp-to-perm contract. So if all you can find in the job market are contracts rather than salaried jobs, don't assume that the temp-to-perm offers are better than those that are presented as merely short-term contracts. Indeed, clients have *more* motivation to make you a job offer when you are earning a high contract rate than they do when you are earning low temp-to-perm rates, since they save more money converting a highly paid contractor to an employee.

The only time a temp-to-perm arrangement might make sense is if you are at the beginning of your career with a lackluster résumé that doesn't leave you a lot of other options.

Job Fairs

You will often see "Job Fairs" advertised in the newspaper. Companies exist whose entire business is running "Career Fairs" dedicated to bringing together employers and technical personnel. Before you waste your time on these you should realize that attending most of them will not do anything for you that you couldn't accomplish by sending your résumé to the Human Resources department. Most career fairs feature booths set up by hiring companies and are staffed either by a few managers—who speak with all applicants for all open jobs, though they are ignorant about the requirements of any but their own departments—or again, by the folks from HR. After standing in line and showing your résumé to the company representative you are usually informed that you will hear from them or are given an application to fill out. The résumé or application is sent to the company HR staffer who handles résumés and in many cases that is that. The most frustrating feature of these career fairs is that you usually cannot get answers to the simplest questions about what positions are open in the company, what qualifications the company requires, and what the salient facts are about the company's IT setup.

A few companies run their own *open houses* at a company facility where managers interview people for actual openings. In this case you can tour booths belonging to different departments, speak to the actual hiring managers, and learn a good deal about the positions that are currently open at the company. These open houses are an excellent opportunity to learn about a company, and you should make an attempt to attend even if you are only mildly interested in changing jobs, since they are usually only held once or twice a year.

Job Postings

Many companies use a system known as "Job Posting." This means that any open position within the company must be advertised to the company's own employees before outsiders can apply. Usually the jobs are listed on bulletin boards around the company, but other companies might list them on-line or make you go to a HR office and look at a notebook. Usually the posting will list the job title, the job class, the offering department or manager, and finally the qualifications needed to get the job. Often these are broken into two groups: the qualifications that must be met for an applicant to be considered and those which would be nice extras.

Watching the posting boards—starting from your very first day at work—is an excellent way to keep tabs on the kinds of jobs that are available within your current organization. Most companies have strict guidelines about how long you must be in a position before you are eligible to "post out." In most you must stay in a job for at least a year. Sometimes a longer period is required. Find out as soon as you enter a company what those guidelines are.

It is very unlikely that, at the time you become eligible for a new job within the organization, the very job you want will come open. But you can still use the posting boards to help you find a position you'd like. Here's how: Long before you are eligible to post out you should familiarize yourself with what qualifications are required for the different open positions and the different job grades your company has. You should also note the names of the managers or departments who have listed jobs over the year that have interested you. When you are ready to switch jobs, the smartest thing you can do is call those managers whose departments have had the interesting openings in the past and alert them that you will soon be eligible for a posting. Ask them if they have anything opening up or, alternatively if any related departments might have something appropriate for you.

By staying abreast of the job postings you will not only get a jump on job hunting within your own organization, which is almost always the best way to get a more interesting and challenging job, but you will also be able to notify friends working at other companies when a position that might interest them is available. Many companies will pay you a cash bonus for such referrals.

How to Contact Companies Directly

When you contact a company directly you must pay close attention to the way you write your résumé. Remember that the person who will first read it and decide whether to pass it on or throw it away will in most cases not be a person with any technical background. Since this person rarely can understand what they see on a technical résumé they usually resort to reading it looking for an exact match with keywords specified on job orders submitted by hiring managers. In some large companies where a single job ad can result in a flood of thousands of résumés, your résumé won't even get to the clerk until it has been processed by scanning software which will search for keywords to decide which résumés deserve to pass before human eyeballs.

So when you write your résumé you must make sure that you include as many as possible of the keywords that appear on the ad you are answering, exactly the way they appear in the ad. Do this even if at times you have to stretch. The time to go into detail about your experience and its limitations is when you are sitting face to face with an interviewer who has enough technical background to understand what you are talking about. If your résumé is too detailed it might just go over the head of the gatekeeper.

Obviously you should not lie about your experience. But if you have extensive database experience using a database that is very similar to one requested in an advertisement and light exposure to the actual one stipulated, you would be wise to mention that light experience. This way it will be the hiring manager, not an HR functionary, who makes the call on whether your skills are a close-enough match.

When answering ads it is almost always a complete waste of time to phone first. The number in the paper will always be that of an HR administrator who will politely request that you send your résumé to the address featured in the ad.

Be aware too of another strange phenomenon. You will from time to time see advertisements that list extremely detailed job qualifications. These usually demand a high educational level and offer a low salary. The explanation behind these is found in immigration law. In many of these cases employers are planning to sponsor a foreign national for a green card which allows them to apply for citizenship or an H-1B "guest worker" visa. The law requires that in these cases the employer must make a good faith effort to determine that the job the foreign national will fill could not be filled with an American citizen. The advertisement is designed to fulfill this requirement while discouraging all U.S. citizens that could fill the job from answering it.

Get Multiple Interviews from Multiple Sources

If you are really trying to optimize the results of your job hunt, the single most important thing you can do is to make sure that you line up several interviews for yourself, not just a single one. Once you begin to interview there will be a lot of pressure on you to quickly accept any job offer that is made to you. If you haven't interviewed for several different job opportunities, you will have to make your mind up about whether to accept the first job offer you get without knowing if it really was the best job you could have gotten.

Job placement recruiters will be no help to you here. In fact, most will only feed you one job interview at a time, because having more than one to choose from might lessen your sense of urgency and encourage you to raise your salary demands. From a recruiter's perspective the worse possible candidate is one who is confident that there is strong demand for their skills—who might turn down a job offer or prevent one from being made to them by asking too high a salary—thus denying the recruiter their commission.

So if you are to have a choice of jobs, you will probably have to work with several competing recruiters, network with friends in the industry, and contact companies directly—all at the same time. Then you will have to schedule your interviews within as narrow a time period as possible and stave off demands that you make a decision on any one job offer you receive until you know how many other job offers you will have to choose from.

When you do this, you go into your next job knowing that it really is the best job you could have found. This is yet another reason why it is best to job hunt while you have a job, rather than wait until you are in a crisis situation. Interviewing for a new job every now and then will keep you abreast of the market too, so that you have a better idea of where you fit in and can take advantage of the relatively rare truly great opportunities that come along.

CHAPTER 8

At the Interview

You've done it! You've gotten an interview with a company that has what sounds like exactly the job you want. What now? Obviously it is time to dust off your interview suit and comb your hair, but what else can you do to make the most of the opportunity now before you? In this chapter we'll show you how to make the best impression on a potential employer. We'll introduce you to the important issues you must consider when evaluating a new job and we'll examine the kinds of questions that will give you the critical information you'll need to determine what the work in the new job would really involve.

These questions may be the most valuable part of this book. While most career books teach you how to impress the interviewer in your job hunt, few take on the far more important task of showing you how to determine, while you are busy impressing that interviewer, if the job being offered is one that you really should take.

This is a shame. Taking a poorly chosen job can set your career back for years or even end it. The hour or two you share with a potential employer is usually your only opportunity to ask your questions and tour their premises and get the information you need to figure out what exactly you would be getting into if you took their job. So it becomes vital that you use this time to ferret out the information you need to have if you are to avoid career disaster.

Making the Best Impression

The best thing you can do to enhance the impression you make on any interviewer is to take your time, listen politely to everyone you meet, and hold back your very natural tendency to tell them just how wonderful you really are. There is a subtle line between confident pride in your competence and obnoxious arrogance. Unfortunately, a great many peo-ple who interview computer professionals on a regular basis report that these professionals all too often cross over that line.

Often what appears as arrogance in computer professionals is really something else—frequently it is overcompensation for the job candidate's natural shyness or discomfort in new social situations. But interviewers cannot know that you are really a modest and helpful person who is overreacting because you're nervous. They judge you only on what they see in the interview situation and if what they see is someone who inter-rupts them constantly, who brags inappropriately, or who seems rude to peers in a team interview, you may never get a chance to show them who you really are.

The best way to control a tendency to overcompensate is to make yourself *listen*. If you have done the homework we'll describe in the next chapters, you'll have a lot more motivation to listen, because there is a lot you will have to find out, and it is tough to find things out while you are the one doing all the talking.

One helpful strategy is to avoid giving interviewers information about yourself until they ask for it. Most interviewers will want to spend a lot of time—often far too much time from your perspective—snowing you with how wonderful their company is. They'll tell you about its founder, its history, its products and its glowing prospects for the future without getting around to any of the subjects dear to your heart—like what their plans are for future software projects or how much they can afford to pay you. But the key to succeeding in the interview is to listen to this introductory material with as much attention as you can muster. By listening intently you can build a non-verbal connection with the in-terviewer. Eventually they will get around to asking you about yourself and what you do and give you a chance to ask them your questions. If you've made a good connection while they were expressing themselves, they'll now be much more open to hearing what you have to say.

If it turns out that you and an interviewer have business acquain-tances in common—perhaps the interviewer once worked with your current manager or for your current employer—avoid making any nega-tive comments about them. While sharing a laugh over your current em-ployer's stupidity may seem like a quick way of establishing rapport, you really can have no way of knowing what the interviewer's real feelings might be about the people you are discussing. What you *do* know is that demonstrating your disloyalty to current or past employers is *not* the way to impress someone you'd like to have as your next employer!

If you are currently employed, interviewers will ask you why you are leaving your current job. Be careful! This is a loaded question. An-swers that will be sure to raise questions in the interviewer's mind are "I'm bored there" or "I'm not getting paid what I'm worth." Until you know a great deal about the job you are interviewing for, there is no way you can know that it pays more than your current job or offers more challenge. By the same token, you should never say you are leaving because your current manager is an idiot or because your true worth isn't being appreciated. No one wants to hire someone—no matter how good their skills—who appears to be unable to get along with others.

Perhaps the best answer to the question of why you want to change jobs is to explain that you have gotten a lot out of your current job but feel that it is time to move on. This is one situation where being vague will not get you in trouble.

The Technical Interview

As part of the interview process you may be given a separate technical interview. This is especially likely if you are interviewing for a job that requires heavy technical skills. Technical interviews may be conducted by a team of technical people with skills similar to your own or by a single team leader. If you find a technical interview on your schedule, be prepared to answer questions designed to verify that you have the skills you claim and to describe your current project in detail. It is here in the technical interview, rather than during the interview with higher management, that you can flaunt your technical expertise, though it is still a good idea to pause from time to time to make sure that the people you are talking with are keeping pace with you.

Unfortunately, many people report that the questions they were asked by technical interviewers were more like trick questions meant to trip them up than valid attempts to confirm their expertise. The interviewer may have asked them for the meaning of an obscure error message of the type that you usually look up in a manual rather than memorizing it or they may have given them pieces of tricky but basically silly code to interpret. Sometimes these technical interview questions sound like they were copied directly from a programming textbook review section.

The reason you may run into these kinds of questions may be that the people asked to run the technical interview don't actually share your identical technical skill set and have had to hit the books to come up with questions they think might reveal your knowledge—or lack of it. They may be people from a related department who are technically knowledgeable in something else or they may be lower level managers whose technical skills are rusty. These can often be the most disturbing interviews, especially if you feel that you are being asked questions that don't fairly allow you to display your experience.

Another reason you may encounter interviewers who ask intensely probing or even hostile questions may be that the interviewer is an immigrant from a different culture who, though technically knowledgeable, is not aware of the subtleties of American social interaction. Or the interviewer may be trying to disqualify you, so that they can "prove" that no citizen with your skills is available and justify granting an immigrant visa. Sometimes hostility from an interviewer is the tip-off that an internal political battle is being waged over hiring someone for this job.

If you find you self being peppered with inappropriate technical questions, take a deep breath and don't let yourself become defensive or rattled. If the question is one where you would look up the answer in a manual, it is perfectly reasonable to explain how you would do just that. If possible, complete your response by giving an example of something similar that you encountered in real life and how you handled it.

If your interviewer is obviously from another culture, remember that they are probably as uncomfortable interviewing you as you are being grilled by them. Again, avoid getting defensive or anxious and do your best to radiate confidence in your abilities.

Some companies will even go so far as to give you written exams that are out-of-date or expect you to be familiar with the kinds of obscure product-specific trivia that most of us just look up when we need to know them. That a company would hire staff using this sort of poorly designed exam is the tip-off that its management is woefully ignorant about computer technology and that you would probably not enjoy working for them.

A STRESSFUL TECHNICAL INTERVIEW

"The subject matter was C. The guy gives me this bizarre verbal pop quiz to see if I understood some bulls*** obscure obfuscated code in which he was assigning the result of a strcpy() to a char pointer variable that was being incremented inside the pointer dereference. i.e., something like:

```
*(p++) = strcpy(some_crap_var,some_other_kaka);
```

"It wasn't all that arcane for a seasoned C developer (although it was the kind of garbage I don't like to write myself) but it was evident that the guy was overcompensating to make sure that I knew he regarded himself as a guru and was all knowing and all seeing. And he kept jumping all over the place in speaking with me so that I couldn't really focus on the question he was asking. It was like, 'You have five seconds—are you done yet? Well you seem like a good guy, here's the answer. Now here's another question... '

"He liked me and recommended that they hire me which they did. This same manager had an earned reputation in this outfit for both demanding and doing 100 hour weeks himself."

Likewise, if a person who cross-examines you with irrelevant questions meant to trip you up rather than show your competence might end up being your team leader or co-worker, this too might be a sign that—unless you like a Mensa-like environment where test taking is more important than achievement—this is not the place for you.

What You *Must Learn at the Interview*

When you are in an interview situation, especially early on in your career, you should assume that you will be a bit flustered or "hyper." Since in that state you can't remember very much, focus on the essential: You should try to emerge from the interview able to answer the following two questions:

♦ What is the role of the person I am talking with and what relation does it bear to my possible future position?

♦ What will I actually, specifically, be doing?

These might seem like obvious questions, but they are not. All too often new hires jump to conclusions about the answers to these questions that lead to real unhappiness on the job.

Who Am I Talking To?

I wish I had a dollar for every new hire I've met who has told me that they took one job rather than another because they liked the personality of the person who interviewed them for that position best.

This is probably the worst mistake you can make. Any experienced corporate employee can tell you that the chances are good you will never again have anything more than a nodding acquaintance with the person who interviewed you.

This is because in most companies the interview is not conducted by the person who will be your boss but by that person's boss. It is their job to see you and evaluate you. But once they decide to hire you, they will assign you to the team leader in whose group they feel you can make the best contribution, and you will have little more to do with them directly.

When you interview at some companies you may be introduced to the person who will actually direct your work and you may get to speak with them briefly, but this is by no means the rule. You may also have a team interview with technical people whom you are told will be your coworkers. But even when you are interviewed by a supposed boss and coworkers, the nature of business is that things change. Often by the time you are ready to begin your job this boss has been transferred to another department and the development team reorganized.

So you should always take the time to determine what role your primary interviewer plays in the organization you are interviewing with.

The interviewer will take this as a sign of intelligence on your part. If they pull out an organizational chart, study it with interest. It can tell you a lot about the situation you are getting into. Many applicants are so eager to impress an interviewer that they plunge into descriptions of highly technical achievements before determining if the person they are talking to is a technical or administrative person. It is very embarrassing to discover that the person you are snowing doesn't begin to understand what you are talking about.

If the interview is going well and your interest in the job is growing, feel free to ask if you can meet the person who would be your actual boss. Just remember that there are no guarantees. What you should be looking at is not the personality of the individuals you are introduced to but what their characteristics tell you about the organization. Do they seem intelligent? Do they seem harried or overburdened? Do they respond to their own boss with relaxed friendliness or with wariness and forced joviality? Even if the actual people you get to work with are not the ones you see at the interview, you will usually find that the company's style remains the same.

If you are favorably impressed with what you are learning about the job opportunity, it might be a good idea to ask a simple question or two about the people you will be working with. But keep your questions generic. Are there a lot of recent college hires? Is the place staffed mainly by short-term contractors? Have most of the people in the department been with the company a long time? The only specific question you should feel free to ask is what happened to the last person who had the job you are interviewing for. If that person was promoted into a higher-status job you will usually be told about it. Otherwise you will be told that you are filling a newly created job or given a vague answer.

Keep your eyes open as you walk through the building. Look at the décor people have in their cubes and compare it with what you would have. A place full of motivational posters is going to feel quite different from a place where all you see is extreme sport trophies—or diplomas. If you see nothing that shows personal taste at all, that in itself tells you something about the company's personality.

You might ask whether the pleasant—or not-so-pleasant—offices you are passing are where you will be working. More than once I've been told no, the department I'm interviewing for is located in the basement.

By making no assumptions during the interview process you will save yourself from getting some nasty surprises.

What Will I Be Doing?

It would seem that you should expect to be told what a job you are interviewing for is all about, but all too often you are not. And, all too often, because they aren't told, interviewees jump to dangerous and damaging conclusions.

We discussed earlier how the person who interviews you is rarely the person who will be your boss. Unfortunately this means that they rarely know what you will actually be doing. Frequently, interviewers who are upper level managers share with you their own broad view of the project—the broad view that they must have to run the project. Often this results in the interviewer telling you about the more interesting features of an entire project that involves forty or fifty people at all levels. They may mention a new development effort that is planned or tell you about a new state-of-the-art technology that the project employs, like a cellular palm-based interface to a database on their server. Unfortunately the portion of the project they have *you* slated for has nothing to do with this interesting stuff. It will be done by old-timers who have worked in this project for years. You are being interviewed for a job that involves doing boring maintenance tasks on an older system so that the people moving to the new project won't have to do them anymore!

This is not necessarily a conscious attempt to mislead you. Project managers will always be excited about the most interesting parts of their projects. The truth may also be that they have no idea what they will have you working on. It may take many months of waiting and reams of paperwork before managers can get permission to hire new people. So smart managers often stock up on new staff while they can, even if they have no specific role in mind for them. They figure that after they have met you and the other applicants they will be able to figure out who they want to hire and what they would best be suited for.

Because of this you are in something of a quandary. If interviewers really don't know what they are going to have you do, you can't very well pin them down. If you demand specifics they will often tell you something off of the top of their heads, but you can be sure that it is not what you will be assigned to when you show up for work.

At other times the job to be filled appears to be very clearly defined. The only thing that can go wrong here is that the department may be reorganized, as occurs about twice a year in many businesses, and the job you were originally hired for may be eliminated and replaced with another.

Again, your best bet is to look at the broader picture of the project and determine the flavor of what is going on. If you can see a couple of different jobs within the project that would interest you, the chances are that you could eventually get one of them even if the job you start out with is less than ideal. However if you are shown a wonderful-sounding job but the work the rest of the people on the project do seems drab, be careful! You might easily end up with one of their jobs, rather than getting the bait the interviewer held out to you.

Finally, if you know anyone who works at the company, pump them for information. Usually the company grapevine can tell you something about the people and the jobs in the area you are interested in.

If you forget to ask an important question at the interview you will have a second chance to ask it after an offer is made to you. Don't feel you must instantly respond to a job offer when you get a phone call. Instead ask if you can contact the person offering the job. Most companies will be happy to let you phone that person. Then finish up the interviewing process and try to get the answers you need to make sure that this really is the job is for you.

If you get a strong, hard-to-quantify feeling of unease during an interview, no matter how appealing a job may seem, take it seriously. You may be picking up on some subliminal issues that months of experience will only confirm. Try not to talk yourself into something just because you are desperate to make a change and don't want to have to keep interviewing. None of us gets that many chances to change jobs, and each job you take has a major impact on your future career development. You owe it to yourself to find a job that you feel good about, and finding such a job may take some time.

The Issues that Define Your New Job

If you consider the following issues *before* you go to the job interview you will enter the interview aware of what you need to find out to determine whether this is going to be the job that gets you where you want to be or one that you should turn down. To understand some of these issues you will need to do some homework before you get to the interview. This will involve researching some facts about the company and checking things out with people who have worked there. In other cases, you will get the answers you need during the interview itself.

In "Appendix A" at the end of this book you will find twenty-five sets of questions. These questions were selected to show you the kinds of things you should consider asking about during an interview. Each of them relates to a topic covered somewhere in this book. Naturally you won't be able to ask all or even most of them, but by familiarizing yourself with the list you should be able to spot troubling signs or, conversely, the selling points of a job you are considering. Decide before the interview which of these questions are the most important to you, then make sure that you don't get so carried away by the heady atmosphere of the interview situation that you forget to ask them!

Taking the following issues seriously and using them to shape the interview process will give you two advantages. First of all you will be able to exert some control over your future by selecting your job, rather than, like most people, letting it select you. The second advantage is that if you do the research you should do before the interview, you will come across to an interviewer as more aware than the other people you are competing with, and thus, more likely to be hired.

Some of the issues we will cover relate to the nature of the company you are considering. They concern structural features of the company and the more elusive characteristics that make up its personality. Others relate to the kind of work the company can offer you. We will look at the software environment from several different perspectives and we will look at what effect the application area you work in has on your subsequent career. We'll find out some surprising facts about the impact of where a project fits into the project development cycle. Finally we will talk about the ever-fascinating subject of money and how to be certain you get offered as much as possible.

No job is going to be perfect. For that matter, few jobs will turn out to be exactly the way they were described at the interview. But if you define what issues are the most important to you, you should be able to find a position that embodies the issues you care about in a way closest to what you want.

If you are starting your job hunt fresh out of school and your credentials are far from breathtaking, obviously you cannot afford to be too highly selective. You may well have to do the best you can with whatever job you can find. But you can still have some minimal standards that will keep your from accepting a job that will frustrate all your career hopes. And even if you are beginning with less than a running start don't forget that in two years, if you follow the guidelines we laid out in Chapter 2, "Your First Job," you should have an experience level that will open up a far broader range of possibilities. You can apply more rigorous standards then.

If you are a more experienced person now, you can afford to be choosier. You must also, unfortunately, be more suspicious. The more qualified you are, the more hiring managers will tend to exaggerate and bend the facts to attract you to what they know is a mediocre job. This makes it that much more important that you come prepared to ask the revealing questions that will expose the truth. And don't just analyze the new job in terms of these issues—look at your current job and at your current company as well. Be certain that you cannot attain your long-term goals by making minor adjustments in your present situation before committing yourself to making a major and irrevocable change which will expose to far greater levels of uncertainty than you would face in the job you know.

Building your career is not easy, but you are way ahead of most people as soon as you take into your own hands the responsibility for shaping that career. If you devote to your job search the same energy and hard work you gave to doing well in school and on the job you will find the high paying, high satisfaction jobs that will build a lifetime of career satisfaction.

Now we'll turn to examining the critical issues you need to look at, one by one.

CHAPTER 9

The Size of the IT Shop

The size of the IT shop where you start your career can have a tremendous effect on the shape of your career — far more than you might realize when you start the job hunting process.

The term "IT Shop" may not appeal to people who like to think of computer programming as a professional occupation. The word "shop" brings with it a certain proletarian tinge. It sounds tough and gritty and has overtones of people doing real work as opposed to the glorified puzzle solving we computer professionals do. However this is a term used, particularly among recruiters. What it refers to is the total computer environment of a company, taken as a whole. The important fact to grasp is that as a computer professional you need to be more concerned with the size of the IT shop within the company than the size of the company itself. Many people are surprised to discover that some large and well known companies employ only a small number of IT staff, while another outfit they have never heard of has many times more.

This is not to say that the size and strength of the company as a whole is not important. It is. You should have some idea of any potential employer's fiscal health as reflected in its most recent quarterly reports. The best job in the world is worthless if the company folds, and this does happen. I have personally witnessed not one but two situations where companies in their death throes went on hiring binges and brought on board expensive experienced programmers who were relocated from other parts of the country in the vain hope of salvaging the company. A month or so later management gave up on the divisions that these programmers were brought in to serve and fired them all, leaving them facing a grim job search in a city undergoing an economic downturn.

While you should try to work for companies with a history of quarterly earnings, not losses — or in this age of dot.com mania, at least companies that might reasonably be expected to someday, somehow have earnings — don't confuse the earnings, size, or importance of a company with the size and importance of its IT shop.

The size of the company's IT shop is reflected in two statistics: the number of programmers, technicians and computer administrators working within the company and the number of custom computer applications that the company has installed. Just counting computers will not tell you what you need to know. There are companies with a PC on every employee's desk that run nothing but off-the-shelf commercial software and need nothing from their IT department but routine tech support.

How Large is Large?

One industry that uses a great number of computer staffers is the insurance industry. What insurance companies sell is their ability to track huge numbers of customers, claims, investments, and agents. All these things lend themselves to computerization, and the insurance industry was among the earliest to computerize. So a large insurance company can easily have a thousand programmers, technical administrators, and technicians working for it. Some of the largest insurers have more.

At the other end of the spectrum, a manufacturing company that uses computers only for bookkeeping functions might have only a dozen programmers. As you move down the scale you will find a good number of smaller companies, many of them producing products or services with brand names you recognize, that have small mom-and-pop-style IT shops. In such a company you might find only three people supporting a PC network or minicomputer system that performs billing and accounting functions. These systems will run off-the-shelf software rather than systems designed and coded by their own programmers. Some companies of this size will advertise for a system administrator who is responsible for running programs, customizing packages, answering user questions and restoring their files. The job title for a job like this might even be "IT Manager."

The number of computer staffers employed by a company tells you a lot about the size of its shop, however, it doesn't tell you the whole story. A vital statistic is how many *custom systems* the shop has developed and what kind of networks those applications are running on. A typical large shop would be one where the company's servers run custom database, inventory, retail, warehousing, EDI, sales force management, and product engineering applications that support thousands of in-house users on workstations or Web connections. These many different custom applications each require continual updating and enhancement, which call for the presence of a large, permanent programming staff.

Variety of Systems

Another determinant of the size of a company's IT shop is how many *dissimilar* computer systems the company maintains. A large insurance company that has five hundred people supporting its personal lines insurance products might actually be supporting fifteen different versions of one base system. There might be a daily batch system for homeowner's insurance, and a daily batch system for car insurance in a set of states that have similar legislation governing auto insurance, and yet another daily batch system for car insurance in the state of Massachusetts, and there might be yet more daily batch systems for individual and for group health insurance. In moving from one system to another you would discover that each of these systems is doing the same things the same ways as the others because they were all cloned from the same base system many years before. Only the details relating to the business side of the application will vary.

Although this is definitely a large shop, compare it to another company that employs two hundred programmers in a manufacturing environment. This company might have an inventory system that uses terminals in the warehouse to collect data and send it to databases on the company server. It might have computerized accounting systems that run through a large daily batch cycle with an on-line query system that executives use to track their operations. This company might have floor control systems that monitor and control the manufacturing process and collect performance data on the manufacturing equipment. There may be computer aided design systems (CAD) utilizing state-of-the-art hardware and software. There may be EDI systems for keeping inventory records up-to-date with vendors and with the distributors who sell the company's products. Even though there might be fewer programmers in this environment than there are the insurance company cited earlier, this is clearly a much larger shop since the variety of different computer applications that the programmer could get involved in is much greater.

There are advantages to working in small shops and advantages to working in the larger ones. Let's look at the good and bad of each.

The Advantages of a Large Shop

The best thing about working for a company with large, diversified IT operations is that the chances are that, if you don't find your first job compelling, you will be able to find something different to do within the same company without having to quit and lose the benefit of the reputation you have built up within the company. Very big companies sometimes act like collections of loosely associated smaller independent companies. In big companies like this each individual IT area often has its own distinct personality. This can mean that moving from one part of the company to another can feel like moving to an entirely different company.

Many Companies in One

When I worked for IBM I found that switching jobs within IBM divisions exposed me to radically different ways of doing things. When I changed jobs within the company, everything changed, from the way I was expected to dress to the frequency with which my paycheck was issued. Because of the size of the company, the different divisions had substantially different corporate cultures, although certain fundamentals, like IBM's famous policy of respect for the individual, were unchanging no matter the location.

For example, at my first job at IBM it was expected that when you received a promotion you would give your coworkers a treat. At lower levels it was donuts all around. As you progressed up the ladder the treats got more expensive. Entry into middle-level management could entail joining other newly promoted managers in hosting an open bar for one hundred programmers after work on Friday. At the IBM location I moved to next, such behavior would have been looked at askance. However at that location you could always expect that the achievement of any project milestone would be followed by a company-paid luncheon at an upscale downtown hotel and the awarding of gewgaws.

At the first location, a factory located in a remote rural location, dress was casual, programmers wore hiking boots, and even managers wore suits only if they had an important meeting scheduled for the day. At the second location, an urban regional marketing center, everyone dressed like the famed IBM sales force. Programmer dress there was carefully scrutinized and managers had been known to call programmers to task for wearing "inappropriate," casual, footgear.

These differences demonstrate the way a large company gives you opportunities to change your environment radically without having to quit. And this means that the reputation you build within the company, your most valuable personal asset, remains undiluted.

Multiple Locations

Some companies offer geographical diversity. If you would like to move around the country or work in other nations this is a real possibility with such a company. This is particularly true if you select a company that has far-flung operations and does not centralize its IT services. If a company has twenty plants and each has its own independent IT system you have a good chance of moving during your career with that company, whether you want to or not. Companies that sell IT services, such as large consulting firms or larger software vendors, also provide travel opportunities for technical professionals who prove themselves within the organization.

This "advantage" works both ways. When you are interviewing for a job with a company that has widespread IT operations you need to ask some explicit questions about how likely you are to remain at the location you are being hired into. Some companies will tell you that you will be expected to move when and where they need you and will let you know that the job you are being hired into is part of a project that is going to wind down in two years and require you to move to an entirely different part of the country. Other companies are not so forthcoming — or may not be able to foretell the effects that changes in their business will have on where they locate their staff. When Electronic Data Systems of Dallas was bought by General Motors a large number of its programmers around the country suddenly received orders to move to Detroit and Indiana where General Motors plants were located.

Obviously, if you are tied to a particular part of the country you would do best to stick with a company that has its IT functions centralized in one or two locations, as do many insurance and financial giants. This issue is particularly important if your spouse has a career too. Many companies boast that they have programs to aid spouses when one of the couple is relocated, but these efforts usually boil down to paying for help in writing up the spouses résumé or paying employment agency fees. If your spouse is also building a professional career and your lifestyle depends on both salaries, then being forced to move to an area where the spouse can not find a good job can cause you economic hardship and generate resentments that can harm your marriage.

If you are attracted to a company because it has technical people working at locations that you find particularly appealing, but you are not interviewing for a job in one of those locations, make sure the job you would be getting will give you the skills that would be required for a job at the location you would like to be transferred to. Often companies have radically different skill requirements from one installation to another, and you might find that the transfer you had hoped for is impossible.

Though caution is in order when companies lure you with the promise of work in exotic locations, it does happen. I have known programmers who were sent on long term, all expense paid assignments to Hawaii and London. Indeed, many computer professionals value their profession because it offers them the ability to live in almost any urban center they choose. The trick here, as with so much else in evaluating a job, is to know what you are getting into before you make your decision.

A Rich Software and Hardware Environment

Besides offering physical diversity, large shops can offer exposure to a much wider range of hardware and software. If you want to develop your skills as a technical programmer you should pay attention to any opportunity to work in an environment where the company has installed—or even better is in the process of installing—hardware and software from a number of currently hot mainstream vendors.

Not only do larger companies have more computers and computer applications installed than smaller ones, they also have more money to throw around experimenting with new approaches. They are more likely to have several development projects going at once as well as pilot projects that are testing new technologies. Working within such a company, you might get training in a state-of-the-art software environment that is being tested at the company before the vendor releases it to other companies. This way you get a jump in adding a potentially hot item to your "bag of tricks." Vendors of high-end packages in niches like ERP (Enterprise Resource Planning) choose certain good customers with whom they have a comfortable relationship as beta test sites. This means that the vendor gives the customer site a pre-release version of the software and then works closely with the company's technical staff to deal with the bugs that emerge as the software is used. This way vendors get to do the final debugging of their software in a real-world environment and the customer gets to have the most advanced technology first.

If you are lucky enough to be associated with the beta test of a high end product that becomes a success, the dollar value of your knowledge is enormous. You will have the ability to work in almost any company that is thinking of implementing the software you have mastered. If you are thinking of being a consultant you can charge the highest rates for this kind of knowledge. Packages such as SAP/ABAP or PeopleSoft are examples of this kind of large-shop software that you can only get trained on if you happen to work for a large shop that implements it. People with only one or two years of experience in the field whose first jobs involved working with these kinds of packages have reported long term contracts to the Real Rate Survey that pay up to $150 per hour!

If you have decided that you want to become a system or database administrator you have very little choice except to work for a company with a large shop. These are the only companies that train people in system or database administration. Generally, smaller companies have only one or two such administrators on their staffs and they do not have the resources to train people in these areas. Typically they raid larger companies for the people they have trained, luring them with high salaries.

The larger shop with its "cast of thousands" might just have a cast of twenty database administrators. Often these companies have evolved training programs designed for applications programmers who have demonstrated technical aptitude in their earlier assignments. If you yearn to be a supertechie you might consider building your reputation for technical wizardry in a large shop environment where you can be rewarded by being offered this kind of training.

More Opportunities in Management

Large IT shops also offer advantages if you have decided that your career goal is to develop into a manager. This is simply because a larger IT shop needs more IT managers than a small one. In a small IT shop you might have to wait until the three current managers quit, get fired, or die, whereas a large growing IT shop will be creating new projects and new project teams which, in turn, creates new management slots you can fill.

Large companies with huge bureaucracies also tend to have formalized paths for developing management personnel that include classroom training. Large companies also are forced to pay a little more attention to equal opportunity issues.

In an earlier chapter we've looked at the advisability of going into IT management, and again I caution you against expecting to ever reach a truly "executive" level coming from a technically oriented computer development or IT background. But if you yearn for a career that leads to middle management, the more IT managers there are in a company you work for, the better your chances are of breaking in.

Better Benefit Packages

Large IT shops have other advantages. They may offer better benefit packages—although many larger companies have, in the past few years, been cutting benefits back. A company-matched 401K plan might not set your pulses racing when you are twenty-two years old and contemplating your first job, but in fifteen years you might be grateful to know that there is a little something waiting for you when you hit the end of your working years.

Large shops often have formal education programs. Some have whole education organizations with classrooms and professional instructors whose only job is to teach technical courses. Much of the technical training that can set you up for a career as a top dollar consultant is taught in these courses, and often these courses are given to applications people as a reward for doing an especially good job.

The Difficulty of Getting Training in the Large Shop

The very diversity and size that makes the large shop so attractive creates some problems too. While the company may teach just those courses you want to take, getting your management to send you to them can prove almost impossible. Managers are not stupid, and they know what is of value on the open market. So they are not likely to provide you with a new skill set that will substantially improve your marketability to their competitors until you have proven your loyalty to the company in concrete and time-consuming ways.

Usually when you are interviewed for a large IT shop, the hiring manager will promise you that you will be sent to two or three courses a year. Some companies go so far as to make it a requirement that each employee at a professional level get a certain amount of annual training. Unfortunately what usually happens is that in your first year you get a lot of training in the nuts and bolts stuff you need to know to perform your job. For example, you might get a class in how to use the company's chosen code editor and development libraries or what the company's procedures are for moving programs into production. But when your second year rolls around, instead of getting the technical classes you crave you will find yourself going to workshops on "Stress Reduction," "Improving Business Communications" or even "Creative Parenting for the Working Parent." The closest you will usually get to a technical class might be a seminar on the principles of software design, which would be great if you were ever permitted to use what you were taught on the job!

The frustrations of working in a large company often boil down to the fact that, although everything you might want is right there somewhere, the company is so big that you can never find it. You will need to be very sharp and very devoted to controlling the direction of your career to avoid being pushed down career avenues that are useful to the company but not in line with your own goals.

The Herd o'Techies Environment

There is another problem you may encounter in large IT shops. It stems from the way that some large IT shops organize the work they do. A company that employs one thousand programmers faces formidable numbers when it looks at job turnover. Since such companies often can't afford to pay high salaries, they accept that large numbers of people are going to quit every year. They also accept that they will not be able to recruit and keep one thousand geniuses to work on their systems, or, for that matter, even one thousand people who understand computers.

What such companies often do is divide up the work so that low-skill low-salary staffers can do the bulk of the grunt work while a few highly paid people figure out what the grunts should do. This is defensive programmer management. In this situation management tries to arrange things so that no single stupid programmer can screw up more than a tiny part of the system. This is done by making sure that the same "stupid" programmer has access only to a tiny portion of the system and by keeping their job clearly defined and limited.

In a company organized this way you will often find herds of clerk-like programmers, each assigned responsibility for a small set of programs. Other departments take responsibility for talking to the user group and defining the requirements for program changes. In mainframe environments, other departments take responsibility for creating the JCL that runs the "stupid" programmer's code or defining the files their on-line program updates. Other departments might even write the modules that the "stupid" programmer uses to retrieve and write data from the database. The poor old "stupid" programmer gets to do one thing: they change the code in their assigned modules exactly the way they are told to and pass it down the line.

While this system might allow companies to employ people of limited ability and pay them poorly while still keeping their systems afloat, it creates an environment that is painful to work in not only for the poor slob on the bottom, insulated from ever learning more than the minimum amount needed to keep their job, but also for the more talented people throughout the organization who have to function in an environment where only the minimum is ever expected from anyone.

If you are an ambitious, intelligent programmer interviewing for a job in a company that employs a large number of programmers, be very certain that you are not falling into this kind of trap—even as a supervisor. The fact that you have impressive credentials that demonstrate your ability and intelligence is not protection against finding yourself assigned to a job designed for the "stupid" programmer described above. This system often produces managers with such limited technical abilities—having never themselves been trained in anything more than the minimum needed to do their jobs—that the hiring manager may not be able to interpret or understand the experience described on your résumé.

If you fall into a job like this as your first job right out of school you are in serious trouble. You will learn a tremendous amount about a few specific programs. You will not get much software exposure. You won't get to observe the systems development cycle, and you won't even learn the business side of your application. At best you will learn how to read detailed specs provided by a systems analyst. And if this is your first job you will have to stay a year because there is usually no way you can change jobs until you have gotten a year of experience. I have seen very bright people spend two or three years doing nothing but updating rate tables in a single set of insurance programs. I have heard of mainframe team leaders whose technical skills were so limited that they could not read a link map—because that was another department's responsibility. I even worked—briefly—in one company where the standard answer to any question was, "Well, maybe there is some way to do that, but we wouldn't know, we're just dumb [company-name]-oids."

Talking to people you meet at work about companies where they used to work or where their friends work now can often inform you about the worst workplaces in your area. But don't be surprised if your friendly neighborhood recruiter tries to sell you a job at one of these sinkholes as a "wonderful opportunity."

THE TELL TALE SIGNS OF A DEAD END JOB

- **Uniform Environment.** Are there a large number of programmers working for the same project in a single large room or a physical environment that reflects uniformity?

- **Segmentation.** When you look at the organizational chart do you see a customer interface group, an I/O group, a database group, and an on-line group all listed as part of the application group? It would be okay to see database support and on-line support appearing in a separate technical support ladder, but not under the same lower-level management. Of course, you might not see these groups on a chart even when they exist.

- **Identical Jobs.** Does everyone on the team do the same thing? In a better shop each person in a department will have responsibilities that are quite different from their coworkers. The similarity will be that they are supporting the same user group.

- **No Autonomy.** Will you be responsible for developing your own specifications or is this the task of a higher-level person? In the best jobs you will do the specifications and design yourself for your part of a project as well as the coding and unit testing.

- **Contractors.** Are there a lot of contractors on the project? This does not always mean trouble but often a cluster of consultants is a sign that the company has had trouble retaining employees in this area.

- **Isolation.** Will you have direct contact with the user group? If not find out why not. In the better jobs you are trusted to communicate with the users. In the worst you are forbidden to talk to them.

- **Dumb Interviewers.** Do interviewers ask questions that show that they don't understand the technical stuff you have listed on your résumé? This is not relevant for college students who often list weird software they picked up in college. But if you have been working with commercial software in the business world and get the feeling that you are losing the interviewer when you explain what you did in a previous position, this is a pretty good sign you might not be happy in an assignment they might give you.

The Small Shop

There are several different types of environment that make up the population of small shops. The traditional small shop may be a medium sized company that has a small number of custom computer applications running or one which uses standard off the shelf PC products for its IT needs. Another variety of small shop, quite different from the traditional small shop, is the software or hardware start-up company.

MY BEST CAREER MOVE

"I was fortunate in that it was a small company and that the CEO was interested in the Internet. In fact he decided to launch his own National ISP and arranged for himself, me, and another engineer to get some basic IP training. From there I ran with it on my own through reading etc.

"After a couple of years I decided to switch permanently and landed a position at a local network integration company. Through a lot of study, I would say at least 20-30 hours per week on top of working full-time and over a period of all but two years, I was ready to sit for the Cisco CCIE test. I passed the written and about six months later passed the lab.

"So here I am today. It has been great. My present compensation is just shy of being six times what I was making at the previous dead-end job. In just three years I went from $32K to $176K including bonuses. It was a lot of work, but it was worth it for both me and my family. All of us sacrificed for those two years and now we all reap the rewards."

Advantages of the Small Shop

Almost everyone who has worked in a traditional smaller shop has said that the best part of the job was the friendly, intimate atmosphere. If large corporations can be like big cities with different neighborhoods and a lot of traffic, a company with a small shop can be very much like a small town. In a small shop you may often have a nice summer picnic and a big Christmas party which you might actually enjoy since you recognize everyone there. In a small shop, too, you know who is in charge at all levels, since there is a simple management structure to deal with and not as much moving around from department to department.

For many people the more personal environment of the small shop is its major attraction, outweighing the career advantages available in the larger but more anonymous big shop.

The smaller software development shop offers some specific advantages to people who are just beginning a technical career. Many of these run the same software that the larger shops use. What they don't tend to do is compartmentalize your work as much. Since they have fewer technical staff to work with they cannot afford to limit their scope of action the way that the larger companies often do. What this means for you if you are a programmer is that if you have responsibility for a set of programs you will be expected to talk with your user when they have any problems with those programs or want changes made. You will probably get to do your own analysis and design in consultation with more experienced programmers. You will do coding and testing. You may very well get to go into the operations area and walk the staff through any procedural changes you must make to a system. This breadth of exposure is invaluable. You may very well get to do a little of everything in the first few years if you work in such a shop.

In a traditional small shop environment another benefit to the new programmer or administrator is that you will usually be kept very busy. This might sound like a strange sort of "advantage," but it is not unusual for new people to be brought into huge shops and then find themselves sitting around for weeks, or even months, waiting for something to break so that they can get to work fixing it, with nothing but busy work to keep them occupied. This is extremely boring and is a lot less likely to occur in a smaller shop that has a tight budget for personnel.

In the smaller shop you may also end up feeling a greater sense of accomplishment. You will usually get to see "your" users using "your" software. People from other parts of the company often will know who you are and what systems you support.

The Disadvantages of Traditional Small Shops

Unfortunately, there are limitations imposed by the smaller size of the small shop. The very intimacy that makes some small shops so appealing can make others hell. Negative personalities or abrasive management styles have a greater impact here. If your IT manager is a stinker you can't just switch departments to escape. You may have to quit. Likewise, if your users are a total pain in the neck, you are probably stuck with them if you want to keep your job. So it is very important that you choose a small shop that has a personality compatible with your own. A friend of mine used to work in a small mainframe shop where the boss took all the programmers out once a month to a restaurant that featured all-you-can-drink lunches. For some people this was heaven. Others found it intolerable.

The other main problem is that the chances for promotion and rapid salary development may be limited. If there are only a few IT managers in a company it is going to take a lot longer to break into management. If there are few development projects you won't be able to get experience with new technologies just coming into the marketplace. In the worst case situation, where you have a small shop whose systems are mature, you might get almost no technical experience at all, since the company sees no reason to spend money enhancing what it sees as satisfactory systems. Finally, most small shops cannot afford to pay high salaries.

The last reason more than any other is the reason that most programmers I've met cite for leaving smaller shops. For a small company, keeping overhead low is not an abstraction. It is often the difference between survival and bankruptcy. Remember, computer support is overhead! As a result, many technical professionals leave the smaller shops for rich large companies awash in waste and fat, where they spend their lunch hours telling their buddies how much better they liked working at the small shop job they used to have.

Software Start-ups

While you may also find yourself extremely busy and exposed to red-hot technology in a software start-up, the main reason programmers are attracted to them is the possibility of getting stock options should the company make it to the IPO stage. Stock options are such alluring bait that many programmers are talked into taking jobs with start-ups that offer mediocre pay and very poor working conditions just because they are promised these options.

Unfortunately, for every computer professionals who gets in on the ground floor at a company like Microsoft or Netscape, there are thousands whose stock options turn out to be worthless. Indeed, the majority of programmers I've spoken with who have taken stock option deals report that they were a huge mistake. In many cases the companies are poorly managed, the working conditions atrocious, and the product never hits the marketplace, or if it does, the company fails before the initial stock offering. Even when the company does make it to the IPO stage, programmers often find out that due to various manipulations that company owners indulge in before the offering, their stock's value has been diluted to where its market value is far less than the money they would have received had they been getting paid a market-rate salary for the time they spent working at the start-up.

Start-ups can be spectacular opportunities or they can be scams run by people hoping to cash in on the latest business craze. It is not easy to determine what you are getting into when a company has no track record, no assets, and no product. Even companies like Amazon.com that are considered the superstars of the start-up world are prone to massive layoffs. Brand new companies may run out of money weeks after hiring you and often do.

If you are considering hiring into a start-up, make sure you will be happy if the only payment you receive is your salary. Check into the history of the people running the company too. What previous experience do they have with software or hardware new product development? Don't be shy about running a business credit check on them if you have any question about their ability to meet a payroll.

QUESTIONS FOR A START-UP

- How many shares are there and what fraction will you be getting?

- Will these shares be diluted at some later date?

- How long will you have to wait to vest?

- What's your gut feel on how likely the product is to succeed?

- How far are they from going public and how long after that would you have to wait to cash in/out?

- How much would you be loosing in earnings over the length of time it took before you *could* cash out?

- How many rounds of funding do they expect to have before they go public?

- What kind of hardware and software do they actually have up and running—not including vaporware?

- Do they realize that no more than ten percent of all tech ventures are successful?

A BAD EXPERIENCE WITH A START-UP

"I work at a start-up in the Boston area. For the first six months, they did not know what they were doing and wasted a lot of people's time with 'grand visions' that lacked any type of solid foundation.

"Recently, they have sort-of settled on an idea, with no clear statement about how they expect to make money with it, and a ridiculous deadline about three months away.

"They are expecting the employees to work fifteen-hour days (all are salaried, of course.) The guys who make 100k/year are bitching that the guys making half that aren't there on the weekends. The idea still mutates on a bi-weekly basis, so it's like trying to shoot a moving target.

"They hired a 'project lead' who had everyone start coding for coding's sake, with very little real design effort. He also likes to code himself and produces some real garbage. As a result, after only a couple of months the code is a complete disaster. The management trusts the 'lead' because he makes it looks like something is happening even though things are a real mess underneath. The project feels doomed.

"I stay there 'til 7 or 7:30 each night and these guys bitch I am not there enough."

CHAPTER 10

The Software Environment

Once you have gotten a year or more of experience, when you look for a new job an interesting thing begins to happen. No one cares what your grade point average was in college. Few interviewers even care if you *attended* college. No one wants to know if you are an efficient programmer or write elegant code. Few people will ever even look at your code. No one cares that you came in twenty-three times last year at 3 A.M. to fix production problems or that you got promoted to associate programmer before anyone else in your training class.

What they do care about, deeply and passionately, is whether you know Java, Solaris, VC++, VB, DB2, Oracle, or a host of other acronyms and product names that describe the skill set of the experienced computer professional.

These are the names of best-selling software products used in the IT world and which ones of them appear on your résumé is the single most important factor defining your usefulness to a potential employer. Sometimes a product name alone is all you will see in the description of a job being advertised in the Sunday classifieds or on a Web job site. If you visit a job placement firm, they will very often run down a checklist several pages long asking if you have experience with each of a large number of software products and how much. If you apply for a consulting contract, the match between the acronyms on your résumé and the client's job description is all that will get you the interview. Because this factor outweighs all others and because it is just as easy to learn how to use software that is in great demand as it is to learn software that no one is interested in, it is of paramount importance that you be able to put some useful software product names on your résumé.

Why is Software Experience so Important?

There is a simple reason why hiring managers consider the acronyms on your résumé the single most important factor in evaluating you for a position. These acronyms indicate the software environments that you have worked in. They reflect real hard-won experience acquired hour by hour working with arbitrary, balky, and sometimes out-and-out absurd software products. More importantly, they represent knowledge that cannot be acquired intuitively. No matter how smart you are you cannot be productive using a new computer language, database, or operating system or even a new code editor or debugging tool without having first absorbed a large body of trivial but essential details, each one of which can eat up hours of your time.

As we mentioned earlier, most students come out of school thinking that the software developer's main skill is writing programs. But after a few months on the job most people come to realize that writing software is the easy part. The hard part is understanding software written by other people, and a big part of the software you need to understand is a set of infrastructure software—software that provides the tools that working software developers use as the foundation for writing their own software.

This software environment includes programs that fall into several families. In one group there are the operating systems. An operating systems is the lowest level of software that loads into the machine when you first turn it on. It directs the flow of applications programs through the computer and makes sure that each program that executes has access to the hardware resources such as memory, video display, files, and printers that it requires.

Most operating systems now include shells, or session managers, such as the Unix Bourne and Korn shells or the IBM mainframe command language, TSO. These are sets of commands that allow you to manipulate files and system resources online in real-time. These shell environments often include interpreter languages like Perl, AWK, or REXX that enable programmers to code up "quick-and-dirty" tools for themselves or their users to use in managing files and other systems resources. Some shells like those found in Windows or Linux's GNOME provide you with a full screen graphical interface.

Associated with the operating system are file access methods. Access methods get your programs the records they need from data files that are organized in different ways. VSAM is an access method for the IBM mainframe while FAT-32 is one found in Windows. More complex methods of storing and retrieving data held in files are called database management systems (DBMS). These are sets of programs that use complex indexing schemes to provide the ability to rearrange the relationships of data elements independent of the structure the actual files the data is stored in. Database management software may include data dictionaries, data query command languages, and application generator software. Oracle and Sybase are databases that use the SQL data query language. Data dictionaries centralize information about the data contained in a great number of files used for many different applications.

Application generators streamline often-required functions, such as report writing, so that instead of having to code an entire program every time a new report or screen is needed the programmer can feed parameters to a generic, all-purpose master program that produces the customized output. SAS is an application generator.

The software environment also includes teleprocessing programs that control networks of computers and the browser-related software that the programmer uses to produce screens that display on-line. There is also a whole set of software tools whose only function is to simplify the job of programming itself. In this family we find code editors which are tools software developers use to type in and modify source code. There are also commercially produced libraries of subroutines or class libraries for object oriented languages. These free the programmer from having to continuously recode routines that are already available. But knowing what routines are available in a library and how to use them involves mastering another layer of trivia. There are also interactive debugging aids that let developers observe programs they are testing while they execute. These let the developer stop an executing program, examine storage values, and even change program logic on the fly.

Some of these infrastructure programs are simple to understand and use. Others are not. But no matter how well designed these programs were when they started out, after years of quick fixes and got-to-have-it enhancements most system software is a nightmare of special cases and nasty tricks. What infrastructure software products all have in common is that they are all entirely arbitrary. While similar types of software usually provide similar function, they do it in whatever way their authors decided to design them.

For example, most code editors provide you the ability to do a global change. That is, they let you use a single command to change one character string into a new character string everywhere that the string is found in a file. If you are an mainframe programmer using IBM's ISPF editor and want to change the string "FIELDA" to "FIELDB" everywhere in the file, you will have to type in at the top of the screen "CHANGE 'FIELDA' 'FIELDB' ALL". But if you were to move to a different mainframe system that uses IBM's VM/CMS operating system and its XEDIT editor instead of ISPF, the command above would only generate an error message. To do a global change in that system you would have to know that you must type "C/FIELDA/FIELDB/ * *". The only advantage you would have as an experienced programmer confronting a new editor is the knowledge that some sort of global change command probably exists somewhere in the editor software. Actually locating it in an unfamiliar environment could easily take you ten minutes or more.

This example illustrates a very minor difference between two similar software products. When you work with database management systems or different operating systems, the differences in how you accomplish similar functions become enormous, and it can take weeks or even months to master the details.

Managers hiring what are supposed to be experienced people don't want to have to pay for those days and weeks of training, and it is precisely for this reason that they are so picky about what software you have already worked with and learned in detail. Employers do expect to spend a certain amount of their IT budget on training classes. But almost universally they want to reserve these classes as rewards for loyal employees. If they are going to have to pay for training, it does not make sense to them to bring in outsiders who have not proven their worth to the company. The only exception to this is, of course, the college new hire who may have to be trained in the use of some software in order to be productive, since colleges rarely provide up-to-date training in the software generally used in the business world—which is the reason why many companies won't bring in college hires.

Getting Software Training

All this should make it clear that your first job represents a never-to-be-duplicated opportunity. It is often the only time that you will receive software training that substantially improves your employability—if the software environment of your first job is well chosen. After the first burst of training most computer professionals will find that they have to wait several years before they receive any further software training that would be of value for building their résumés, and that training is generally only awarded, if it is awarded at all, to programmers who have been star performers using the first training they received.

The reluctance of managers to train new people in valuable software skills is so strong that you should be very cautious whenever an interviewing manager holds out the lure of immediate software training to entice you to take a job. The sad fact is that the only time managers will provide training to an experienced person at the start of a new assignment is when one of two situations exists: The first is that the company is using some obscure software products unknown outside of the company. These might be homegrown products. If some misguided manager let a local genius write his own operating system or database engine fifteen years ago, the company may have such a huge investment in the code that rides on top of this software that it must continue to support it, even though maintaining homegrown code is always a nightmare. Home-grown software seems to be an occupational hazard found mostly in large, bureaucratic companies with more money than sense, and large, often idle, programming staffs.

If a manager promises to train you in "database internals" make sure that it isn't the on-line internals of the JUNQUE database written by Joe Smith in tech support. The theoretical mastery you acquire by learning a home-grown software product is useful to you personally in enhancing your understanding of how systems work, but it doesn't buy you anything when you go out looking for your next job.

The second situation in which you might be offered training is when a company is using vendor software provided by a vendor who has a very small market share. In this case you might be looking at an opportunity, but then again you might not. In a case like this you might have the chance to learn something that is used outside of the company that is interviewing you, but the chances are that you will have to look long and hard for other companies that have this product installed and are looking for programmers or administrators who know how to use it.

If your résumé suggests to your employer that you might be a good candidate for training in a brand new software product they are about to install that no one else in your market has experience with, you might be offered training at the start of a new job. In this case you must do a little market research of your own. Read the surveys found in the trade press to find out how many companies are using the software you would be getting trained in and find out what industry watchers think the long-term prospects are for this product.

Training Yourself in New Software

If hiring managers are not going to train you in the mainstream software that could mean money in your pocket and a wide choice of career options down the line, what can you do?

The first thing you can do is decide what kind of software exposure you would like to have, based on your future plans. Look at what kind of software is being used by people doing the kind of work you'd like to do in the industries you'd like to work for. Browsing the Real Salary Survey at www.realrates.com can help you get a good overview of the software that makes up the skill sets of people who are currently in demand. When you identify the software you would like to be able to put on your résumé, some of it may be stuff you can buy and install on your own computer at home and learn with the help of books. If that is the case, buy it now and start teaching yourself what you can. If you need help, there is plenty available on the Web especially in newsgroups and bulletin boards dedicated to the particular software tool.

Having done this, get the best entry-level position you can find in a company that has an installation featuring the other software components you want to master. When your credentials are poor you may not be able to be very picky about the job you take first, but if your first, or failing that, your second job puts you in an environment where the software you want to master is installed and used by a couple departments, you can do a great deal on your own to learn it, even if you are not immediately assigned to a project that uses that software.

There are several ways to do this. First of all, you must build up a reputation for competence doing whatever it is you were assigned to do. The next thing you should do is locate the manuals for the software you want to learn and browse through them at any opportunity. Sometimes when new versions of manuals come in the old ones are thrown away. Ask if you can keep some of these older editions for your own use. Although they may not have the very latest features described, you can still learn a lot about the product.

If you can get to program listings online, download them and study them in your spare time. Get to know people who do work with the software you are interested in and ask if they can let you have old copies of listings of applications that use the software. These old listings are worthless to them and can give you the concrete examples you need to look at to learn how the software works. Also let these people know you are interested in moving into their area. When a position opens up they might even suggest your name.

You should also take advantage of education benefits your company may have. Many companies will pay for work-related courses. See if you can take relevant technical school courses and get your tuition covered. And finally, after you have worked for your current manager for at least nine months and done a terrific job, let them know that when it is time to move on you are ready to move into the area that uses the software you have been working so hard to master.

The Well-Rounded Résumé

There is no prescription for the "right" software combination for your résumé. You can have an excellent career specializing in a single product, learning its internals and becoming the resident guru, or you can flourish, especially as a consultant, by having a broader, more superficial exposure to several popular software packages.

If you are planning to go into management, you might never have to learn any of the "hot" packages at all, but might just demonstrate business skills and leadership working in a so-called dead end software environment and rise on the strength of your management skills alone.

The table on the next page shows you some of the software skill sets reported by computer professionals who reported salaries over $75,000 per year to the Real Salary Survey in the first quarter of 2000. Use it to get an idea of what kinds of software tools are used in a single job.

Some Skill Sets reported in 1999 to the Real Salary Survey with Job Titles, Industry, and Salary

SKILL SET	JOB TITLE	INDUSTRY	SALARY
Access97/VBA	Sr. Developer	Government	$98,000
aix,solaris,hpux,sp2	Systems Administrator	Banking	$94,610
AS/400 / EDI / Webmaster/Java	Developer	Transportation	$80,000
ASP/VB/SQL Server/UNIX/	Sr. Programmer	Retail	$96,800
Assembler/COBOL/CICS/DB2/IMS	Sr. Programmer	Computer-Software	$87,500
C / C++ / Asm Embedded Systems	Software Engineer	Other	$87,500
C, 4Test, MS SQL, Sybase, NT	Testing/QA	Custom Software Dev	$78,000
C/C++/Ada/Ada95 VxWorks	Sr. Software Engineer	Engineering	$93,000
C/Solaris UNIX & HP UNIX/METRI	Consultant	Software Consulting	$122,000
C/Unix/Cisco	Network Engineer	Telecommunications	$120,000
C/Unix/Sybase	Sr. Software Engineer	ISP	$82,000
C++,Java,CORBA,Telecom	Sr. Developer	Telecommunications	$96,000
C++,java,macintosh,nt	Sr. Programmer	Computer-Software	$95,000
C++,PERL,JAVA,UNIX	Sr. Software Engineer	Consulting Firm	$87,500
C++,VB,ASP/NT	Architect	Telecommunications	$76,000
COBOL/DB2/AIX/MVS	Sr. Software Engineer	Computer-Software	$86,000
DB2/CICS/IMS/COBOL 2	DBA	Retail	$150,000
DHTML/VB/SQL 7	Sr. Developer	Computer-Software	$87,500
Lotus Notes Domino	Systems Administrator	Automotive	$81,000
NT, SQL Server, IIS, COM, ASP	Team Leader	Web Site Design/E-Commerce	$85,000
ORACLE / VB / SQL Server / PB	Sr. Developer	State Gov. etc	$90,000
Oracle 7&8	DBA	Computer-Software	$83,000
Oracle 8.04 pl/sql & reports	Sr. Developer	Other	$85,000
Peoplesoft Financials	Team Leader	Financial	$90,000
PeopleSoft HRMS	Consultant	Government	$150,000
PeopleSoft/Oracle/PowerBuilder	Manager	IT Consulting	$91,000
Perl, SQL (Oracle), html,	Sr. Software Engineer	Web Site Design/E-Commerce	$80,000
SAP ABAP	Team Leader	Consulting	$95,000
SAP/ABAP/SAPscript	Sr. Programmer	Health Care	$80,000
SAS/ALPHA/Financial	Consultant	Financial	$77,500
VB/SQL/Oracle/Java/Web/MTS	Consultant	IT	$79,000
VC++/ATL/ASP	Sr. Programmer	ISP	$92,000
Visual Basic/Human Resources	Business Analyst	Financial	$80,000
Visual Basic/Windows NT	Sr. Software Engineer	Computer-Software	$82,770
Visual C++/Oracle/Internet	Sr. Programmer	Financial	$82,000
Visual C++/Visual Basic	Sr. Programmer	Telecommunications	$78,000
Visual FoxPro	Team Leader	Computer-Software	$80,000
VM CMS REXX	Sr. Software Engineer	Other	$90,000
VMS systems	Systems Administrator	Telecomm	$130,000
WEB DESIGN/ASP/GRAPHICS/DHTML	Sr. Developer	E-Commerce	$83,500
XML/SGML	Sr. Programmer	Other	$81,000

Remember, too, that business conditions change and today's hot item may suddenly become tomorrow's dud. By the same token, new products can appear whose success can radically change the market-place.

The software you will need to master to be in demand with employers falls into several categories. The most important ones are described on the pages that follow.

FROM IBM MAINFRAME TO ORACLE/JAVA

"I started out in PL/1, IMS, RPG and VSAM. Today, I code PL/SQL, Oracle 8i, Javascripting, & Java, and command appropriate market-competitive rates.

"In making the transition, it became clear to me that 'there was nothing new under the sun' and the leap from the procedural world into the OOP world was not that great from a conceptual standpoint. I have never taken any formal classes although I read everything I can get my hands on, immerse myself in Web sites, downloads, code examples, books, magazines, and manuals.

"For me, entry to the client server world came not through language as much as databases. I had some background in DB2/SQL, which I then segued into Paradox, Access, and then Sybase, and finally Oracle.

"The key thing is to approach new technology with intellectual curiosity and flexibility, looking for hooks between what you do know and what you must know, and then by systematically filling in the gaps through personal initiative.

"My MO in general is to buy two or three solid 'bibles' from different publishers from the local bookstore, download as much production code as I can get from the site I am at, often thousands of lines of code, create a 'hello world' application, expanding on it with additional operations or classes as the case may be, and then going out to the Web for all FAQs, tutorials, and downloads that may be out there—and there is a vast amount.

"Without being too arrogant about it, I truly believe there isn't a language or system that I cannot master within a month by using this approach. I do realize some people need the structure and the security of a classroom, but for me a 'university of one' is the way to go. And you can't beat the tuition! "

Development Languages

These are the languages you use to code in and those currently in demand included C++, C, Java, Visual Basic, Perl, and Cobol. Rarer languages are RPG, used on IBM's AS/400 systems and Smalltalk, the original object oriented language which had a vogue in the mid 90s but never earned the market share of the object oriented market that C++ did.

Databases

These are the software tools that store data, often on servers or mainframes. Those currently in demand include Oracle, Sybase, SQL Server, DB2, and Access. Being a database programmer means more than knowing your database access calls. It usually means knowing how to design the database intelligently and how to use calls efficiently so that they don't bog down the system. Database administration is a career path in its own right, and one that can be very well paid. Companies often hold out the promise of training in database administration as bait to attract programmers to dull maintenance jobs, which use the database but do not include any real innovative work.

Operating Systems

Currently, the major operating systems in use in the business world are Microsoft's Windows, particularly the NT version; Unix, including the HP version, Solaris, and Linux; and, for mainframes, MVS.

The operating system with which you get your early experience will be extremely significant as your career moves forward. A C++ programmer working in the Unix world will accumulate a great deal of platform-specific knowledge different from that which a Windows C++ programmer picks up. Because of the highly specific nature of employers' demands when they hire a new programmer, as your career advances you will find it increasingly difficult to get hired to work on a different platform than the one you have been working on.

Though Microsoft operating systems currently dominate the business market, the future is cloudy for those who would like to predict which operating system to specialize in. At one end Linux is showing serious signs of becoming a standard for servers as client/server systems grow to where they are once again beginning to resemble the centralized mainframes of the past. At the other, handheld devices such as the Palm handheld computer are becoming a serious client platform competing with PCs. While I might have suggested four years ago that you couldn't go wrong basing your career on a Microsoft operating system, that is no longer true. In fact, programmers who have committed their careers to Microsoft platforms are in a position very similar to that of IBM mainframe programmers fifteen years ago. It is unlikely that Windows will go away completely, but it may cease to be the major platform for new corporate development. The inefficiencies of Windows have become very expensive to corporate IS departments which are continually forced to upgrade their huge hardware bases just to be able to continue to run the currently supported version of Windows.

Vendor Packages

Some of the highest salaries reported to the Real Salary Survey on Real-rates.com are reported by programmers who work not with languages like C++ or Cobol, but with application-oriented vendor packages like SAP, Lotus Notes, or PeopleSoft. These are expensive—sometimes extremely expensive—packages used only at huge wealthy companies. What these packages have in common is that their expense or the size of the network required to run them is such that you, the programmer, can't just buy and master them at home as you can with a lot of other PC-based software. The only way to learn these packages is to work for a company that has installed them and will send you to vendor-sponsored training programs.

Programmers who want to upgrade their own skills often see the hefty salaries being paid to specialists in these packages and figure that one of these must be what they need to add to their skill set. But this can be short sighted. The reason for this is that upper management tends to adopt these packages as "magic bullets." They enthuse over them for a few years, assured by vendors that once installed they will address all their IT needs, simplify maintenance, and allow them to cut programmer costs. A few years later management discovers that these new solutions are no less troublesome than their older solutions. They still require maintenance and, because of the rarity of people with the skills to work on them, they may increase rather than cut maintenance costs. Invariably new management comes in and decides to cut its losses by jettisoning the discredited magic bullet of the past—and, most likely—installing the latest *new* magic bullet technology, which they expect to simplify maintenance and cut programmer costs. When this happens demand for people experienced with the old package drops to zero and they can find themselves in a difficult career predicament.

Development Tools and Libraries

Another software category that is easy to ignore is development tools. Because of the extreme specificity of many job requirements, the development tools you use can become another, highly significant part of your résumé. This is particularly true in complex C and C++ software development environments where knowledge of a particular library may be as important as paid experience with the language.

Software Complexes

When you answer a job ad that calls for specific skills, to get an interview you will need to have experience with all, or nearly all, the software tools cited in the ad, not just a few. That is because the skill sets that employers look for are generally a combination of a language, database, operating system, and set of system tools. For example a dot.com company advertising for a C++ programmer will specify not only that they need someone with heavy duty C++ programming experience, but probably also paid experience with other languages like Java, HTML, or Perl; an operating system, Unix or NT; the Web server CGI interface; and a specific SQL database like Oracle.

It is a very good idea to start reading the help wanted ads in your local newspaper, or to scan Web job boards long before you begin your first job search to become familiar with the software complexes that are in demand in the region where you would like to make your career.

Proprietary Software

One pitfall all new programmers should be aware of is proprietary software. This refers to languages, operating systems, databases, and software tools, which, in some fit of madness, a company has had developed for its own use. These are rare, but not unheard of, and wasting time mastering one of these will contribute nothing to your future career development, no matter how interesting and complex it might be to work with, or what a test it might be of your brilliance as a programmer. Mastering this kind of software tool ties you to a single employer, often to a single department, and makes it very likely that you will be out on the street with no job and a very difficult job hunt when the company gets around to replacing its proprietary junk with something more standard.

What Software Should I Learn Next?

The most common question I get from visitors to `Realrates.com` is "I'm trying to upgrade my skills. What software would you recommend I learn next?" Because software changes so quickly, programmers who have committed their careers to products that are falling by the wayside often find themselves confused as to which direction to take next. Should they jump on the latest bandwagon and learn whatever the trade magazines are trumpeting as the next hot development language or environment like Java or Linux or should they put their time and money into mastering things like C++ or Windows NT that have already established themselves as standards?

Unfortunately, there is never an easy answer to this question. Sometimes the best step you can take is to abandon your previous skills and learn whatever is the latest buzz-tool—especially if you can get in before everyone else in your predicament does the same thing. At other times, you would do best to analyze the skills you already have, including the business and applications experience, and look for a new technical skill that will let you keep using your rich experience in the environment you are familiar with.

When a new software standard emerges it can offer a huge opportunity to programmers and technical administrators who get early paid experience with it, since there won't be too many other people with that skill to compete with. This can mean high salaries early in the career and the opportunity to earn far higher consulting rates further on. But at the same time, committing yourself to a new software standard that despite early promise does not achieve a significant market share may leave you unemployable, or at best employable by the very small number of companies that have built systems using the technology which they now must maintain.

While it is true that the people who keep their careers and salaries growing are those who keep abreast of technology, read the trade press, and take the initiative to learn promising new software wherever possible, even if that means paying for their training themselves, it would be unfair to suggest here that keeping your skills growing is easy. Every long-term professional I know has wasted time mastering some tool that turned out to be a dead end. For the serious computer professional, education and re-education must be an ongoing and sometimes frustrating process — one that must continue while you work those sixty hour weeks on your current job.

No one who isn't a self-promoting hypester will attempt to predict where technology will go in five years. Even predicting what will happen in two is a stretch. So committed professionals can only do the best they can, accept that they will make mistakes, and keep on reading the trade press, buying books that explain new software technologies, acquiring new hardware on which to install their new software, and fooling around with emerging technologies, in order to keep their careers viable.

But while it is hard to spec out the pathway that will lead to success, it is easy to describe the one that leads to almost certain failure. That is the path pursued by people who blindly accept any job offered simply because it offers a higher salary than their current job or involves working for a prestigious company, who wait for the company to give them paid training, who save money by refusing to keep an up-to-date computer at home stocked with the latest software tools, who stay in a single job for years because it is easier than learning something new, and who look for new jobs only after they've been fired from their old ones.

Can You Fake Software Experience?

I don't like lying, so I don't think I would ever claim to have worked with a software product I'd never seen. However, after several months of having my résumé thrown out because the people reading it did not have enough experience themselves to comprehend the skills my unusual experience represented, I did start rephrasing my résumé so that it more accurately reflected what I really could do. Many experienced programmers are forced at times to follow a similar strategy.

If you have good technical skills there are a lot of software products that you can master in about ninety minutes, since the new products closely resemble other products you have worked with. Unfortunately, managers whose experience has been limited to a single software environment rarely understand this and may reject you for a job that you could easily fill with distinction.

The problem is knowing which skills you can claim experience with, with some stretching, and which you cannot.

I've seen people try to fake skills in things that they really had no experience with and look like fools. I worked with not one, but two, characters who claimed to be IBM 370 Assembly Language programmers when it was obvious they had never written a line of assembly language code. While it is true that you can often pick up a new high level language pretty fast if you know a couple of others, assembly language coding is quite different from coding in higher level languages like C or Cobol and is not something you can fake. Both these guys got canned.

I've also heard of a young woman who claimed to be an experienced Cobol programmer who was greatly confused when she got a S0C7 data exception. This is something any IBM mainframe Cobol programmer would have encountered in the first two weeks of their training. She, however, was not canned, so strong was the local demand for programmers!

One team leader told me of a contractor who was baffled by her inability to get a programming change to take effect. The team leader looked over her shoulder and saw that she was making her changes to the program's compiler listing, not to the source code. When this was pointed out to her she said she *still* didn't understand why the change wasn't going in!

These were people who were really out of their depth. But I've also met people who faked CICS experience and pulled it off. In every case they were seasoned professionals who knew enough about other teleprocessing software to have a very good idea of what sorts of things were going on in CICS even if they did not know the details. They also claimed only to have "light experience" a phrase that will cover you the first time you do something really dumb.

Since each company uses software products a little differently than do other companies, you may actually have experience with a product but find it installed differently in a new environment. Because of this, even experienced people are given a little leeway to make mistakes at first.

So if you have a good understanding of systems fundamentals and have worked with several software configurations, you may be able to exaggerate yourself into a rewarding job that lets you use software you have always wanted to learn. If this is truly the case, you will not be doing an employer a disservice in exaggerating your experience in this way, because you will be able to do the job, often better than a person who doesn't understand the "why"s of what they are doing with the software.

The key thing to ask in a situation like this is "what skill level does the hiring manager really need?" If they are asking for Oracle experience because they need someone to design an Oracle database from scratch, this is not the place to extrapolate from your experience with Sybase, another SQL database. But if they are looking for someone to maintain existing application software, you might be perfect for the job. In this case you will be making small changes to existing programs and the chances are that you will rarely have to do much altering of database queries. You will have time to read the manuals and look at existing programs to learn how things work in this new environment. Best of all, because you are learning something new, you may find the job a lot more interesting than a more experienced Oracle programmer would and will be less prone to quit in a few months.

Another question to ask if you are considering stretching your résumé, is whether there will be some skilled people available to you as a resource or whether you will be on your own. Clearly, if you are going to be teaching yourself new software as you go, it will be a lot easier if there is someone who can answer your questions or help you when you get stuck.

With the brighter managers you won't have to stretch the facts to get a position like this. They should be able to understand what you have already done and know that at a certain point an IT professional can easily learn software similar to what they've already worked with. Obviously, you would also be happier working for a manager who had this kind of intelligence. But if you can't find one of these and are forced to exaggerate your skills, make sure that you know enough about the software that you are claiming to know to be sure that you will be able to learn it quickly.

CHAPTER 11

The Application Area

Unfortunately no one hires computer professionals just because they're fun to have around or to marvel at their elegant code. Businesses bring in technical people only when they need to solve some kind of business problem. The area of the business that your problem solving efforts will address is what we call the application area. If you are a developer, once you become experienced, employers are as likely to value you for your knowledge of how their particular type of business works as they are for your technical skill.

The Application Matters

This might sound pretty basic, but many developers go through life as if the application area they were working in was irrelevant to their career. They choose a company because it has a good reputation or offers excellent compensation or because it offers a lot of IT education and the opportunity to work with state-of-the-art hardware and software. What most don't consider is that when you develop software for a specific application area you are going to find yourself spending a tremendous amount of time learning the business details of the application. In fact, to be a successful applications programmer, you may have to have almost as much business knowledge as your users do in order to help them design the system that they really need.

There is little difference between the skills needed to write an Oracle database query for an insurance company database and those needed to write an Oracle database query for a database used by a retail store. But most people find that there is a tremendous difference between thinking about insurance all day as opposed to thinking about inventory control, real estate investment, electronic mail, or hospital patient tracking, all applications areas in which I have worked. If you would rather think about hospital patients getting better treatment as a result of the pharmacy management system you are writing, rather than learn all the formulas used to rate drivers in a specific risk pool, then the extra money you might make working at an insurance company might not be enough to compensate you for the boredom you'll experience in the daily contemplation of insurance trivia.

Since many programmers begin in one applications area and never move out of it, they often are unable to separate their feelings for the application area from their feelings for programming. Many of the programmers I've met who tell me that they feel burned out in their careers appear to be people who are bored by the application areas they have mastered.

Therefore when you are looking for your first job you must think carefully about the application you will be working on. You can expect to learn a tremendous amount of trivia about it in the years to come, and the extent to which you enjoy learning that trivia will have a lot to do with how well you succeed on the job. In fact, you should treat the application area as your second career!

Applications Families

Applications tend to fall into families, and after you spend four or five years working in a single family of applications you may find it hard to move out, particularly if your experience has emphasized systems analysis which is heavily applications oriented, as opposed to more technical concerns. However even with this degree of specialization, it is a lot easier to move into a new applications area that uses your existing technological skill set than it is to move into a completely new software environment.

The one exception to the above statement occurs when your applications area and software expertise merge together, as is the case when you are working intensively with a widely used applications package. Examples of this are the Human Resources or Financials packages sold by PeopleSoft or BAAN and SAP ERP modules. In this case your value to a potential employer is not just your applications knowledge but your very specific knowledge of how these application-linked software packages work. Thus the impact on your career of taking a job where you learn one of these is stronger than most application level decisions usually are.

Sometimes applications are grouped by industry. You will see advertisements for e-commerce programmers, insurance programmers or banking programmers, even though the software environments may be quite varied from one bank or insurance company to another. This is because in many financial service applications the level of technical skills needed is low but it is very important to understand fairly complex financial service concepts.

Manufacturing applications form another related group. These range from robot control to cost accounting, but again, many employers value your applications experience here as much as your technical background.

The fact that you suspect that your technical skills are by far your most important asset will not make much difference if the manager interviewing you has worked only in manufacturing and doesn't realize that your insurance experience has taught you how to design and code just about anything that needs input definition, processing, and output definition.

Other times you will see applications grouped together by their function within a company rather than by industry. For example, inventory applications, accounting applications, billing applications, and Web page design applications will be grouped together since it is assumed that if you have worked with accountants or graphic artists in one situation you can work with them in another. Yet another specialized set of applications are engineering and scientific applications like telephony, embedded systems, and computer-aided-design and manufacturing (CAD/CAM). For these, as we've mentioned, your applications knowledge is often the major qualification you need, since in order to do program definition in these areas you need to be able to understand the kind of highly advanced mathematical or engineering concepts you would only have learned by getting the same training as your users.

The application area you choose can also have major repercussions on how high a salary you can earn in future jobs because some industries and the application areas closely related to them pay a lot better than others. Traditionally education and state government have paid the poorest salaries while the entertainment and the investment industry pays the most. We'll look further at the issue of how money and industry relate to each other in Chapter 14.

Poor Choice of Application Area Leads to Conflict with Users

Choosing an application that is harmonious with your personality is a key factor if you want to find yourself happy fifteen years into your career. It is tough to work with people who are talking all the time about things that bore you! Beside that, if you treat the application as secondary, you run into another source of strife: conflict with your user.

Misunderstandings and out-and-out bad feeling between the users of a system and its computer support staff are so widespread in IT that many people assume that it is just a natural outcome of having technical people try to support people who are not interested in understanding technology. However the real problem is often the technical people's deep dislike of the very thing most central to the user's life: the application.

If you are interested in your users' field of endeavor you will be much more likely to listen closely to them. Furthermore you will be more likely to think through the details of their system and understand how it will appear to them. This enables you, in effect, to save them from themselves during the all important system design phase. The developer who can say to a user, "This screen that you said you wanted here is going to be a real pain in the neck because you will often want to look at it when you are in the middle of this other screen here" will not have to redo the screen flows late in the project after customer testing, which is when the customer who is unused to using a computer system may first discover the problem. The only way that the developer can come up with this kind of useful suggestion is by having a very good idea of how users think when they are doing their work. And the only way I know of really getting that understanding is to be interested enough in what the user does that it is fun to walk in their mental footsteps.

In contrast, the developer who is bored by the application — and, by extension, by its users — will often spend just enough time with the user to get the rough specifications for a project before running back to the systems department where they can begin doing what they enjoy — programming. When their program is done and demonstrated to their user, the chances are very good that the customer will not be satisfied with the end product and will explain in a testy way all the things that ought to have been put in the program in the first place. The developer feels cheated because, for crying out loud, they did just what the user told them to do, and the user feels irritated because developers can never get anything right!

It is very hard to do good work for someone you consider to be a boring jerk. For this reason and because it is unrealistic to expect your users to understand the problems that developers must deal with, you will do the best work — and work that is most highly praised by your users, when you work in an area that captures your interest.

If you intend to become an entrepreneurial software developer and design software packages for business, it should be quite clear that the applications area you master in your IT apprenticeship years will either strengthen your ability to come up with a viable product or hinder it. You are not going to pick up applications knowledge at the depth necessary for creating a successful niche product except by working with that kind of application in a business environment. So if you want to become a software entrepreneur, it is worth being especially careful that you choose an applications area you can enjoy and one you are prepared to spend several years mastering.

About the only people who can ignore applications completely are systems administrators. This is because in their case the application is the technology itself. If you believe that you are the kind of person who would find just about any business application area uninviting but who loves working with computer systems, you probably should take the steps necessary to move into a tech support area as soon as you can.

How Important is the Application on This Job?

When you are interviewing for a new job you should pay a lot of attention to the way the interviewer discusses the applications area. It will give you some clue as to whether you are looking at an environment in which most of what you learn will be application-related or whether technical computer skills are stressed. I have had interviews with IT managers who sounded much more like users than programmers and who went into great detail about the business aspects of the system they were developing. I've also worked for other managers who hadn't an inkling of how users would actually use the systems they were building but who obviously had very sophisticated technical skills. It is very important for your future happiness that you find a good match here.

But a word of caution: This doesn't mean that if you love to fish you must work only for a boat manufacturer! We all have our little oddities. For example, you might not think of yourself as a person who enjoys accounting but you may still get a feeling of satisfaction or even pleasure when you balance your checkbook or prepare your own tax return. If so, you may find working with an accounting or financial application quite tolerable.

I myself have always enjoyed working with manuscripts. As a result I enjoy any work that creates attractive documents, whether the application involves writing a word processor or creating an HTML page generator. I also enjoy thinking about real estate and therefore found working on a real estate investment system much more interesting than working on an insurance system in the same company, though to many people the demands of the two systems might have seemed very similar.

You may need to spend some time taking inventory of your proclivities before deciding whether the application area a new job will introduce you to is for you. If everything else about a job seems inviting except the application involved you might give yourself the benefit of the doubt and take the job in the hope that the technical component will outweigh the importance of application itself.

But if you find yourself hating your job, before you conclude that you hate working as a computer professional and decide abandon your computer career entirely, you owe it to yourself to try to move into an entirely different applications area. In choosing your new job, try to find one in an industry that is more closely aligned with your personal interests or hobbies. Making that kind of change may be all that it takes to revive your interest in computer work and connect you back up with the excitement you felt when you first started working with computers.

CHAPTER 12

Your Place in the Development Cycle

Somewhere among your college computer science courses you undoubtedly studied something called the Systems Development Cycle. Your textbook detailed an orderly process by which the user's original need was analyzed, designed, coded, tested, implemented, and maintained — in that order, with neat demarcations between each phase.

In real life, particularly in companies whose primary business is not software product development, the life cycle of a system is a lot messier, and it is often difficult to tell at what "phase" a project really is. Nevertheless if you are embarking on a career that involves software development you need to understand where a system is in its overall lifecycle before taking on an assignment with it, because this, too, is an issue that can have some important ramifications in the development of your career.

Because college courses tend to focus almost entirely on the creation of new systems, most new college-trained programmers tend to glamorize "development" and shy away from "maintenance." Development is seen as the opportunity to do something new and exciting, preferably with state-of-the-art techniques. Maintenance, on the other hand, is viewed as drudge work, that at best involves fiddling with old software, an inferior kind of work to be avoided at all cost.

Hiring managers know this. As a result almost no interviewer will ever tell you that the job you are being hired to fill is a maintenance job. They know that to tell you this is to fatally discourage your interest in a position they very much need to fill. So instead they will characterize what you will be doing as "small development projects" or perhaps label it with that useful catchall "enhancement."

The Hidden Benefits of Maintenance

Young developers who buy into the stereotyped view of maintenance versus development may actually miss out on the jobs that could best prepare them for a successful future. Why is this so? Let's look at what experienced programmers know about "development" and "maintenance."

Working on new software development projects can provide excellent career advantages — for the experienced programmer. However, for a person fresh out of school, development groups can be the worst possible environments in which to make a start. This is true for a number of reasons.

First of all, college courses generally focus on teaching the student how to write individual programs. Even courses that are titled "Systems Analysis and Design" usually present you with an oversimplified system for which the student writes five or six interrelated programs, often working alone, or, in a more enlightened class, with a few like-minded classmates. This exposure leads to new programmers entering the work force with the illusion that they understand systems design and have some experience in it.

The reality, of course, is that real business systems consist of hundreds of program modules with a multitude of interactions. And most new systems have to relate to other, older, systems that are already in place. In order to be in a position to work on designing even a small part of such a system you must have several years of experience that will enable you to understand this kind of large intertwined system — not only how it functions, but the long-term issues it will face, such as data integrity, security, and the ability to be easily modified so that it can adapt to the changing nature of the company's business needs.

How do you get this experience? Not by writing small pieces of code assigned by an experienced systems analyst on a true "development" project. The new programmer becomes a professional by working on existing systems in a way that allows them to observe these large systems as they function. In short, the very best training for becoming a systems designer is doing maintenance on older, in-place systems.

In my first year as a trainee, a small part of my job was maintenance responsibility for a system that maintained secretarial mail logs. These mail logs were stored on a mass storage device (MSS), an oddball cluster of data storage cartridges accessed from a centralized index. One day this mass storage device malfunctioned, erasing the index to the volume our master file was on. The operator who tried to restore the volume from the master file backup had his mind on other things. Thinking he had completed the restore he carelessly answered a system prompt with a response that told the system to destroy the index to the backup volume! At this point I received a phone call from the operations area telling me that my master file had been destroyed. Naively I told them to load the tape backup for the file, only to be told that there was none. The file had been backed up on the same MSS volume it resided on—the one that the operator had just destroyed. Since it turned out that once the index to an MSS volume was gone no device on earth could recover the contents of the volume, I had no recourse except to spend the next week calling up each of my users, one by one, and after explaining to them what had happened, try to convince them that they really didn't *need* the data that they had stored in this system after all.

Since many of them did, our data entry department was kept busy for the next few months keying in a new master file that we reconstructed from the users' latest printouts. Even worse, this system belonged to a user group that our management was trying to sell a far more complex and sophisticated email system that would handle not only their mail logs but all of their intracompany correspondence!

This experience with a system that was entirely in maintenance mode taught me more about data integrity than anything else ever possibly could. Years later you can be sure that any system I design has frequent and religiously observed backups and that these backups don't involve making a single copy of vital files. I don't take just anybody's word that the backups are being done, either—I check it out myself. And I am always interested in knowing what mechanisms a system contains to enable files to be reconstructed should integrity problems be discovered. No system I designed would ever erase its transaction input files two days after they ran through batch—as one system I've seen did—in a system with no meaningful journaling! But of course, this was a system designed by people whose previous experience had been mainly in new development.

In the maintenance environment you will constantly experience episodes of petty disaster which gradually teach you the principles of good file structuring, good program design, and good operations procedures. That many of these will be teaching you by bad example is irrelevant. The lessons will be indelibly inscribed on your mind.

Maintenance experience will train you to think in terms of daily operations. It will sensitize you to the kinds of procedures that cause problems with operations personnel. It will train you to develop code that is easy to maintain, for example, code in which similar modules use identical field names for the same fields and identical titles for subroutines. It will teach you to leave room for expansion in your files so that you are not faced with the need to go through tedious file conversions affecting many programs every time your user has a new idea. Most important, it will sensitize you to the fact that if anything can go wrong on a production system, it will—especially if you are trying to give management a demo!

In contrast, programmers who go directly into development groups from college have no way of understanding the huge number of changes that even the best-designed systems will undergo in coming years. And, having had little day-to-day interaction with the people who use computer systems, they also often fail to appreciate just how hard it can be for their users to use the best designed systems. Instead they think that if they do a great job using all the enlightened principles they learned in school, the system won't need modifications in the future. If you've been paying any attention to the rest of this book I think by now you will agree that this is not, in fact, the case.

Experience in maintenance also gives the programmer insight into the communication problems we've mentioned earlier: the problems that arise when users attempt to explain to programmers what it is that they want the programmers to do for them. The experienced maintenance programmer has learned that, in most cases, the user can describe only a part of what they want, since they assume that much of what they need will be provided in any new system, simply because it makes sense to them that it would be there. Through working on a series of smaller changes and fixes the experienced maintenance programmer comes to a far better understanding of the way their user group thinks and the way they use their existing systems.

The Pitfalls of Development

Maintenance is starting to look a lot better, isn't it? I think so. You should be very suspicious of any organization that would bring in new hires and put them on true system development! Very few would. What they are more likely to do is put new programmers into the lowest level jobs on development projects where their task is to code small sections of code to rigidly designed specifications provided by more experienced systems analysts.

And this, I can assure you, is where you really encounter drudge work. The new maintenance programmer may actually have a fairly exciting life. They usually find themselves in an environment where staffing levels are sparse and they are encouraged to do as much as possible on their own. They must design solutions when users demand immediate system modifications. They must develop their own test environments. They must test their programs well enough to ensure that they are not roused from a warm bed at three in the morning by a hot systems failure. Often the maintenance programmer develops a good relationship with the user group employees whose system they support.

In contrast, the so-called "development" new hire may often spend months doing nothing more than writing subroutines that follow the detailed specifications written by more experienced people and then testing them with data supplied by others. Often this development programmer has no idea what their routines do in the larger system. They may not even get to participate in the next steps of the testing cycle, the integration and system tests.

And this is if all is going well on the project! Many programmers I've seen hired into development projects have not even been given the opportunity to show off their coding skills. Instead they have found themselves sitting at their desks for long periods of time with absolutely nothing to do! This is caused by another characteristic of development projects that is seldom covered in college systems development textbooks: true development projects are frequently canceled. This cancellation often occurs after anywhere from three months to two years have been spent on the project. Sometimes new projects escape cancellation but suffer catastrophic shifts in direction and major reorganizations that result in everything the programmer has done up until that point landing in the trash.

This is a natural part of systems development, since often during the detailed systems analysis and design phases it becomes apparent that it is going to cost a tremendous amount of money and effort to achieve what the user has asked for, and the user — who, after all, has to pay for it — will decide that the project isn't worth what it will cost.

In a well-managed project this decision should occur at the high-level design phase. But life does not imitate systems analysis textbooks. Since many managers demand that programming start before the analysis phase is truly complete, it is not at all unusual to see a project canceled only after the programming departments have coded — and tested — enough of the system for the customer to see a demo and get a hazy idea of what the system will actually look like. It is only at this point that the user realizes that the system as it has been designed — and often signed off on by themselves — omits some absolutely vital feature, which they may have forgotten to mention in the design phase — without which the system is, from their perspective, junk.

It is at points like this that managers scurry around trying to find ways out that leave everyone looking good — every manager of course — and developers find themselves with time on their hands.

It is no picnic for any programmer to see their work get thrown away, and I know of one development programmer who wrote programs for five solid years without seeing a single one ever get to implementation. But for a new person with no track record at the company, it can be devastating. You could easily find yourself at the end of your first year with the company having nothing whatsoever to show for yourself. Since raises and promotions come as rewards for having demonstrated your worth to the company, a situation like this leaves you with little leverage. Your chances of having something to brag about are a lot better working in a maintenance environment.

In contrast, the programmer who demonstrates real talent and a flair for handling the routine insanity that maintenance represents can build a strong reputation within the company. This reputation is what leads to joining the quality development projects — and to joining them in a design role too. Furthermore, if that maintenance programmer is you and if you have been paying attention to what is going on in the company around you, you should have a pretty good idea of who in your organization is likely to lead a successful development project and who is not. This may protect you from even getting involved in the development projects destined to crash and burn.

Good Management's Impact on Development Success

If you are seriously considering joining a development group the most important thing you should do is look at the people leading the project and assess how sharp they really are. I'm referring here to the managers, not the team leaders, architects, or programmers. In my experience the development projects that were the most destructive to programmer careers were those heavily influenced by middle managers who had weak or nonexistent technical skills. It is these managers who force programmers to waste time trying to modify outside vendors' software to serve purposes it was never intended for. It is these managers who fall for the timesaving gimmicks that almost always result in horrendous time losses, and it is these managers who, worst of all, exhort the troops to follow whatever is the latest buzzword in development methodology, but then tell them there is no time to create the flow charts, design the object classes, make the walkthroughs, or pursue whatever else it is that the methodology actually requires be done during that most important system design phase.

Sadly, there are some development managers lurking out there who are real losers. If you become a consultant, many of the assignments you will find will involve cleaning up the devastation left in the wake of one of these. As an example of how bad it can get, I observed one project that managed to reach its fourth year without written specifications. The different portions of this project had been assigned to managers who were in different warring chains of command and therefore under no pressure to get along. Each group designed its part of the system without having to have it reviewed by the others. The upshot was that, a few months from implementation, this system consisted of a front end that collected data and put it in a logical order, a database interface that destroyed this logical order, a database that stored the data using logical relationships which were not those used by the report writer routines which accessed it, and finally, the piece de resistance, an almost incomprehensible homemade application generator — the details of which resided only in the head of one person whose strong point was not communication — which attempted vainly to compensate for the rest of the system's destruction of data. Since the dominant concern of each manager was to defend their section of the system against the managers in the other groups, programmers unlucky enough to be lured to this project quickly learned to keep their heads low or look for new jobs.

Contact with a development project such as this one is unlikely to do much for your career. But it is exactly because you are not in a position to know anything about the people in charge and the history of a project in a new company that joining a development team can be so dangerous, even to the experienced programmer.

It is somewhat cynically said by the old-timers that the time to join a development project is when the end of the project is in sight. Usually by this time the project's originators are gone, having taken the blame for all that went wrong throughout the project's life cycle, and the people who take their places can continue to blame their predecessors for anything in the system that is not what it ought to be. Besides that, they get to enjoy the glory of reaching implementation and the corresponding banquets and awards. Sadly, experience would tend to bear this out.

So look with fond indulgence on the interviewer who promises you that a new job is "sixty percent development and forty percent maintenance." They know it's not true. You know it's not true. But at least you can feel better knowing that in entering the typical maintenance shop, which experts acknowledge makes up fifty percent to eighty percent of all programming environments, you are placing yourself in a very good spot to spend your IT apprenticeship.

Maintenance Losers

There is really only one kind of situation in which maintenance may not offer you the benefits detailed above, and you should try to avoid it at all costs.

I'm talking about the "casts of thousands" maintenance environment, which I described earlier, where management has had to hire a large number of poorly trained people. In this environment the maintenance programmer's assigned task may be to maintain a tiny portion of a large system and their area of exposure will be tightly limited. Here a programmer usually does not get to learn the larger system their programs are part of nor do they get to deal in an ongoing manner with users. Coding off of other people's specs in an isolated cubicle is not the way to develop a career that goes anywhere. Make sure when you look at a maintenance job that it is one where you do your own analysis and design and that you are not merely the coding arm of a more experienced person.

The other thing to look for when choosing a maintenance/enhancement kind of job is to get that job on a system which offers a rich complexity of function and, ideally, good exposure to a popular set of software tools. Even if your original assignment is not in the more interesting parts of a system, you are way ahead in the long run if the system you start out on uses a database and communicates with a server. This is because no matter where you start out in this kind of system, by demonstrating competence you can usually move into the more interesting parts of the system. Plus, you can put those coveted acronyms describing in-demand software on your résumé, since you now have paid experience using them, which can move you into more exciting work with the same software suite. The richer the system you are working on is in its function and software tool dependencies, the more you can learn without having to job hop within or outside of the company.

CHAPTER 13

Corporate Culture

You might find a job that allows you to learn a tremendous amount of technology, pays you reasonably well, exposes you to an application you find interesting, and yet still leaves you seething with frustration at the end of every working day.

The reason for this is that, in addition to all the issues mentioned previously, when you consider a new job there is another major issue you must consider, one that is much harder to describe. What we are talking about here is what students of business call "corporate culture."

Anyone who has worked for a number of companies can tell you that no two companies feel the same. Each company has what might be described as a personality. This personality is reflected in obvious things like the way that the company promotes — whether they promote from within or prefer to bring in outsiders, and how they motivate — whether the emphasis is on giving rewards or causing fear. It is also reflected in a host of smaller details — whether managers eat lunch with the people under their control, how workers are treated when their children are sick, the availability of vacation time, and whether you must inform your manager any time you leave your work area or are considered responsible enough that such scrutiny would be demeaning.

Sometimes the corporate culture is consistent throughout the company. Other companies are made up of many subcultures and you might find that moving from one department to another feels like changing companies.

The important thing for you to realize is that the corporate culture and the way that the people in the corporation manifest this culture to each other will have a tremendous amount to do with whether or not you like working for the company. Your chances for success are much higher in a company whose personality is compatible with your own.

Often I find that computer professionals who are feeling burned out are suffering not because they are ill-suited to their jobs, but because they assume that the features of the corporate culture where they have been working and which they hate would be present at any other company. Unsuited to that one particular culture they begin to feel hopeless.

It would be impossible to detail all the different kinds of corporate cultures you might encounter. Instead what we will do in this chapter is describe some of the extremes that you may encounter as you move from company to company. We will look at how each type of corporate culture affects the computer professional's life and work. This should help make you more aware of elements of the corporate culture that is in place in any company you might consider.

If you are a highly experienced person who is contending with burnout, this discussion might help you recognize the hallmarks of the dominant culture at your current employer and help you see that much of what irks you about being a computer professional is really what irks you about being a computer professional working within your current employer's toxic corporate culture.

The Macho Shop

In a macho shop people brag about how they brought in their sleeping bags and slept under the desk all week—if they slept at all—to get the project completed by its deadline. People in macho shops will also brag about how they had to cancel their vacation plans at the last minute or how they were back at their desks the day after their wife had the baby— or two days after they had one themselves!

Macho shops are by no means staffed only by men. I've known plenty of women who flourished in this kind of environment. To the outsider such shops can seem baffling, especially when the outsider discovers that these people are not being paid any more than their counterparts at other, more humane, shops. In fact, the managers in the macho shop sometimes realize that a certain type of individual is so well rewarded by being given the opportunity to prove how tough they are that no further rewards are necessary, so in this kind of shop rewards, including raises and promotions as well as the corporate gewgaws and the free dinners other companies provide, may be few and far between.

If you come into a macho shop prepare to work like a slave. Often in the macho shop management has calculated that employee overtime is cheaper than rewriting aged and limping systems. In the worst situation you will be immediately promoted to an "exempt" job class, one in which the company is not required by labor law to pay you overtime for overtime hours worked, and then find yourself on-call one or two weeks a month for systems that are guaranteed to fail each night.

Being on-call for this kind of system is horrendous. When you work for a macho shop, your cell phone or beeper will go off at some excruciating hour every night, and when you call in you will be told that the system has encountered some problem that demands your presence on-site—a problem that, of course, no one currently on site can articulate or explain. Or, instead of having to come in, you might just have to answer questions at forty-minute intervals throughout the night, every night, including Saturday and Sunday. Some companies confer a laptop with cellular modem upon you as if it were a great mark of honor, though, of course, it merely means that you will have no excuse not to work on the system twenty-four hours a day. After a few weeks of this kind of duty you will probably begin to hallucinate from lack of sleep, your judgment will be impaired, and you will begin to appear demented.

A gentleman I once worked with, who was known for his sense of humor, once substituted the phone number of a well-known IT Job Placement firm for his own on the on-call list, as a hint, perhaps, of what the company could expect if they called him too often. Though this is not a strategy I would recommend it does make a point.

Being on-call is not a feature particular to macho shops alone. As a programmer you should expect to be on-call at various points in your career. The only way to avoid it is to work only on systems that get turned off in the evening or on development projects that don't make it to implementation. For anyone who ever deals with mainframe batch systems or networks, it is part of the job. This is particularly true if you have been responsible for making a lot of changes to the production system recently or if a development project you have worked on finally goes live. There is a certain thrill in being at your desk while the city sleeps—for the first couple of nights—but where corporate culture comes in is in how often you are on-call and how difficult it is to repair production problems when you are on-call.

When you interview for a new job you should feel free to ask how often you can expect to be on-call and you should listen closely to the answer. Some people are afraid to ask because they don't want to appear lazy to the interviewer. However a brutal on-call system can be a source of misery to people who do not get ego gratification from proving their toughness through exposing themselves to endless hardship. It can also wreak havoc with your family life.

Macho shop managers will tell you that "of course" you will be on-call once a week, or one week every month, or more. It is part of the job, and they're proud of it. Non-macho shop managers will tell you of the steps that management has taken to minimize as much as possible the need for being on-call. They will brag about the high quality of their test system and how it ensures that system changes are tested in an environment so like the production system that production failures rarely occur. How different from the macho shop where people actually brag about not even having a test system!

Overtime is the other big issue that defines a macho shop. In a macho shop you are told that overtime is expected, with the hint that people who go home after a mere forty hours of work are sissies. If you work in this kind of shop you will receive this message not only from management but from your coworkers who will be decidedly hostile if they see you heading home at 5:00 PM even if you have completed all your assigned work. Alas, after the huge wave of downsizing that occurred in the late 1980s and early 1990s, when fear replaced reward as the incentive of choice in most companies, industry has gone overboard in demanding overtime from all employees. So you may now encounter this attitude in many if not most of the jobs you interview for.

In fact, a major reason why so many programmers were attracted to contract consulting through the late 1990s was that it was only by being a contractor that could they get paid for the overtime they knew their employers would demand. And because contractors were getting paid for the extra hours while salaried employees were not, this expense often served as a brake on how much overtime managers would demand from contract staff.

I urge you to feel free to ask at an interview about a company's attitude toward overtime. You will have to live with the answer. If overtime is not something that you want to deal with as an everyday rather than as an every-so-often thing, it is better to know about it up front.

And don't be afraid to turn down a job — particularly if you already are employed — because of the overtime demands. There do exist companies — only a few, alas, nowadays — in which the ongoing need for overtime is considered a sign of poor planning by management. You might just be happier in one of these. Some managers have found that staff who work fifty and sixty hours a week every week for long periods of time produce sloppy work that requires even more effort to fix or that the long-term effect of this kind of schedule is constant job turn over, as people "tough it out," but secretly look for other, less spartan environments.

Nevertheless, there are individuals who flourish in the macho shop because of their own values and personality makeup and who would be miserable in what they would perceive as the lax environment of a "country club." The key here of course is to know your own personality and what you would be happy with.

The Political Arena

Most people, when asked, claim that they hate office politics — they just want to do their job. In reality, of course, people vary greatly in the degree to which they enjoy playing the games that make up office politics.

As a new hire you will probably be shocked at the extent to which "politics" rules what happens in any company; and to a certain extent, becoming aware of the real role of politics in business and learning how to work within the framework of politics is part of moving from being an inexperienced trainee to becoming a seasoned professional. Technical people tend to be very logical and have a lot of difficulty with the artificial, but very important, rules and rituals that are followed in the game of business. To the technical person these rules often seem like fripperies that make it harder to get the job done. But because of this outlook, the brightest technical people often ignore important business game rules and set their careers far, far, back.

For example, you need to understand that the placement of offices relative to other offices on a floor is really a code that tells you people's relative positions within a company. Otherwise you might choose an office that had a nice computer in it but is so far from the rest of your work group that it signals that you are "out of it." You also need to understand the signals you send out with your office decor, so that you don't express your individuality in a way that subtly signals you are not a team player. Most important you need to understand the concept of the team and what you must and must not do when functioning as a team player, so that you do not find yourself in a position analogous to that of a catcher who stomps out to the mound and pitches the ball himself since the pitcher is doing such a lousy job.

Technical people often make the worst mistakes because they fail to take politics seriously, and their reward is to have power withheld from them because they have demonstrated to those in control that they are dangerously unaware.

The truth is that you are going to have to deal with a certain amount of politics anywhere you work, since what politics really is, is the codified, ritualized way people have evolved to enable them to function in groups.

But there are politics and there are *politics*. Companies vary widely in the extent to which playing politics is the company pastime. In a company in which politics have been minimized there are well-publicized standards guiding all managers and employees, which, most importantly, everyone knows.

A wooden desk or a corner office might be the signal that you have attained a certain level of power in the company, but it is clear to all people in the company what you have to do to get that wooden desk. In a well-run company what you have to do to get that desk is to do your assigned task well and demonstrate initiative, identifying and solving problems without needing to have them pointed out to you — when they fall within the scope of your current position.

In a company where politics has gotten out of hand, nothing is straightforward. The company may be riddled with mini-empires and little fiefdoms. Workers in such a company will tell you that the only way to get ahead is to ally yourself with the winning group in the ongoing power struggle. In such an environment it is not at all unusual to hear workers exchanging conspiracy theories to explain otherwise inexplicable management moves.

In a place where allying yourself with powerful individuals has taken the place of demonstrating competence as the method for getting ahead the person who is not adept at political maneuvering is in for a grim time. In this kind of situation people routinely shift blame for project failure onto the backs of powerless scapegoats—often the unwary technical person. Chains of command may be complex and functionally very difficult to understand, reflecting as they do not a simple scheme for getting jobs done, but power alliances forged over many years.

If you have never worked in this kind of place my description probably sounds extreme and exaggerated. But I warn you that they really do exist, and if you should stumble into one you must watch your step. Most importantly, pay attention if more than one person tells you early in your career in a new company that politics is the name of the game there. One or two complainers are the norm in most departments, but if three people tell you that the place is a snakepit—it usually is!

The environment in which politics is the most likely to get out of hand is the company where managers and employees are not moved around every few years to new jobs. Current management theory suggests that this kind of movement is a good idea because it keeps people from getting overly possessive about the things they work on and coming to feel that they "own" a particular project.

The worst company I've ever seen in terms of politics was one in which managers managed the same department for ten or fifteen years and programmers remained in the same departments for similar periods of time. A system in this company was not just a system, it was Joe Smith's system, and any suggestion that something could be improved in the system was interpreted as an attack on Joe Smith, causing him immediately to rally his supporters and those who owed him favors in order to resist the change. Not surprisingly this company had in place some of the stupidest systems I have ever seen in business.

The key thing to remember when working in a politicized environment is that decisions will never be made on the basis of technical expertise and common sense. Nor will your career progress because you are excellent at what you do. Instead, you will see foolish decisions being defended because of who made them, and those who are the best at making friends with petty autocrats will be the ones receiving the promotions.

Good management minimizes politics for politics' sake and also minimizes the impact of personal relationships in the workplace. But I know people who flourish in an environment of shifting alliances and nefarious plots who would probably find an environment where only software development was going on very dull.

A word of caution: You will not be able to determine the political atmosphere at a potential job site from the interview, since absolutely no interviewer will tell you that their company is ultra-political. So don't make a fool of yourself by asking.

The only way you can get some idea about the role of politics in a company is by talking with people who have worked in that company. If you are looking for a job in a town where you have lived for a while you have probably already heard things that should tell you something about what a company's corporate culture is like, particularly its internal politics. The mistake that people make is that they don't take seriously the things they are told or they think that they can somehow remain immune when entering a politicized environment because they themselves intend to stay out of politics.

If you are a member of a minority or other group that is prone to being discriminated against, you should pay particular attention to hints of political problems at a company you are investigating. If you hear that a company makes it hard for women, workers over forty, orientals, or blacks, and hear it more than once or at most twice, take it seriously — there is probably something to it.

If you are looking for a job outside your home territory, it is harder to gauge the political climate at an unknown company. Try to find someone, through friends, old school acquaintances, or Web Bulletin board regulars who can tell you something about the culture in place in the company before you leap into a job with an unknown employer, particularly if it involves relocation.

The penalty for getting in over your head in a company where office politics rules is to find your career completely stymied, because no matter what you do, you will get mediocre evaluations and no raises. In the worst case you might even get fired.

Emotional States

Companies have very different emotional climates. Some places are pressure cookers where people are obsessed with deadlines and emotions run high. People yell at each other in meetings. Doors slam and people burst into tears at their desks. This sort of situation can result when management, for whatever reason, gets out of its depth and makes impossible demands on the people working for the company.

A different emotional situation is the one where there is an ever-present undercurrent of grumbling and complaint that rarely breaks through to the surface but subtly poisons the air. Ironically, you will often find the grumble-heavy environment in companies that treat their employees very well. Aware that they can't duplicate their present salaries, stock options, or working conditions elsewhere, employees sometimes feel trapped by the very job security other people would love.

Because they feel trapped they mutter and complain, knowing that they are not about to do anything about it.

This grumbling may be conspicuously absent in a high turnover situation, since the people who would be the ones to grumble don't, they quit. If a company has a lot of "lifers" (people who have put in ten or more years with the company) or employees who are close to retirement and merely waiting things out, you might have trouble fitting in as a young, enthusiastic, tear-up-the-world sort. If might be worth taking a look around a potential job site to see if there are other people your age or if you would be in a distinct minority.

Not all emotional states are necessary pathological. In some places people just take things very seriously. In this kind of environment everything is very, very important. You don't joke around here, nor do you surf the Net at your desk when things are slow. Three-quarters of the things that cross your desk are labeled "Confidential" and heaven help the person who leaves without locking up their cabinets. In a very different environment the mood might be just the opposite—you might not fit in there unless you could find the weirdest new Site of the Day or get your question featured on SlashDot, and a person without a sense of humor would be at a distinct disadvantage.

I know of one shop where you would have to really enjoy boating and fishing to fit in, since those subjects dominate all conversation that is not directly work related. There are places that feel like "singles" shops and contrasting shops where no one ever goes out for a drink after work because they all have to get back to the kids. While I would not advise that you to take a job simply because you share the same interests as the other people who work there already, there is no question that you are more likely to enjoy working if you are in an environment with people who have interests, beyond computers, in common with yourself.

The Sweatshop

The sweatshop is similar to the macho shop, except for one difference, in the sweatshop the employees share one common characteristic: they are working there because they do not believe they could get jobs any place else.

Some sweatshops hire people whose credentials are, in fact, so poor that they probably could not get computer jobs anywhere else. In return for hiring them and training them, the sweatshop offers low wages and the opportunity to do endless work. You should be wary of employers who actively recruit people with no IT credentials. In the 1980s one well known company actively sought out college students with no IT background and hired them as programmer trainees after getting them to sign contracts obliging them to work for the company, anywhere the company pleased, for a term of three years. If the employee broke the contract they were liable for some $9,000, which the company claimed represented the cost of the "education" they had received. If the programmer was relocated during this time they signed a further contract that made them liable for all relocation costs should they and the company part ways — including if the company fired the programmer. On the salaries this company paid it was very hard to save up the money to pay back these costs.

This same company also made people hired through job placement firms responsible for paying back the job placement firm fees the company incurred in hiring them if they left the company within a year. This was true even if the company fired the individual, which they were prone to do. The enforceability of these types of contracts varies from state to state, but remember when dealing with any large corporation that a large company can afford far more expensive legal services than you can.

A company that operates like this thinks nothing of massive forced relocations, compulsory permanent overtime, and may use tactics that verge on intimidation to keep programmers in line. And of course, when employees can't quit, there is little incentive to give them raises. People who left the company described above after their three-year contracts ended told me that they easily doubled their salaries with the next job.

In the early 2000s, many sweatshop companies now turn to third world countries in the search of captive programmers and system administrators. Congress's passage of laws allowing hundreds of thousands of new H-1B "guest worker" visas has greatly encouraged this practice. Workers who come into the U.S. on these visas must stay with the employer who sponsors their visa, many of which are consulting firms — a situation which constitutes an open invitation for abuse.

A February 21, 2000 *Baltimore Sun* article for which the paper claimed "hundreds of court records and government documents were reviewed and dozens of recruits interviewed" quoted Indian programmers brought to the US by abusive body shops who reported being crammed in fourteen to a small house, not paid the wages they'd been promised, denied health care, and in general being "treated like a bonded slave." The *Sun* investigation found that in violation of federal law, visa holders often collected a small fraction of the salaries they've been promised while doing make-work projects. If workers quit, they were frequently sued by employers claiming damages of $30,000 or more. Workers who challenged employers were routinely threatened with being sent back to their homelands. To top off the indignity, the body shop operators who employed these captive workers regularly billed U.S. companies at rates three to four times the salary they were paying these foreign workers.

Though the huge increase in the number of H-1B visas has greatly magnified the number of foreigners falling prey to such scams, the strategy is not new. Back in 1982, a coworker who had immigrated to the

United States from India told me that he had been contacted by a group of Indian programmers who had been recruited by a well-known American retailer and offered salaries that were very impressive to them by Indian standards—salaries under $10,000 a year. Once in America they found that these salaries were not enough to support the most meager of lifestyles. At the time he heard from them, they were being kept in barracks and forbidden access to telephones.

If you are an ambitious would-be computer professional, you want to avoid the sweatshop if you have any other alternative. If you have resolutely avoided getting any training in programming and a sweatshop offers you your only chance to break in, go ahead. It might beat carrying air conditioners up and down stairs for a living. But if you have any credentials at all why do this to yourself? In particular do not, repeat not, sign any contract ever that makes you liable for money if you leave or are fired. This is setting yourself up for serfdom. Decent companies do not charge employees for education either, no matter how great it is supposed to be, so don't fall for that enticement either.

I would also give a wide berth to any company where programmers have been actively trying to unionize. I have great respect for unions and what they can do for their workers. However unionization only becomes an issue in engineering and software development shops when things are very bad indeed, since the shortage of skilled staff over past decades has meant that dissatisfied computer professionals can and usually do vote with their feet. Unionization attempts occur in situations where staff are being intimidated, where long-term employees are having their benefits stripped away, or where people who have a stake in the company have become the targets of other exploitative behavior. Why get involved in a situation like this?

The Country Club

The country club is very different from the other environments we've discussed so far in this chapter. Here management has addressed the problem of high employee turnover by making the project fun. I worked at one self-proclaimed "party project" where the company provided free donuts every Wednesday morning. Not only that, we had a birthday party once a month, a Halloween party complete with costumes, and the company sprang for an all-you-could-eat shrimp and champagne buffet when a project milestone was achieved. At Christmastime I found a little Christmas stocking filled with candy at my desk, compliments, of course, of management. I also got a personalized "thank you" note when I did something out of the ordinary. as well as a lovely key chain with my initials on it when our project went live. And I was not even an employee on this project, just a contractor!

Not surprisingly, most people on the project loved working there, even though the tasks that had to be done at this phase in the project's life cycle were at best routine and at worst, drudgery. There was such a good team spirit in place with all the festivities that turnover was almost nonexistent. People stayed because they liked being there. I myself returned as a contractor later on, turning down the opportunity to take a much better paying contracting assignment at a macho shop.

Management also made the attempt to give employees the education and opportunities to learn new skills that they wanted. When overtime was required, which was quite often, as this was the last stage of acceptance testing of a large project, management paid for pizza or brought in brownies. More than that, every effort was made to see that the overtime that was worked was the minimum amount humanly possible. The dollars spent on shrimp and donuts in this project were saved over and over again in the dollars not spent training new people to replace people who quit.

At another "country club" company in a different part of the country everyone got Friday afternoon off when daylight-saving time was in effect. That company gave generous Christmas bonuses and turkeys to its employees. Along with these frills the company also provided generous raises and gave programmers the opportunity to take on as much responsibility as they could handle. Yet another company I've heard about takes all its staff to Nantucket for a weekend for a periodic "morale boosting" fest.

The only way I've ever found to locate places like these is by talking to coworkers about other places they have worked. Nobody advertises "Free Donuts and Parties" in the Sunday Classifieds. And, if they do, don't trust them. Ironically, many macho shops use advertisements that project a phony image of fun, free food, and a party atmosphere as bait to attract the under-thirty, unmarried, socially inept supertechies they need to get working eighty hours a week to meet their project deadlines.

You are more likely to hear about the real country clubs from those who actually work in them. Keep your ears open and you might be able to find a convivial environment, which might restore your feelings of fun in what you do. On the other hand, you must know your own nature. Perhaps the limited technical nature of the work available in such an environment would outweigh the team spirit for you. Or you might even have to accept that you were not comfortable working somewhere where people tried to have fun during working hours!

The Physical Environment

On a slightly different tack, as a prospective computer professional facing your first interview, you should be warned about the physical environment that you might encounter and how to interpret it. The sad fact is that many software development environments appear pretty grim to the neophyte. You will often be given a desk in a tiny cubicle defined by paneled fabric walls. Usually you will not get to sit anywhere near a window or have your own office until you have achieved some administrative rank, at least that of team leader.

Although you might be getting paid thousands more than a manager in the user department you are supporting, you will not have the physical perks they do, simply because most companies reserve physical comforts—and that includes natural daylight—as rewards to be distributed to managers. There is some range of variation to be found. While some highly paid programmers work in subbasements, some new hires have their own offices with doors that close. In the latter case it is usually because the programmers are part of a small support department associated with a user group that has heavy customer contact and thus needs impressive office space.

Since software development and support areas are usually not a stop on the tour of the premises given to prospective clients, most programmers and administrators work in unimpressive office environments reminiscent of—because they are derived from—the accounting clerk environments of the past.

If you are interviewing somewhere that has particularly luxurious office space this may well be a signal that the programming effort going on here is unimportant. Perhaps it is a very small part of what the division you would be programming for does and that is why the office space is a reflection of the user's other functions. Often the places where you will find a lot of programming activity along with the kinds of diversity and training that lead to a bright future are housed in a drab, more traditional, type of programmer work space. My first job, which was a terrific learning opportunity, was housed, because of a space shortage, on the second floor of a building in a tiny shopping center, directly over a supermarket.

CHAPTER 14

Money

Whatever other gratification you receive from your job, the salary that you receive for doing it has got to be a large part of your motivation for showing up every day. And it is no secret that the salaries paid in the computer field are among the highest available. The January 2000 Real Salary Survey Report showed that the median salary of all computer professionals with two or less years of experience in 1999 was $47,000 and that a majority of the people in that group earned salaries that ranged from $35,000 to $58,000. The same survey showed that the median salary of all computer professionals with three to five years of experience was $60,000, with salaries for people in that group concentrating in the range between $41,000 and $84,000.

But statistics only go so far. How do you make sure that when it comes to negotiating your own personal salary it ends up at the $84,000 end of the spectrum, not the $41,000 end? In the rest of this chapter we are going to examine this question in detail and show you how you can make sure that, when you find a job you like, you get offered the best salary possible. That way when you start your new job, you won't, like many people new to the corporate world, find out too late that people far less qualified than you are making far better salaries.

Your First Salary

The salary you are offered when you take your first real job is extremely important, particularly if you would like to build your career in that company and not leave it. That is because most companies are bound by formulas which specify the maximum salary increase any employee can receive. In some companies these formulas are explicitly stated. Other companies claim that they don't use formulas and that all salaries are awarded according to merit, but the experience of old-timers in these companies contradicts this. In one such company a friend of mine had responsibility for the software that did budget planning for the IT area. She told us that the software had a series of routines that multiplied current salaries by percentages to estimate future salary needs. The percentages used were precisely those that the old-timers had told us were used to arrive at raises, with appropriate calculations introduced to estimate a range of performance ratings.

This means that no matter how good a job you do as an employee of a company, your manager can only give you raises that fall within these percentage ranges. So no matter how high a score you get on your performance evaluations, you might find yourself paying dearly over many years for a moment of naivete at the job interview.

Sad to say, many people coming to the marketplace for their first professional job prepare themselves for every facet of the job interview except the question that will certainly be asked by the interviewer: "How much do you want?" Some interviewees are afraid that if they appear too interested in money they won't be offered the job. Others, accustomed to the school system where you generally get the grade that you've earned, assume that they will be offered the best salary possible because of their qualifications.

When the student who had a 4.0 average discovers over lunch one day that the big mouth down the hall whose credentials are nowhere near as impressive as theirs started out at a salary $10,000 higher, it is a nasty, but illuminating, surprise.

There is no easy way to come out on top on the money question. If you ask for an amount that is way out of line with what the company starts people at, you might indeed lose the job. On the other hand if you ask for an amount that is less than the hiring manager had planned to offer, they may offer you a little more than you asked for to make you feel good and hold back the rest. After all, you said you didn't need it!

How then can you figure out what the appropriate figure to ask for would be? To start with, you must do some research.

Determining the Salary Range for your First Job

Your employer's industry greatly influences your potential salary. Companies in some industries tend to make much more money than those in others and so can afford to pay their employees better salaries. Survey data from the January 2000 Real Rate Survey Report, which you'll find graphed on the next page, showed that the financial industry, the entertainment industry—in particular those companies developing Web Sites—the consulting industry, and the telecommunications industry paid salaries that clustered in a higher range than other industries. In contrast, education, banking, and insurance paid salaries that clustered in a much lower range.

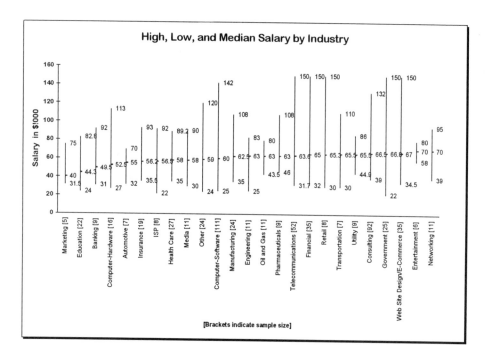

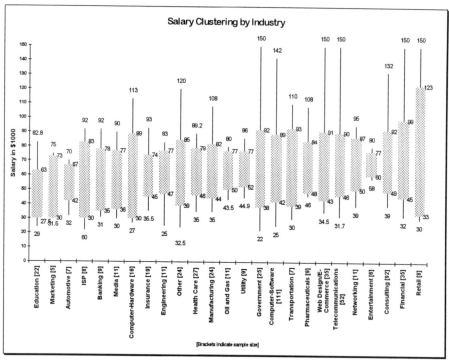

Source: January 2000 Real Salary Survey Report

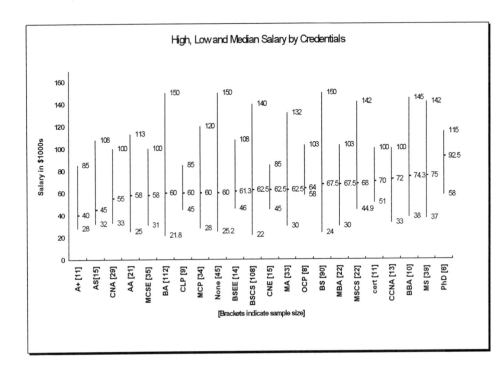

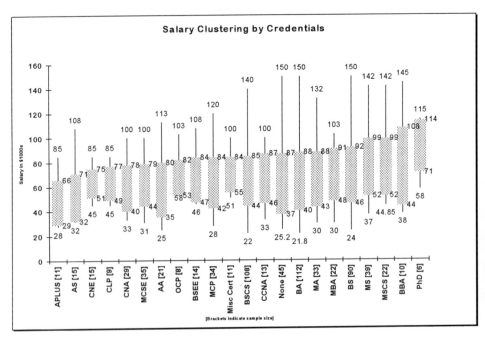

Source: January 2000 Real Salary Survey Report

The job's geographical location will also have an effect on the salary you may be offered. Obviously you will earn more working in New York or Chicago than you will at a factory in the rural South. But even cities in the same state may have very different economies. For example, you might be offered $120,000 a year in Boston for a senior level Unix system administration job because Boston has a huge number of software development firms that spur demand for technical staff coupled with a very high cost of housing that deters many people from moving there. A technically identical System Administrator job a mere 100 miles away in Western Massachusetts might pay only $70,000, because the presence of universities cranking out CS grads, a scarcity of employers, and more modest housing costs mean there are more people looking for such jobs.

Another major determinant of what kind of salary you can get for your first job — but not necessarily for any future one — is your educational level. The graphs on page 192 illustrate this. The lowest starting salaries are paid to two-year college graduates, the next higher to four-year college graduates, higher still are the salaries paid to people with master's degrees in a computer-science-related field, and finally at the top are the salaries paid to those with PhD.s. While this sounds as if going full time for a master's degree would be a great idea, you must remember that the extra years spent in school earning that degree balance against the salary increases you would have made had you been working each of those years. You might also be surprised to find that in many companies the people with the two-year degrees are making salaries quite close to the people with master's degrees after five or six years. This is because the salaries at that point in your career are affected much more by the quality of your technical experience and the job class you are in rather than by your educational attainments. After five years the competent person with the two-year degree — or a college degree in English — may well have been promoted beyond their more educated coworkers.

There is only one real problem you might encounter if you do not have at least a bachelor's degree. Some companies have policies that require employees to have a four-year degree in order to rise into certain job classes or offer management jobs only to people with at least a four-year degree. If your credentials are weak, find out a company's policy on education before you commit to it, as there are still plenty of employers that do not base promotion on your education level.

Many programmers I've met consider a master's degree in computer science — particularly the business-oriented master's rather than the engineering-oriented one — to be an almost worthless credential. It is true that it may get you an initial offer of several thousand per year more when you are hired in from school — if you know how to negotiate — but if you acquire a master's degree while you are already employed by a company where you would like to remain, it almost never will get you a significant salary increase. Our January 2000 Real Salary Survey data showed that the median salary for people with a Masters of Science in Computer Science, $67,500, was only $500 higher than that of people with Bachelor of Science degrees in majors other than Computer Science, and $5,500 higher than the median salary for people with the BSCS.

You rarely see a Master's degree in Computer Science listed as a necessary qualification in ads for any jobs except low-paying, part-time college teaching jobs! This may be in part because so many university Master's degree curricula are out of touch with the reality faced by people working in the field, and the courses that students take in these Master's degree programs do not significantly increase the contribution they can make to a business.

The situation is different for those with PhD.s. The Real Salary Survey's 1999 data showed that the median salary of PhD.s was $92,150 — far higher than the median salary for the group as a whole, which was $62,000. And the salaries of the PhD.s as a group concentrated in a range between $71,000 and $114,000 which was much higher than the range of $42,000 to $88,000 where salaries concentrated for all salaried computer professionals as a group.

To find out what would be a reasonable salary for a person with your skills, in your industry, in your region, at your job class there are several steps you can take. The first is to look at survey data. Our Real Salary Survey, which you will find on the Web at Realrates.com, is the most detailed salary survey available on the Web. You can search it for free online or download the data for a small charge. Other places to get some idea of realistic salaries for entry-level programmers are the various salary surveys published by the IT trade magazines such as *Computerworld, Information Week*, and *Datamation*. Many of these are available on the Web and can be searched for your particular specialty. You can find more salary information by visiting the big Web job hunting sites like JobOptions.com and Monster.com. These have "resources" pages that will point you to a good selection of salary surveys.

But surveys are only the first step. You should also talk to people currently working in the field in positions similar to yours or in the kinds of positions you would like to be hired into. If you are currently in college, in the spring, when the college recruiting season is in full swing, listen to what students a year ahead of you claim to have been offered. Everyone in college loves to brag about their salary offers, and some may even be telling the truth!

If you are already working and getting ready to look for a new job, the best approach is to ask friends who work in other companies in your industry what they think the range might be at their company for someone with your skills. But please — be aware that it is extremely rude to ask people what their *own* salary might be. Confine yourself to talking about ranges. This gives people a way to give you the salary information you need without revealing what they are currently earning.

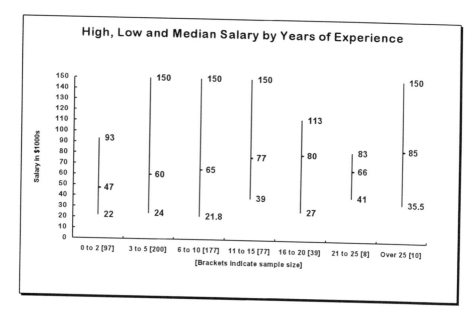

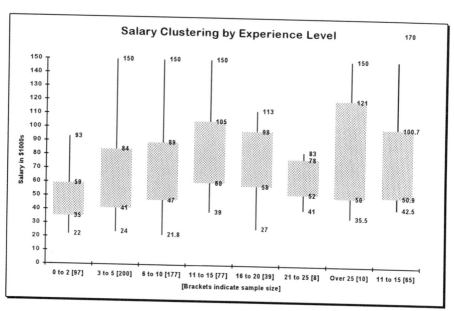

Source: January 2000 Real Salary Survey Report

A final source of information about salaries is job placement firms. Unfortunately, these are the worst places to find out what you could be earning. Placement firm recruiters only get paid if they find you a job. Since it is a lot easier to place an employee who is asking for a low wage than it is one who is asking for a salary at the top of the scale, recruiters will often try to talk you into believing that anything above the lowest salary for your job class is "unrealistic." If you've done your research and have statistics to back up your claims, you have a much better chance of getting the salary you really want.

Bonuses

An important factor in calculating the real value of a salary is whether or not the company pays bonuses, and, if they do, how they are calculated. In the 1990s, many companies started to offer annual bonuses in lieu of raises. This was a cost cutting measure, since a bonus could be offered to an employee who had had a good year but did not have to be repeated the next year the way a raise would have been. Bonuses reported to the Real Salary Survey have ranged as high as $43,000 with the median bonus in the first quarter of 2000 being $5,000. Bonuses may be based on performance or may be given to all employees as a percentage of their base salary. Be sure to inquire how the company you are interviewing with handles any bonuses it may offer.

Another kind of bonus you may encounter, once you are an experienced employee is the "sign on" bonus. You will be paid this bonus—which can range from $1,000 to as much as $20,000—simply for taking the job, usually when you hire in directly so that the company avoids paying an employment agency fee. Typically there will be a significant waiting period until you receive this bonus, anywhere from three months to a year. If you are promised a bonus of this type, be sure to get the offer in writing. Unscrupulous companies have been known to make it hard for employees to collect on some of these. And don't get talked into taking an otherwise unattractive job with a mediocre regular salary just because you were offered a hefty bonus. Unless the job contributes to your long-term employability, the extra money you get now in the bonus will be offset by the difficulty you will have getting your next job and the one after that when this job does nothing to strengthen your résumé.

Benefits

An important piece of the salary equation doesn't show up in the dollar figure that you see listed in the surveys or hear quoted when the recruiter calls you with a job offer, and that is the package of benefits the company offers. The company's benefit plan deserves a long hard look before you make up your mind to take a job. In the old days most companies offered very similar benefit plans and many paid the entire cost of health benefits. But that is changing. As the costs of these plans escalate, companies are forcing employees to cover an increasingly large share of the benefits' cost, or else they are offering employees a choice among benefits rather than the whole set.

For example, it is not at all unusual now for employees to have to pay $150 or more each month for family health benefits. Some companies even make new employees wait ninety days before they are eligible to receive health benefits or their health plans exclude a pregnancy already in progress when you start the job. If you have a family, the difference between a completely company-paid plan that covers all your health expenses and one for which you must pay $840 with a high deductible and a twenty percent co-payment can add up to a several thousands of dollars a year. And you don't even want to think about what an uncovered, complicated pregnancy could cost you!

Parking is another important benefit, since you may have to pay for parking if your office is downtown, which can cost you another $500 a year or more. So take a good look at the company's complete benefit plan. Feel free to phone the employee benefits office and ask exactly what you would have to pay for any benefit you are interested in, and if benefits like discounts, supplementary insurance, savings plans, and group travel rates are offered, ask yourself whether you would be likely to use them.

Frequently a company will offer employees a deep discount on or free use of their own product or service. If you can use this benefit, it can sometimes be very valuable. For example, airline employees may get free vacation flights or college employees may get free tuition at the college for their children. Other valuable benefits some companies give their employees include the use of a company car, the home use of company laptops or other hardware, paid trips to major industry conferences or conventions, and generous matching of the employee's contribution to their 401K plan. Other benefits reported by computer employees to our Real Salary Survey include free meals, free membership in on site health clubs, flexible hours, recruiting bonuses paid for finding other new computer hires, and the availability of an extra week or two of vacation.

If the job you are considering requires that you move from another part of the country, find out what kind of relocation assistance the company will provide you. A generous relocation package can be worth $20,000 or more and pay for hotel bills, movers' fees, temporary housing, and even the cost of selling your old home. However, companies have become much more stingy about offering these packages in these cost-cutting times, so you should not assume you will be offered any help with a long distance move. If you are not, the costs of the move can easily eat up any significant raise in pay you get on the new job.

Salary Secrecy

Some companies will be very open with you about what range of salaries they pay at each job class and will even show you graphs of their salary scales at the interview. In other companies the salary scale is a deep, dark secret. In the 1980s, Electronic Data Systems even went so far as to tell new hires about to begin work that revealing their salary to another company employee would be grounds for immediate dismissal. Be suspicious of any organization that makes a big production about keeping salaries secret. You can assume that this kind of secrecy is needed to cloak the fact that in these companies people doing the same work are receiving widely different salaries. Other companies, while not expressly forbidding such discussions, have corporate cultures that make discussing your salary a faux pas. However, you will often find that once you get to be good friends with coworkers in this kind of workplace salary information is often exchanged.

In one company I know of, where revealing your salary was frowned on, but not completely unknown, a group of programmers discovered in whispered conversations that no matter what salary they had individually started out at and no matter what their performance ratings, they were all making within $1,000 of each other after a few years with the company. The only difference was that those programmers who had started out at lower salaries and received huge raises felt much prouder of themselves than the ones who had started at higher figures and had, as a result, received only modest raises.

Other Important Factors Affecting Salary

Besides your starting salary there is another important factor that affects how your salary will grow, and that is the frequency of salary reviews. Usually a new employee is given an appraisal and a salary review anywhere from six months to a year after being hired. The frequency of these reviews in subsequent years varies greatly. In some companies you might continue to be reviewed every six months, but in others you could easily wait eighteen months for your next review. This is important because it is only after a salary review that you generally are eligible for a raise.

In a company with frequent salary reviews a person who does a fine job has more opportunities to get a raise. Since typical raises in your first years can be anywhere from five percent to twenty percent of your current salary — and the Real Salary Survey data showed that twenty percent was the median of *all* raises computer professionals reported receiving in 1999, although this statistic included many raises achieved by changing jobs. But clearly, getting salary reviews on a regular basis can mean a lot to your salary development.

Find out, too, how long a person can be expected to remain at each job class in the company. Most managers will tell you something to the effect that you should expect to remain at a trainee grade for a year and then spend three years at the next level and another four years at the next level, after which you might become a team leader and, two years later, reach a management entry-level job class.

This information is important because each promotion represents an opportunity to get a larger-than-usual boost in salary. Many companies confer promotion bonuses on top of your usual salary hike; these can amount to five percent or ten percent more. A company that has regular merit reviews and steady promotions can provide you with the opportunity for dramatic salary growth and may end up paying you better in the long run than a company that starts you at a higher salary but gives out small raises sparingly thereafter. This is particularly true if you are a dazzling performer.

Check out the Cost of Living

An additional word of caution is in order when you are interviewing for positions outside the region of the country you are familiar with. Be sure to investigate the cost of living where your new job might be before you accept a job offer. If housing costs are much lower where you currently live than where you are thinking of going, the salary that sounds quite adequate to you now may turn out to be woefully short of what you need to live a middle class life in your new home. Usually salary ranges reflect the cost of living, so be sure that you do not cheat yourself by asking for an amount that is less than what you will need to earn in your new location.

There is a Cost of Living Salary Calculator available on the Web at `http://www.homefair.com/homefair/cmr/salcalc.html`, which is useful for getting an idea of how your salary will be impacted by the cost of living in a particular area. Be sure to visit it before you negotiate salaries for a new job.

Your Salary when you Change Jobs

When you apply for your first job, all you need to know is the range of starting salaries for the kind of job you want. But once you are an experienced programmer there are a few more issues to consider.

You should still attempt to figure out what the prevailing ranges are for your geographical area and for the kind of business you are working in, and, as the graph of Page 195 shows, you should expect your salary to rise with your years of experience, but there is a new factor to be added in: your current salary.

If you look in the classified section of your local Sunday paper, at least if you live in an urban area, you will see many advertisements for computer professionals listing dollar amounts. If you are interested in seeing advertisements for jobs outside of your local region you can find these in the back pages of *Computerworld* and, occasionally, in special professional employment supplements of the *New York Times*. You can also find salaries listed in some job postings on Web job boards though many will simply say "DOE" which stands for "depending on experience." However, you should take any salaries you see in such ads with a grain of salt, and never assume that you could get the top figures listed when you see a range. These numbers are put in the advertisements by recruiters who make them high enough to catch your attention without seeming completely out of line. Generally the salaries mentioned in these ads will hint at the relative salaries paid for different types of experience, but only rarely are they the actual salary you could command. That is because the actual salary you will be offered will almost always be figured based on your *current salary*.

However you now face a Catch-22 situation. The sad fact is that in the interview situation everyone will ask you what your current salary is and everyone will assume that you are lying when you give them an answer. That may be because almost everyone *is* lying when they state their current salary. But there is good reason for this: the salary you are offered when you change jobs is almost always a figure that is ten percent higher than your current salary. So, if you don't inflate your salary when the recruiter asks you about it, the interviewer will often mentally lop off ten percent and assume that the diminished figure is your real salary!

The result of this is that if you are an honest soul you might find a job you really like, only to be offered the job at a figure identical to your current salary. Meanwhile, the person making you the offer assumes that they have just given you a whopping ten percent raise!

I'm not sure what the answer to this situation is. I've tried being completely honest about my salary and received offers lower than the salary I was currently receiving! I've tried inflating the figure too and concluded that it works better, but I hate having to do things this way. I'll leave it to you to decide, but sometimes I've wished I could just pull out my last paycheck to make my point rather than have to give in to a system based on the assumption that would-be employees are all dishonest.

In a market where demand for technical personnel is unusually strong some people find it useful simply to tell recruiters "What I'm currently making is irrelevant. I'm here talking to you because I want to find a new position that pays $X." When faced with application forms that have a field for "current salary" or "desired salary" these savvy folk simply write, "To be discussed." This kind of strategy may work very well, as long as you've done your homework to determine that the $X you are asking for is a reasonable salary for someone with your skills and experience. If you do take this approach, be prepared to encounter some recruiters and hiring managers who will refuse to negotiate with you without a firm "previous salary" number. But if you are willing to sacrifice some opportunities in the hopes of finding the one job you need that meets your expectations, and if your current salary is much lower than the market rate for your skills, this may be the only way to rectify the situation.

Salary Problems Moving To A Lower Cost of Living Region

There is one other situation in which you should be extremely careful when you are asked about your previous salary. That is if you must relocate to another part of the country whose economy is less robust than your current region. While you can get seriously hurt by moving to an area where the cost of living is higher than it is in your current home, once you are an experienced salaried worker you can also get hurt doing the reverse.

For example, if you were an experienced programmer working in a high cost area like Silicon Valley where your salary might be over $100,000, and needed, for personal reasons, to move to a region like North Carolina where salaries were much lower, telling an interviewer the truth about your salary could result in the rapid termination of the interview. There are places where no salaried programmers make more than $60,000 a year. If you move to one of them you will have to "exaggerate" your salary downward or you may not be able to find a job at all.

That is because many HR departments establish company policies that say that managers may not hire in new people at salaries that are lower than what they earned in their previous position. The reason behind this is the belief that a person who takes a steep cut in pay is likely to leave as soon as they can find any job that pays them their old salary. Whether or not this is true in your case, you may find yourself shut out of jobs you might want if your previous salary in another region was much higher than what the company pays in your new home.

You face a similar problem if you are trying to go back to work as a corporate employee after having worked as a contractor or consultant. Most people in this situation, when asked their previous salary, will give their hourly consulting rate, which can be $75 per hour or more. An interviewing manager will usually multiply this out by the number of work-hours in a year and arrive at the figure of $150,000 for your previous annual earnings. Since even their own salary is unlikely to be this high, to say nothing of what they pay employees at your level, when this happens, your prospects for being hired are slim.

The smart thing to do in a situation like this is to remember that the figure you should give the hiring manager who asks about contracting income is your *net* annual earnings. Calculate how much money you ended up with over the whole year after figuring in sick days, holidays, time without work, and after deducting for insurance payments and other expenses you ran up while running your business. After doing these calculations you will probably come up with a more modest figure to present the would-be employer. If the number is still too high you have some hard thinking to do. Will you really be able to live at the reduced standard of living this salaried job represents?

Will Ex-Employers Report Your Previous Salary?

For those of you who are wondering, a potential employer cannot call your old company and find out what your salary really was. If you've ever applied for a mortgage, you've seen a permission form which must be filled out by an employee before a company will divulge salary information. Without this same form an employer or ex-employer cannot give out information about what you were paid. However they can, if they choose to, tell someone what your old job class might have been, although many choose not to. Since most managers and recruiters have a pretty good idea what the salary range should be for each job class, at least in local companies, lying about your salary in a big way will be spotted and probably result in your not being considered for a job. But if you provide a salary number that corresponds to a reasonable salary for your actual job grade no one will be likely to challenge it.

How to Negotiate Money

You will discuss money several times throughout the job hunting process. If you work with a job placement agency, the recruiter will ask you what you want almost as soon as they contact you. Try to get recruiters to come up with a figure first, before you tell them how much you'd like to earn. If they try to get you to name a number before they do, during that initial contact it is best to simply specify a general salary range, until you see what kinds of interviews the agency can turn up for you.

If you've done your homework and know what the range is for your skills and are forced to come up with a number, it might be safe to ask for an amount towards the high end of that range. If your salary is currently a good one for your skills, and the market for those skills is hot, asking for an amount that is twenty percent higher than your current salary is another simple way to come up with a number. But if you have to come up with a salary figure make it clear to the recruiter that it is just a ballpark figure and that you are looking for the very best salary you can find—and ignore any pep talks they give you on the theme of how salaries are tight now and your demands unrealistic. Recruiters almost always try to talk employees down about their salary expectations since people are much easier to place if they are asking under-market salaries!

If you are looking for a new job because your skills are outdated and you are trying to change your technical niche or because you have been unemployed for a while, you cannot be aggressive about salary at this stage. In this case accept what the recruiter tells you they can find. The time to negotiate will be later, after you've made a strong connection with a potential employer.

Once you get an interview with a potential employer, someone there will be sure to ask you how much you want. If you got the interview through an agency, they should have given you some idea of how much the employer is willing to pay. But it is quite possible that they have actually given you a lower figure than what the employer is prepared to offer. Recruiters will sometimes tell you before an interview that a job pays less than it actually does because this puts them in a position where they can offer you a nice "surprise" if an offer comes through. This surprise might give you the psychological boost that encourages you to take the job. It also keeps you from asking for a too high salary at the interview—one that would preclude your getting the offer.

So when the would-be employer asks you what salary you want, you need to be even more careful. Ideally, you should try to get the interviewer to state a salary figure first, to make sure that you don't start out asking for a figure lower than what they have been considering. Again, you should have done your research before you get to the interview so that you can ask for a number that is towards the high end of what you have already determined is a legitimate range for the skills you have in the job you are seeking.

However, when you enter these negotiations, it helps to remember that recruiters and managers have much more experience than you do at negotiating and that you are unlikely to be able to trump them by using negotiation tricks you read about in a book the night before the interview. Negotiation is tough and many technical people are very bad at it. So don't expect yourself to pull off miracles in a very stressful situation. Experienced salespeople and managers will probably finesse you into revealing how much you would be satisfied with before they divulge what they are willing to pay. That is why, if you don't have prior experience negotiating, it is often best to avoid complex negotiation maneuvers and focus on the essentials. Before the interview, do your research and determine what the *highest* salary is that you think you can get. Then decide what the *lowest* salary is that you would be happy earning. At the interview, give the highest salary when asked for a salary figure and make it clear that you will not take anything less than the lower number you decided on. Be stubborn about sticking to your lower limit. This way you aren't likely to get talked into taking a salary you'll later regret.

Before your salary discussions with potential employers conclude, be sure to remember to ask any questions you have about the benefit plans, bonuses, and the frequency of salary reviews.

The last time you will get a chance to negotiate the actual salary that you will get in a new job is after the company informs you, either directly or through a recruiter, that it wants to make you an offer. The best strategy to pursue when this happens is to hear out the company's offer, warmly thank the recruiter or the hiring manager for it, confirm the details of salary, the actual job itself, and the start date, and then, before anyone can subject you to a hard sell, explain that you will get back to them the next day to hammer out the final details. Then hang up!

There are several reasons for doing this. One is that you do, in fact, need time to think. The offer might be so exciting that you can't think clearly and may forget to negotiate for some important perk—like relocation expenses or, if you interviewed for several positions at one company, you may not have been told whether the job you are being offered by the company is one you would prefer. The other is that, if you've been wise about your job hunt, you should have several other interviews pending and you will now need to contact the people involved with these to make sure that there isn't something better available at one of them. You are never as appealing to a potential employer as you are when someone else has made you an offer, so unless you very strongly prefer one company over another, don't hesitate to use the leverage your current offer gives you to improve your prospects elsewhere.

If you have no other options and want the job, call back the next day and accept it. It can't hurt to ask for a slightly higher salary than what is being offered. You may be told, "No" but it is unlikely that asking for a bit more money will result in the offer being withdrawn. This is easier to do if you are negotiating directly with the hiring company, rather than with a job placement firm.

One you've accepted the offer, it is appropriate to ask that the offer be sent to you in writing, particularly if you hear about the job offer from a job placement firm recruiter. It is a big mistake to give notice at your old job until you have a firm offer in hand—faxed or mailed by the hiring manager, not just the recruiter. Even the best-sounding job offers have a way of evaporating in the wake of some business reverse. And some unscrupulous recruiters have been known to jump the gun on telling you that you have the job to keep you from going elsewhere, when the hiring company is actually not one hundred percent sure they will make you an offer.

Once you have given notice at your old job, don't be surprised if your manager makes you a counteroffer of more money in order to get you stay on. Unfortunately, it is usually a mistake to accept a counteroffer, no matter how attractive the money might be. By giving notice you have marked yourself as someone who is dissatisfied with the current job, so if you stay on, you may find yourself, despite your new raise, under continuous, negative scrutiny, and bypassed for the assignments and promotions you'd want.

APPENDIX A

TWENTY-FIVE QUESTIONS
YOU MUST GET ANSWERED
AT THE INTERVIEW

The following is a list of twenty-five sets of related questions that you might want to ask an interviewer when you are being interviewed for a computer job. They are drawn from many different chapters of this book. After each set of questions is the number of the chapter or chapters where topics related to those questions are discussed.

Browse the list before you go to an interview and try to select the five questions that would be most important to you, given your personal career goals. If you read these questions and plant them in the back of your mind, you are more likely to spot both the trouble signals and bonuses of any job you investigate.

THE QUESTIONS

1. What is your position in this organization?   [Chapter 8]

2. How many programmers, [or administrators, technicians, etc.] work for the company? In this division? In this department?   [Chapter 9]

3. What kinds of applications does the company have computerized? The division? The department?   [Chapter 9]

4. What kind of courses do you give staff in-house? At outside training centers? How often?   [Chapters 4 and 10]

5. What kind of a hardware and software does your network and server use? Does the rest of the company use the same kinds of networks and servers? Are there any plans to do a conversion in the next few years?   [Chapter 10]

6. What operating system are you using? Are there plans to migrate? If so, when?   [Chapter 10]

7. Does the system I will personally be working with use a database? Which one? Will I get classes in it? Does a separate department write or maintain the database and code the database query subroutines?   [Chapters 9 and 10]

8. Am I being hired for a stand-alone or networked system? If stand-alone, are there plans to move it to a network or server? Will I be sent to any classes to learn how to program in the server environment? Does a separate tech support group debug the complex and interesting systems problems?   [Chapters 9 and 10]

9. What will I actually be responsible for on this system? Is this definite or liable to change? What jobs in this company could I evolve toward working with this system over a number of years? [Chapters 3 and 7]

10. What does the person who used to do this job do now? If it is a new job, why are you bringing in outsiders?   [Chapters 4, 7, and 13]

11. How long has this team been together? What is the main manager's background? If this is a software start-up, what other successful products has project management participated in, and in what capacity?   [Chapters 4, 9, and 12]

12. What computer language and development tools do you use here? Will I be sent to classes to learn any of these?   [Chapters 10]

13. If a package from an outside vendor is being used, was this package developed only for your company or is it in general use? Will I be sent to outside classes to learn it? Are you planning to modify the package here? Has the package been delivered and tested or is it still in development mode?   [Chapters 3 and 10]

14. Is this a maintenance phase project? If so, how active is the system: does it require a lot of changes and enhancements or is it fairly stable?   [Chapter 12]

15. If this is a development project, how much coding has already taken place? Would a lot of new people come into the project with me right now? If so, why? How much of the actual design will I participate in? Is the specification phase complete? What kind of testing is

planned? Will I personally work with the system's users? With systems analysts?   [Chapters 9 and 12]

16. Tell me more about the application. Who are the users? Will I work directly with them or through an interface group? What is their level of sophistication as far as computer systems go? Do you encourage programmers to take courses in subjects relating to the application area?   [Chapter 9 and 11]

17. Will I be on-call? How often? Do you give on-call programmers a beeper or cell phone? Do you let staff work on your system from home? Do you allow telecommuting during regular working hours when appropriate? [Chapter 13]

18. How much overtime will be expected of me in this position? Is that year round or just during crunch periods? [Chapter 13]

19. If this is a production system, do you have a functional test system? [Chapters 13]

20. Does the company post job listings? If not, how does a person get a new position within the company? What conditions must be met before a person can apply for a job that is posted?   [Chapter 4, 7, and 9]

21. Do you have formalized performance appraisals? Do they go along with salary reviews? How often do you schedule salary reviews? [Chapters 14]

22. Are certain educational requirements needed for promotion beyond certain job classes on my career path? What are they? Will the company pay for courses needed to improve my academic credentials? [Chapters 1, 3, and 14]

23. Would benefits be effective immediately? If not, how long is the waiting period? Does the company pay my health and other benefits entirely or do I have to pay a portion? Does the company cover my family members without extra charge? If there is a charge, how much is it?   [Chapter 14]

24. Who will be my supervisor? May I meet him or her? Who will be my team members? May I meet them?   [Chapters 2, 8, and 13]

25. Is this where I will work? If not where? If downtown, does the company supply parking? How likely is it that I will be transferred to another location in the next two years? Do programmers move from site to site often?   [Chapters 4, 9, and 14]

INDEX

READ THIS BOOK *BEFORE* YOU CALL A CONSULTING FIRM!

ANSWERS FOR COMPUTER CONTRACTORS:
How to Get the Highest Rates and the Fairest Deals from Consulting Firms, Agencies, and Clients.   **$29.95**

224 Pages

Computer contracting is booming! Contractors around the United States are earning rates of $75, $100, $150 per hour and more! Find out how you can cash in on this hot trend. Drawing on data from the Real Rate Survey and the Computer Consultant's Message Board, this book answers over 300 frequently asked questions about computer contracting. Topics covered include:

- What it takes to be eligible for big money contracts
- The differences between W-2, 1099, and corp-to-corp contracting
- What rates contractors are really earning and for what kinds of work
- How consulting firms operate and how they exploit the unwary
- How to find contracts through consulting firms and agencies
- How to work directly with clients
- How to protect yourself from abusive contract clauses
- What to expect on the job
- How to increase your value on the open market

Reviewers Comments:

"A hard-hitting, well-organized collection of facts and figures about compensation as well as collected wisdom about how to negotiate higher compensation rates. Organized in a question-and-answer format, *Answers* is extremely accessible and easy to use. Indeed, its ease-of-use is almost as valuable as the information it contains. The book encompasses just about every topic you need to know to contract successfully. ... If you contract or plan to, this "Ruhl book" belongs in your library

—Alan R. Earls, *Computerworld*

This is the manual to get anyone acclimated to the basics in the world of contracting.... She explains fairly, carefully, and objectively every aspect of the business of contracting from the perspective of both the contractor and the agency. There really doesn't seem to be an issue that she hasn't tackled.

—Michael Lane, CP Universe Web Site

ORDER TODAY FROM TECHNION BOOKS!
www.realrates.com

FIND OUT WHAT *YOUR* SKILLS ARE WORTH!

Why guess when you can *know* what to answer when an interviewer asks, "What salary do you want?"

The Complete Real Salary Survey database includes a year's worth of salary and job data collected from working computer professionals. You can download it online for only $25!

Each Salary Report includes

♦ Skills: languages, databases and packages, operating systems

♦ Location: city, state,

♦ Employee's salary

♦ Industry

♦ Job description

♦ Source of job

♦ Whether temporary or permanent

♦ Employee's salary on previous job

♦ Length of time at current salary level

♦ Unusual benefits with job

♦ Employee's experience, including years of experience, credentials, and other qualifications

♦ Employee's age, gender, and immigration status (these are optional fields)

♦ Employee's bonus (for salaries contributed after 1/1/2000.)

Download an entire year's worth of
Real Salary Survey data at:
www.realrates.com/down.htm

MASTER ENTREPRENEURIAL CONSULTING

The Computer Consultant's Workbook

277 Pages

TECHNION Books

ISBN 0-9647116-0-5   With 10% online buyer discount   **$36.00**

The Computer Consultant's Workbook leads you through the steps it takes to decide if you have what it takes to succeed at consulting and design an effective marketing plan. It helps you identify your clientele, set rates, develop a marketing message, locate potential clients and convince them you can do the job. It includes meaty discussions, worksheets, exercises, fact sheets, sample letters, contracts, proposals and more.

Computerworld's reviewer wrote, "Although the volume of information Ruhl provides is tremendous, it's easy to absorb and can be immediately useful. Even experienced consultants will find ideas to savor. But those who will benefit most from The Computer Consultant's Workbook are individuals with good technical skills who need a short course in entrepreneurship and self-management. In fact, it's hard to see how someone following Ruhl's savvy suggestions can go far wrong. Almost every page can be quickly translated into a to-do list or the outline of a plan of action. And it's easy to find the information you need, when you need it."

Promote Yourself to Expert

TECHNION Books Audiotape   **$12.95**

60 minutes

Big name consultants don't just appear out of nowhere. You know their names because you read about them in the trade press. This tape shows you how to raise your visibility by placing the right kinds of articles and books in business publications. Learn how to turn yourself into an expert!

Raise Your Rates

TECHNION Books Audiotape   **$12.95**

60 minutes

Learn the secrets of charging a premium rate from consultants earning rates of $100 per hour and more. You'll learn how to improve your skills and image, how to improve your ability to negotiate and how to find the right agency. Reinforces what you've read in this book!

ORDER TODAY FROM TECHNION BOOKS!

www.realrates.com